How to File for Divorce in Massachusetts

How to File for Divorce in Massachusetts

with forms

Sharyn T. Sooho
Steven L. Fuchs
Attorneys at Law

Sphinx Publishing
A Division of Sourcebooks, Inc.
Naperville, IL • Clearwater, FL

Second edition, 1998

Published by: **Sphinx® Publishing, A Division of Sourcebooks, Inc.®**

Naperville Office
P.O. Box 372
Naperville, Illinois 60566
(630) 961-3900
Fax: 630-961-2168

Clearwater Office
P.O. Box 25
Clearwater, Florida 33757
(727) 587-0999
Fax: 727-586-5088

Interior Design and Production: Shannon E. Harrington, Sourcebooks, Inc.

This publication is designed to provide accurate and authoritative information in regard to the subject matter covered. It is sold with the understanding that the publisher is not engaged in rendering legal, accounting, or other professional service. If legal advice or other expert assistance is required, the services of a competent professional person should be sought.

From a Declaration of Principles Jointly Adopted by a Committee of the American Bar Association and a Committee of Publishers and Associations

Library of Congress Cataloging-in-Publication Data

Sooho, Sharyn T.
How to file for divorce in Massachusetts : with forms / Sharyn T. Sooho, Steven L. Fuchs.—2nd ed.
p. cm.
Includes index.
ISBN 1-57071-329-4 (pbk.)
1. Divorce—Law and legislation—Massachusetts—Popular works.
2. Divorce—Law and legislation—Massachusetts—Forms. I. Fuchs, Steven L. II. Title.
KFM2500. Z9S66 1998
346.74401'66—dc21

97-47057
CIP

Printed and bound in the United States of America.

Paperback — 10 9 8 7 6 5 4 3 2 1

CONTENTS

Using Self-Help Law Books

Whenever you shop for a product or service, you are faced with various levels of quality and price. In deciding what product or service to buy, you make a cost/value analysis on the basis of your willingness to pay and the quality you desire.

When buying a car, you decide whether you want transportation, comfort, status, or sex appeal. Accordingly, you decide among such choices as a Neon, a Lincoln, a Rolls Royce, or a Porsche. Before making a decision, you usually weigh the merits of each option against the cost.

When you get a headache, you can take a pain reliever (such as aspirin) or visit a medical specialist for a neurological examination. Given this choice, most people, of course, take a pain reliever, since it costs only pennies, whereas a medical examination costs hundreds of dollars and takes a lot of time. This is usually a logical choice because rarely is anything more than a pain reliever needed for a headache. But in some cases, a headache may indicate a brain tumor, and failing to see a specialist right away can result in complications. Should everyone with a headache go to a specialist? Of course not, but people treating their own illnesses must realize that they are betting on the basis of their cost/value analysis of the situation, they are taking the most logical option.

The same cost/value analysis must be made in deciding to do one's own legal work. Many legal situations are very straight forward, requiring a simple form and no complicated analysis. Anyone with a little intelligence and a book of instructions can handle the matter without outside help.

But there is always the chance that complications are involved that only an attorney would notice. To simplify the law into a book like this, several legal cases often must be condensed into a single sentence or paragraph. Otherwise, the book would be several hundred pages long and too complicated for most people. However, this simplification necessarily leaves out many details and nuances that would apply to special or unusual situations. Also, there are many ways to interpret most legal questions. Your case may come before a judge who disagrees with the analysis of our authors.

Therefore, in deciding to use a self-help law book and to do your own legal work, you must realize that you are making a cost/value analysis and deciding that the chance your case will not turn out to your satisfaction is outweighed by the money you will save in doing it yourself. Most people handling their own simple legal matters never have a problem, but occasionally people find that it ended up costing them more to have an attorney straighten out the situation than it would have if they had hired an attorney in the beginning. Keep this in mind while handling your case, and be sure to consult an attorney if you feel you might need further guidance.

INTRODUCTION

This book provides an insider's view of divorce. Our goal is to provide sufficient information so you can handle your own divorce, or supplement legal services if you choose to hire an attorney. Since 1977, we have represented many men and women in divorce court. Most come into the system with many misunderstandings and fears that we hope to dispel.

We focus on the middle class: too affluent for free legal services and not rich enough for high-priced lawyers. We provide forms and instructions for processing a divorce without an attorney. Handling your own divorce is most easily done by couples without children or significant assets. If you have children, real estate, or pensions, it may be best to confer with attorneys about the legal, financial, and tax implications of divorce. For those readers who do hire a lawyer, this book offers information about divorce law and procedure to maximize the benefits and reduce the cost of legal representation.

Historically, divorce in the United States is controlled by state law. Divorce cases are handled in Massachusetts by the Probate and Family Court Division of the Trial Court Department. As you read this book you will see references to Massachusetts statutes, with a few notable exceptions such as the U.S. Internal Revenue Code and federal laws on employment benefits. Selected portions of the Massachusetts laws relating to divorce are found in appendix A.

In appendix B and appendix C you will find forms commonly used in divorce cases. Appendix B contains sample forms that have been filled in for a fictional case, some with instructions and others that are so basic that only the filled-in form is provided. For a few forms, instructions are found in the main text of the book. Appendix C contains blank forms for you to use in your divorce, with each form being given a number which appears at the top of the form. For each form in appendix C, find the instructions or sample completed forms by looking up the form number under the heading "form, instructions & samples" in the Index. We do not discuss or provide forms for *separate support* cases, the Massachusetts version of a legal separation, because this procedure is rarely used. You and your spouse may live apart without the formality of a legal separation. We also omit any reference to annulment, because few marriages qualify.

We acknowledge that no divorce is truly simple. Each case is akin to a road map of alternative routes, dead ends, short cuts, super highways, and rocky roads. We may convey a sense that there is a straight road from marital separation to divorce because we want to keep our concepts and language simple, but at the same time acknowledge the pain and suffering of divorce.

Newton, MA S.T.S.
1998 S.L.F.

1 Divorce Law and Procedure

Overview

In a divorce, there are basically five matters which are resolved:

1. **Dissolution of the marriage.** This allows the parties to legally remarry.

2. **Division of property.** Massachusetts uses a concept called *equitable distribution,* requiring a judge to divide marital property "fairly," according to a set of factors listed in the Massachusetts statute, Massachusetts General Laws, Chapter 208, Section 34 (abbreviated as "M.G.L. Ch. 208, Sec. 34"). The factors include the length of your marriage and your overall financial circumstances. (See appendix A.) Equitable distribution does not always result in a fifty-fifty split.

3. **Alimony.** Whether you or your spouse are entitled to alimony, and if so, how much and for how long. These matters are determined by the same factors used in dividing property.

4. **Child custody, and visitation rights of the non-custodial parent.** Unless you and your spouse reach an agreement, child custody is determined by a judge based on the best interest of the children. There are no guidelines customarily used by

Massachusetts courts to decide custody or visitation disputes. These issues only concern parents with children under the age of eighteen years.

5. **Child support.** The court applies the child support guidelines [see the CHILD SUPPORT GUIDELINES WORKSHEET (Form 4)], taking into account the needs of the children and the parents' ability to meet those needs. Child support concerns parents with children under the age of twenty-three years. Children over the age of eighteen, however, must be full-time undergraduate students.

Although all of these matters may be decided by a judge, you and your spouse are encouraged to reach an agreement. Judges generally accept anything to which you and your spouse agree, so long as the agreement is fair and reasonable to you, your spouse, or the children. We explain all of these concepts in greater detail in later chapters, and provide completed forms with instructions in appendix B. Blank forms may be found in appendix C. References to forms include the form number used in appendix C. Most of these forms are also included in appendix B as sample completed forms.

BASIC PROCEDURE

The basic procedure for obtaining a divorce is as follows:

1. Prepare a JOINT PETITION FOR DIVORCE UNDER M.G.L. CH. 208, SEC. 1A (Form 1) or a COMPLAINT FOR DIVORCE (Form 10). If you and your spouse have a signed agreement on all of the issues, you may use the JOINT PETITION FOR DIVORCE UNDER M.G.L. CH. 208, SEC. 1A (Form 1). This is more simple than other types of Massachusetts divorces, but by no means "simplified," as in some states. In all other situations, file a COMPLAINT FOR DIVORCE (Form 10), the document which gives the judge the parties' names, addresses, date of the marriage, names and ages of the children, etc. The complaint also tells the court you want a divorce, your reason ("ground") for

divorce, and the issues you want the court to resolve. (Other forms may be filed along with the petition or complaint.)

2. Officially notify your spouse about the divorce, unless you and your spouse file a JOINT PETITION FOR DIVORCE UNDER M.G.L. CH. 208, SEC. 1A (Form 1), in which case you do not need to take any other steps to inform your spouse about the divorce.
3. Ask for a court hearing. The trial clerk then notifies you and your spouse in writing as to the time and date of the hearing.
4. Appear at the hearing and present the necessary information as outlined in more detail in the following chapters.

There are various situations which require special forms and procedures, and these are discussed in more detail in the remaining chapters.

FAULT AND NO-FAULT DIVORCE

In Massachusetts, until 1976, one party had to be at fault before courts granted divorces. If both parties were at fault, the courts refused to grant a divorce to either party. Some states allowed divorce only on the ground of adultery, causing couples to fabricate tales of infidelity. Judges and lawyers knew the allegations were false, but no one objected, leading observers to demand reform to eliminate the deception and hypocrisy. Some observers believe that no-fault divorces hurt women and children because financial settlements are not as generous, but we believe there is insufficient data to support that assertion.

Today, the practical differences between fault and no-fault divorces are generally insignificant. If a husband and wife do not agree on the terms of their divorce, regardless of whether they choose a fault or no-fault divorce, courts listen to and weigh evidence on conduct during the marriage. Most people are tempted to dwell on their spouse's bad conduct. Judges, however, usually discourage a lengthy presentation of marital misdeeds.

The Massachusetts divorce statute require evidence on a number of factors, including:

- length of marriage.
- financial resources.
- both parties' conduct during the marriage.
- standard of living.
- ages.
- employability.
- health.
- homemaker contributions to the family.
- education.
- unmet needs of the children.

If you settle your case, the court reviews the settlement agreement and other documents, including affidavits and financial statements. Occasionally, a judge asks the parties a few questions to supplement the written information. When preparing your documents or testimony, keep in mind that courts do not give greater weight to misconduct. Truly egregious conduct may tip the scale, but in the ordinary case, the usual recital of spousal fault makes little difference to the outcome.

Fault Divorce

Grounds for Divorce

The statutory *fault* grounds for divorce in Massachusetts are:

- adultery.
- cruel and abusive treatment.
- impotency.
- prison sentence.
- utter desertion.

- nonsupport.
- gross and confirmed habits of intoxication.

Historically, divorces were granted to the "good" spouse because of the "bad" spouse's misdeeds. Today we use fault divorces for a variety of reasons, usually to save time. Fault divorces are the swiftest, although none of the Massachusetts divorce procedures are truly speedy.

The faults described in the Massachusetts divorce statute are legal terms, with specific definitions which differ from common usage. For example, *utter desertion* requires one spouse to leave home and stay away at least one year before the stay-at-home spouse files for divorce. Furthermore, the stay-at-home spouse must have not done anything to cause the other spouse to leave home. *Gross and confirmed intoxication* means drug and alcohol abuse of such proportions that the wrong-doer is intoxicated on the day of the court appearance. Except for *cruel and abusive treatment*, most fault grounds are used infrequently because they are difficult to prove.

The most common fault ground is cruel and abusive treatment, which covers a wide range of behavior. When the timing of your divorce is important (for example, if you want a divorce by the end of a tax year) you may want to file for divorce on this ground, giving you the right to ask for a trial date immediately. Asking, however, does not guarantee a speedy trial date, but you do avoid the extra six month waiting period imposed on people asking for a contested no-fault divorce. Sometimes people worry about the negative implications of cruel and abusive treatment. The general public and media believe a spouse must have committed physical abuse. In divorce court, however, cruel and abusive treatment also means verbal or emotional abuse.

SETTLEMENTS

If you settle your fault divorce, meaning you and your spouse have a signed written agreement resolving all of the issues relating to the dissolution of your marriage, you should request a hearing date as soon as you file your settlement agreement. Depending on the county, your case will be scheduled within a matter of days or weeks. If you cannot settle, ask for a trial. Courts are busy, so you will wait from four to nine months for your trial. Whether you settle or go to trial, you and your spouse must wait an additional ninety days after you appear in court before a final divorce judgment will be entered. You may not remarry until your divorce is final. During the ninety-day waiting period, you simply wait and are not required to take any additional steps. The court automatically enters the final divorce on the ninety-first day.

NO-FAULT DIVORCE

Since 1976, Massachusetts judges have granted no-fault divorces because of "an irretrievable breakdown of the marriage." No-fault divorces are either "uncontested" (known as "1A") or "contested" (known as "1B"). If uncontested, the parties do not have to testify about the problems of their marriage, but must file an affidavit signed under oath stating that the marriage is irretrievably broken. Over the years, a "standard" affidavit evolved in support of the request for an uncontested no-fault divorce (see Form 2).

UNCONTESTED CASES

Parties in an uncontested no-fault divorce usually ask the trial department to assign a hearing date as soon as they file their JOINT PETITION FOR DIVORCE UNDER M.G.L. Ch. 208, Sec. 1A (Form 1). Depending on the county, your hearing is set up within a matter of days or weeks. The divorce laws now take a peculiar turn. After the hearing, you wait 120 days for a final divorce, a month longer than a fault or contested no-fault divorce. In 1976, when the first no-fault divorce provisions appeared in Massachusetts, lawmakers were wary of no-fault divorce, afraid that it would break up more marriages, so they built in longer waiting periods.

CONTESTED CASES

Massachusetts also has an additional statutory waiting provision for contested no-fault divorces—you must wait six months after filing your COMPLAINT FOR DIVORCE (Form 10) before you may even ask the court for a trial date. Lawyers call this the *up-front waiting period*. Parties then wait an additional four to nine months for a contested trial date, but waiting does not end with trial. Like other divorcing parties, you must wait ninety days for a final divorce judgment after trial. In practice, the contested no-fault divorce takes approximately eighteen months or longer, making it the lengthiest of the different kinds of divorce.

Tax Implications

A divorce raises certain questions concerning taxes. The following information is a brief summary of some of these tax implications.

Alimony is usually deductible by the paying spouse and taxable to the recipient spouse. Child support is not deductible by the paying parent, nor taxable to the recipient parent. The custodial parent has the right to claim the children as tax dependents, unless that parent signs IRS Form 8332, releasing the dependency exemption to the non-custodial parent.

Property divisions between divorcing spouses are generally nontaxable events, if done in connection with a settlement agreement or divorce judgment.

Your tax filing status is determined by your marital status on December 31. For example, if you are married, but living apart on December 31, you and your spouse may file either a joint tax return or separate returns. You cannot file as a single taxpayer unless your divorce is final on or before December 31 of the tax year in question.

Summary

Massachusetts has fault and no-fault divorces, each of which may be contested or uncontested. The uncontested fault divorce is the swiftest; the contested no-fault divorce the slowest.

The waiting periods for each type of divorce are:

Type of case	Hearing may be requested	Wait for hearing	From Hearing to Final Divorce	Total (Approx.)
Uncontested Fault	Immediately	4 - 8 weeks	90 days	4 - 5 months
Uncontested No-Fault	Immediately	4 - 8 weeks	120 days	5 - 6 months
Contested Fault	Immediately	4 - 9 months	90 days	7 months +
Contested No-Fault	6 months after filing Complaint	4 - 9 months	90 days	13 - 18 months

One variable by county is the amount of time from the date of your request for a trial or hearing until your case is scheduled. According to our experience in 1997, Suffolk County takes about eight to ten weeks to schedule hearings on uncontested divorces, whereas Middlesex County usually schedules such hearings within four weeks. Each county's caseload varies month to month, so ask the trial department of your county court for an estimate when filing your request.

In most divorces you work to settle your case and simultaneously prepare for trial, if you cannot reach a fair settlement through negotiation within a reasonable time. Different people can tolerate the uncertainties of divorce with different degrees of stamina, but most cannot cope beyond eighteen months to two years. Thus, the court system becomes an effective means of resolving your differences. Chapter 4 gives an overview of various settlement techniques, chapter 5 describes the uncontested divorce procedures, and chapter 6 explains contested divorce procedures.

As a rule of thumb, if you do not resolve major issues within four to six months of separating, explore litigation tools and techniques. For example, even if you mediate your divorce, both parties need full financial disclosure. If disclosure is slow, or incomplete and inaccurate, consider using the litigation device of *discovery* to enhance your knowledge of your marital financial information (as discussed in chapter 6).

After reaching settlement, parties often prefer to proceed on a no-fault basis and change or amend the original complaint from a fault divorce to an uncontested no-fault divorce under a JOINT PETITION FOR DIVORCE UNDER M.G.L. CH. 208, SEC. 1A (Form 1). Courts readily allow requests to amend complaints in these cases. (See Form 13.)

2 Divorce—With and Without a Lawyer

Do You Need a Lawyer?

Millions of Americans are divorced each year, although few understand the legal and financial implications of divorce. People often ask: do I need a lawyer? If I hire a lawyer, what does the lawyer do, and how can I prevent legal fees and costs from escalating? This book is designed to help you take control of your divorce by explaining the ABCs of divorce. You may use our forms to process your own papers or simply to organize material for your lawyer's use. In either instance, you may eliminate or reduce legal fees.

If your case falls into the category of a simple divorce, then you should be able to negotiate and prepare a settlement agreement—a mandatory condition for obtaining an uncontested no-fault divorce. You should be aware that a judge may reject your signed agreement. If you choose to represent yourself, you may avoid unpleasant surprises and save thousands of dollars in legal fees by paying a lawyer for the limited purpose of reviewing your divorce papers, particularly, the settlement agreement and financial statements.

The question of whether you should represent yourself should be considered carefully. You represent yourself with little risk if you: 1) have no children, 2) can support yourself, 3) were married just a few years,

4) have a working spouse, 5) have few assets, and 6) can communicate with your spouse.

Even in more complex cases, many people handle their own case, because they cannot afford an attorney or do not want a lawyer. The law says you may represent yourself, some cases are best handled by an attorney. You may want to consider retaining a lawyer if one or more of the following circumstances apply: 1) you were married more than a few years, 2) you have children, 3) you own substantial assets, 4) you cannot support yourself, 5) your spouse is unemployed, 6) you cannot talk to your spouse, or 7) your spouse has an attorney.

Finding and Assessing a Lawyer

Not all lawyers are alike. There are take-charge lawyers who tell you, "Don't worry. Leave everything to me." They do not share information and rarely seek your permission before filing papers. If you leave "everything" to your lawyer, you may pay higher fees and have less control. Be an active participant, since you know more about your family and your needs than any lawyer or judge.

Other lawyers use legal jargon. If you cannot understand what the lawyer is saying and he or she will not explain it so that you can understand, find another lawyer. Some lawyers dislike negotiation, preferring to "fight," push the case to trial, and stir up hostilities—and cost you unnecessary legal fees. Other lawyers avoid going to trial at all costs. They are ill-equipped emotionally to withstand the adversarial atmosphere. If your spouse's lawyer knows your lawyer's reputation for capitulation, he or she may bully you into an unfavorable settlement.

Some lawyers are general practitioners who do few divorces and are unaware of the complexities of divorce law. You are better off with a divorce lawyer, even if your case is uncontested. The specialist knows the ropes and what divorce judges want, which saves you time and money. Whatever you do, never use the same lawyer as your spouse. Any competent, ethical lawyer will decline joint representation.

When looking for a lawyer, speak to friends and family who have gone through divorce, then interview lawyers and find out:

- How many years have they been in practice—the hourly rates should be commensurate with the lawyer's experience.
- What portion of the practice is devoted to family law—"specialists" devote at least fifty percent of their practice to family law.
- Their hourly rate and policy on retainers—ethical lawyers welcome fee discussions.
- Their willingness to advise parties going through mediation—good lawyers should be open to less costly alternatives.
- Readiness to conduct a trial—is the attorney prepared to take necessary action?
- Hourly rates of lawyers and staff (if any) who may work on your case—subordinates should have lower fees.

If you do not find a lawyer by word of mouth, call the bar associations in your area for a referral. A note of caution: Massachusetts does not certify specialists. Do not assume that the lawyers recommended by bar associations are specialists.

Other resources: *Martindale-Hubbell*, a national directory, is available at public libraries and lists lawyers by state, city, and town. The directory also supplies biographical information and an alphabetical rating of legal ability: A (very high to preeminent), B (high to very high), and C (fair to high). All attorneys with performance ratings are regarded as highly ethical. Ratings are determined by a sampling of other lawyers' and judges' opinions. Some lawyers belong to professional organizations, such as the selective American Academy of Matrimonial Lawyers, which is also noted.

Do not choose a lawyer solely on credentials. In the final analysis, your reaction to the lawyer, the staff, and the lawyer's responsiveness to your questions, should determine whether you retain the lawyer. Lawyers with impeccable credentials sometimes have poor interpersonal skills. Chemistry is important. There are as many different styles of lawyering as there are lawyers, so find a lawyer whose style fits your needs.

Competent lawyers have a few questions for you during your first telephone call. Experienced lawyers ask:

- Your name and your spouse's name—to be sure he or she does not already represent your spouse.
- Whether any court action is pending and whether you have a court date.
- Whether there is any physical abuse.
- Whether there are assets your spouse may hide, give away, sell, or use as collateral.
- Status of credit cards, bank accounts, and home equity loans—the lawyer is trying to determine whether assets may be depleted without both spouses' permission.
- Whether there are children involved.

Many lawyers will charge little or nothing for your initial meeting. Most bar association lawyer referral services keep a list of attorneys who will work for a reduced fee if your annual income does not exceed $14,720 for one person (add $4,960 for each child). In 1996 the reduced fee rate was $40 an hour. If your income is low, you may qualify for free legal services at a local legal aid office. Eligibility is determined by federal guidelines. Indigents, as defined by federal guidelines, may speak to volunteer lawyers at the local Probate and Family Court. Volunteers fill in forms and give limited advice or tell you whether a private attorney will take your case because your spouse may be ordered to pay your fees for a private attorney.

Your First Meeting

Now that you have done the preliminary screening, prepare for your first meeting. The lawyer may ask for documents, such as your marriage certificate, tax returns, deeds, bank statements, insurance policies, certificates of title, prior divorce papers, prenuptial agreements, wills, and trusts. Do not expect the lawyer to review the documents at the meeting because more time may be needed, but experienced lawyers spot issues quickly. For instance, if you have a prenuptial agreement, you may be barred from seeking alimony. Be sure to discuss fees, expenses, and payment arrangements.

At the conclusion of the meeting you may want to retain the lawyer or interview others. Many clients like to interview two or three lawyers before making their selection. Sometimes lawyers and clients disagree during the course of their relationship and agree that the client should retain successor counsel. This is an accepted practice, but may be disruptive and possibly expensive, so choose prudently the first time.

Legal Fees and Retaining a Lawyer

In the Boston area, hourly rates range from $125 to $500, with most lawyers charging from $150 to $300. Typically divorce lawyers demand a prepaid retainer of several thousand dollars. They generally bill by the hour and may deplete the retainer before your case is concluded, requiring another lump sum payment. Contested custody cases, where fees can exceed $100,000, command much higher retainers because of their time-consuming nature, where fees can exceed $100,000. You should receive periodic itemized statements of time charges and expenses, including filing fees, sheriff's fees, overnight mail, couriers, photocopies, toll calls, expert witness fees, and other expenses relating to your case.

Some lawyers bill by the "unit"—a newer approach which allows lawyers using computers to work quickly, but to bill a minimum for certain units of work, such as drafting a complaint for divorce. In the pre-computer age, the lawyer spent an hour writing the complaint, had a secretary type it, and then reviewed the final copy. Sitting in front of a computer, a lawyer uses a few key strokes to produce the same document. Lawyers justify unit or value billing because of the legal expertise which enables them to punch out a complaint in five minutes.

Avoid lawyers who insist on a large nonrefundable retainer at the first meeting (this may be prohibited under new ethics rules). If you decide to hire someone else, they will not refund your retainer. They claim this is necessary protection against clients who set up introductory meetings for the sole purpose of creating a conflict of interest, thus ensuring that the lawyer cannot represent their spouse.

The lawyer should provide a written fee agreement explaining the fees, expenses, and billing procedures (see a sample fee agreement at the end of this chapter). Do not feel you must sign the agreement and pay the retainer at the first meeting. Read the agreement carefully, and even consult another lawyer about the agreement before signing. No ethical divorce lawyer charges a percentage or contingent fee, although some fee agreements allow the lawyer to award himself a bonus, if he believes he did an outstanding job. Do not agree to give your lawyer unbridled discretion over fees or any other matter in your divorce.

Courts sometimes make one spouse pay the other's attorneys fees, but you must still pay all fees in excess of the award. As a practical matter, whether you or your spouse write the check for your legal fees, there are fewer post-divorce dollars for the family.

Lawyer Reference and Referral Resources:

☛ Boston Bar Association Lawyer Reference Service	617-742-0625
☛ Lawyers Referral Service of Middlesex County Bar Association	617-494-4150
☛ Massachusetts Bar Association Lawyer Referral Service	617-542-9103
☛ Volunteer Lawyers Project, Boston Bar Association	617-423-0648
☛ Legal Advocacy and Resource Center, Boston	617-742-9179
☛ Dial-a-Lawyer, Massachusetts Bar Association	617-542-9069
☛ Middlesex County Bar Association Legal Clinic, Cambridge	617-494-4150

☛ Legal services at various locations, and *pro bono* (free) services through county bar associations (see your local yellow pages).

Fee Agreement
Domestic Relations Case - Hourly Fee

I, ___Eva Frances Lee Rivers___ of ___Hyannis, MA___ the "Client," hereby agree to retain ___Sharyn T. Sooho___ the "Attorney/Firm," in connection with the domestic relations matter as follows: ___Eva Frances Lee Rivers v. Louis Rivers___

1. The Attorney has received $___2,500.00___ as a partial payment on account. The Attorney agrees to provide legal services in the above domestic relations matter and to keep the Client fully informed of all significant developments, and to send copies of relevant documents necessary to achieve that purpose. The payment received shall be applied against the bills for the legal services and costs as described below.

2. The legal services performed shall be charged at the rate of $___250.00___ per hour for the Attorney. The Attorney may employ associate(s), ___Steven L. Fuchs___ and paralegal(s) ___Steven J. Steinmetz___, to assist in the case. If so, their services will be charged at the rate of $___200.00___ per hour for associate(s), and $___75.00___ per hour for paralegal(s).

3. The time charges include but are not limited to court appearances, including waiting time, travel to and from court, telephone conferences, telephone calls to and from the Client (all telephone calls are billed at a minimum of ___one___/10th(s) of an hour), office conferences, legal research, depositions, review of file materials and documents sent or received, drafting of pleadings, correspondence and memoranda, preparation for trials, hearings, and conferences.

4. The Client may request a report or bill from the Attorney for a current status of the legal fees and costs incurred. Interim billings may be submitted to the Client from time to time if time charges exceed the initial payment on account. All interim billings shall be due and payable on receipt unless otherwise stated. Failure to pay interim billings promptly will permit the Attorney after notice to the Client to terminate the representation of the Client subject to applicable rules of the court.

5. In the event the Client shall discharge the Attorney, or in the event the Attorney determines to terminate the representation of the Client, the Attorney shall be paid for all work performed up to the point of termination of services, and this payment shall include all services which have been completed, as well as reimbursement of costs expended up to the time of termination of the Attorney/Client relationship.

6. The Client agrees that the final bill submitted by the Attorney for legal fees and costs will be due and payable at the conclusion of this matter, or at the termination of the Attorney/Client relationship.

7. In the event that, either on the completion of the within matter or the termination of the Attorney's representation of the Client, the total cost of the legal services performed by the Attorney shall be less than the amount paid on account by the Client, the balance shall be refunded to the Client by the Attorney.

8. The parties understand that in some cases the court may award legal fees to one party and order the other party to pay the amount awarded. Any award of legal fees is solely in the discretion of the court and cannot be relied upon with certainty. In other cases, if there is a settlement agreed to by both parties, thereby avoiding a trial, the settlement agreement may provide that one of the parties contribute to the other party's legal expenses. It is difficult to predict whether either of these situations will occur. In the event, however, that the court awards payment of fees by the other party and/or there is an agreement as to payment of fees by the other party, and such funds are received for the benefit of the Client, then the amount of funds so received will be credited against the Attorney's final bill to the Client. In the event any such agreements are reached or awards entered by the court for payment of the Client's legal fees and/or expenses, and the Client's spouse fails to pay all or any portion of the fees and expenses, then the Client remains responsible under the terms of this agreement for payment. Should the Client decide to attempt to recover such monies from the spouse in the event of the spouse's failure to pay, the Client shall be responsible for any work and expenses incurred by the Attorney in regard to the attempted recovery.

9. The Attorney and Client state that no results have been guaranteed by the Attorney to the Client and that this Agreement is not based upon any such promises or anticipated results.

10. The Client agrees to pay for costs incurred and out-of-pocket disbursements made by the Attorney, including, but not limited, to filing fees, witness fees, travel, sheriff's and constable's fees, expenses of depositions, investigative expenses, expert witness fees, charges for photocopies and telephone, and other incidental expenses. The Attorney/Firm agrees to obtain the Client's approval before incurring any single cost or disbursement in excess of $ 200.00 and incurring total costs in excess of $ 200.00 .

The Client understands and acknowledges that no legal representation, appearance, or preparation will begin in this matter until payment on account as set forth in paragraph one is paid in full.

We, the Client and the Attorney/Firm, have read the above Fee Agreement on this 3rd day of March , 19 96 , and understand its terms and both have signed it as our free act and deed.

Eva F. Rivers — Client

Sharyn T. Sooho — Attorney/Firm

The Client acknowledges receipt of a copy of this agreement.

Eva F. Rivers — Client

Sharyn T. Sooho — Attorney/Firm

This is a legally binding contract. Ask to have each term explained to you so that you understand the agreement. If you wish, seek advice of counsel before signing.

Optional Clauses

1. If the Client fails to pay any bill within 60 days of receipt (simple/XXXXXXXX) interest will be paid at the rate of 14 percent per (year/XXXXX).

2. If the Client and Attorney are unable to resolve their differences on the question of any fee, and or expenses, they hereby agree to make a good faith effort at resolving their disputes. If the dispute cannot be resolved, the Client and Attorney agree to place the matter before the Fee Arbitration Board of the Massachusetts Bar Association, or some other fee dispute resolution body, and agree to be bound by the decision.

The Client understands and acknowledges that these optional clauses are incorporated into and made a part of the attached fee agreement.

We, the Client and the Attorney/Firm, have read the above Optional Clauses on this 3rd day of March , 19 96 , and understand its terms and both have signed it as our free act and deed.

Eva F. Rivers — Client

Sharyn T. Sooho — Attorney/Firm

The Client acknowledges receipt of a copy of these Optional Clauses.

Eva F. Rivers — Client

Sharyn T. Sooho — Attorney/Firm

Documents and Forms 3

The necessary documents and forms depend on the type of divorce you seek, as described in chapter 1 (i.e., contested or uncontested; fault or no-fault). The following information, however, applies to all types of divorces.

Marriage Certificates

When filing divorce papers, you must prove you are legally married, and thus eligible for a divorce, by filing an official copy of your marriage certificate with a raised seal. If you were married in Massachusetts, you may obtain an official copy of your marriage certificate by writing to:

- Massachusetts Registry of Vital Statistics, Department of Public Health, 150 Tremont Street, Room B-3, Boston, Massachusetts 02111 (the fee is about $11.00 per copy); or
- The town or city hall in the municipality where you were married. Massachusetts municipalities typically charge about $6.00 for certified copies of marriage certificates. Some cities and towns fill requests made in person, but call first to find out the preferred method.

If you were not married in Massachusetts, write to a bureau of vital statistics located in the capital city of the state where you were married. Most states charge a fee ranging from $10.00 to $20.00, payable in advance, for certified copies. Massachusetts divorce courts do not accept marriage certificates issued by a rabbi, priest, or minister. If you were married in a foreign country, special rules apply, requiring a copy of the foreign marriage certificate authenticated by the local U.S. Embassy. For example, if you were married in Shanghai, The People's Republic of China, obtain a copy of your marriage certificate from the Shanghai authorities, and then send the document to the U.S. Embassy in Beijing for authentication. If the certificate is not in English, obtain an official translation by arranging with your county Probate and Family Court clerk for a court-approved translator.

Courts allow a delayed filing of the marriage certificate, provided that a MOTION TO DELAY FILING OF MARRIAGE CERTIFICATE (Form 11) and an AFFIDAVIT IN SUPPORT OF MOTION TO DELAY FILING OF MARRIAGE CERTIFICATE (Form 12) are filed. Form 11 is easy to complete according to the instructions in the following section of this chapter; fill in the date, signature, name, address, and telephone information at the bottom of the form. For help with Form 12, see Form R in appendix B.

FORMS

You may use the forms in this book, or forms available at no cost from any Massachusetts Probate and Family Court. We do not include a blank Domestic Relations Summons in appendix C because each court issues its own official Summons with its raised seal. Appendix B contains a sample Summons, but you must use the official court Summons available for $1.00 at your county's Probate and Family Court.

Notice that most of the forms are similar at the top. This *caption* gives information about the county court in which the case is filed, the docket number, and the names of the parties. This section is to be filled in the same way for each form you use. Older forms use "__________SS." for the place where you fill in the county's name, and newer forms use "__________Division."

You may find forms with slight variations, but the same information is required on all of them. For example:

Commonwealth of Massachusetts
The Trial Court
The Probate and Family Court Department

___Berkshire___ **Division** **Docket No.** ___98D-2946-D1___

___Jane Margaret Doe___,
Plaintiff

V. Complaint for Divorce

___Joseph R. Doe, Jr.___,
Defendant

Filing Your Forms

The Massachusetts state courts are organized by county. There are fourteen counties, with the probate and family courts named for their respective counties. For example, we refer to the Suffolk County Probate and Family Court when speaking of the court in Boston. The rule on where to file depends on where you last lived with your spouse and whether either of you still reside in the same county. For example, if you and your spouse last lived together in Middlesex County, and either of you continue to live in Middlesex County, your divorce case belongs at the Middlesex County court. If you move to Norfolk County, and your spouse moves to Suffolk County, you may file in Norfolk County or Suffolk County, but not Middlesex County. If you and your spouse did not live together in Massachusetts, there is a one year residency requirement for the party seeking the divorce, unless the event causing the break-up of your marriage happened in Massachusetts before the end of the first year.

Massachusetts Probate and Family Court Telephone Numbers by County:

Barnstable:	(508) 362-2511 x267	Hampshire:	(413) 586-8500
Berkshire:	(413) 442-6941	Middlesex:	(617) 494-4533
Bristol:	(508) 824-4004	Nantucket:	(508) 228-2669
Dukes:	(508) 627-4703	Norfolk:	(781) 326-7200
Essex:	(978) 741-0201 x317	Plymouth:	(508) 747-6204
Franklin:	(413) 774-7011	Suffolk:	(617) 725-8300
Hampden:	(413) 748-8600	Worcester:	(508) 770-0825

You and your spouse may live together on the day you file your divorce papers. Massachusetts abolished a requirement that parties live apart at least thirty days before filing for divorce, but as a general practice, many judges expect you to be living apart on the day you appear for your trial (contested) or final hearing (uncontested).

Although we refer to the divorce forms as *uniform*, each county has its own version. For example, you see "Suffolk County" printed on forms from the court in Boston, and "Middlesex County" on forms from the court in Cambridge. Courts accept most forms distributed by other counties, except for the Domestic Relations Summons. Each county requires its official Domestic Relations Summons. **Note:** If you and your spouse file a JOINT PETITION FOR DIVORCE UNDER M.G.L. Ch. 208, Sec. 1A (Form 1), do not use a Domestic Relations Summons (see chapters 4 and 5).

Before filing your papers, read all of the instructions on the forms carefully, and refer to the appropriate sections of this book for a more detailed explanation. File your papers in person or by mail, although it is best to go in person, in the event that your papers need changes. The clerk (called the *register*) will review your papers and let you know whether there are any errors or omissions. Clerks are prohibited from giving legal advice, but they may tell you to take corrective measures. For example, if you have minor children named on your COMPLAINT FOR DIVORCE (Form 10), but no Affidavit Disclosing Care or Custody Proceedings, your papers will be rejected and returned to you. You then need to complete the custody affidavit, and re-submit the papers.

Whenever you send or deliver forms to the register, also provide a cover letter listing the documents you are filing. If you mail the forms, also enclose a self-addressed, stamped envelope or postcard, and ask the register to acknowledge receipt of the documents. All filing fees should be paid by bank check or money order, not by personal check. Checks and money orders should be made out to the register of the appropriate county court (for example: "Register of Dukes County Probate and Family Court").

If you cannot afford the filing fee, prepare and file a MOTION TO PROCEED IN FORMA PAUPERIS (Form 17) and an AFFIDAVIT OF INDIGENCY AND REQUEST FOR WAIVER, SUBSTITUTION OR STATE PAYMENT OF FEES AND COSTS (Form 18). Form 17 simply requires the completion of the case caption according to the instructions in the "Forms" section of this chapter, the date, your signature, and information requested beneath your signature. For help in completing the Form 18, see the sample completed Form T in appendix B. If you do not receive public assistance and your income is higher than the established poverty level, but you still cannot afford the fees, prepare and file SUPPLEMENT TO AFFIDAVIT OF INDIGENCY (Form 19). See sample completed Form T in appendix U for further guidance.

Hot Tips on Using Forms

There are *standard* forms designed by the court, such as the COMPLAINT FOR DIVORCE (Form 10), FINANCIAL STATEMENT (Form 5 or Form 6), and the CHILD SUPPORT GUIDELINES WORKSHEET (Form 4). There are also *nonstandard* forms, such as motions, certain affidavits, and a SETTLEMENT/SEPARATION AGREEMENT (Form 8). The nonstandard forms in this book are based on models we use in our office. Use standard forms when available, otherwise the clerk may reject your papers. As for non-standard forms, alter these forms to suit your case, but follow our format, addressing points judges want to know.

HOW TO USE FORMS

The following are some guidelines for using legal forms:

1. Make a few photocopies of the blank forms in appendix C. Fill in the copies, and keep the original blank form on hand in case you make a mistake.

2. Follow the line-by-line instructions in appendix B. Type information, if possible, or print legibly in blue ink. For further guidance, refer to the sample completed form following the instructions in appendix B. Some forms require a deletion of an optional word or phrase that does not apply. For example, some forms give options such as "husband/wife," or "plaintiff/defendant."

3. After completing the form to your satisfaction, sign and date it. Be sure to sign in the presence of a notary, if a notarized signature is required (see instructions).

4. Make two photocopies of your completed form. File the original with the court. Serve one copy on your spouse or your spouse's attorney. Keep a copy for your files.

How to Organize Your Divorce File Folder

Keep everything organized in file folders. Use the following guidelines to organize your file folders:

1. Keep papers in reverse chronological order (most recent papers on top).
2. Keep copies of court documents in one folder, and correspondence and other documents in a second folder.
3. For easy reference, number all court documents with tabs. Make a list and staple it to the inside cover of the folder. The following is a list for an uncontested no-fault divorce:

   - ❑ Marriage certificate.
   - ❑ JOINT PETITION FOR DIVORCE UNDER M.G.L. Ch. 208, Sec. 1A (Form 1).
   - ❑ JOINT AFFIDAVIT UNDER M.G.L. Ch. 208, Sec. 1A (Form 2).
   - ❑ Wife's FINANCIAL STATEMENT (Form 5 or Form 6).
   - ❑ Husband's FINANCIAL STATEMENT (Form 5 or Form 6).
   - ❑ Affidavit Disclosing Care or Custody Proceedings (obtain from the court clerk).
   - ❑ CHILD SUPPORT GUIDELINES WORKSHEET (Form 4).
   - ❑ SETTLEMENT/SEPARATION AGREEMENT (Form 8).
   - ❑ CERTIFICATE OF ABSOLUTE DIVORCE OR ANNULMENT (Form 25).
   - ❑ REQUEST FOR TRIAL—PRE-TRIAL ASSIGNMENT (Form 9).
   - ❑ Notice of Hearing (prepared by the court).
   - ❑ Court's findings (prepared by the court).
   - ❑ Judgment of Divorce Nisi (prepared by the court).
   - ❑ Final Judgment of Divorce (prepared by the court).

How and Where to Find More Information

The following is a list of sources of additional information:

> ***Tip:*** If you have one or two legal questions about your paper work, find the volunteer *Lawyer of the Day* stationed in many Probate and Family Courts. Volunteers generally offer services to indigents, but sometimes courts allow nonindigents to ask a few questions.

1. Use our Glossary if you have questions about legal terms and definitions.

2. If you have tax questions relating to divorce, (alimony may be deductible by the paying spouse, and taxable to the recipient spouse, but child support is neither deductible nor taxable) get a copy of IRS Publication 504 on "Divorce and Taxation," (available for free from the IRS).

3. Most public libraries have a four volume set by Charles Kindregan and Monroe Inker called *Family Law and Practice with Forms*, as part of the *Massachusetts Practice* series. The material is detailed, and written for lawyers by a law professor and divorce lawyer.

4. The Divorce Center, Inc., sponsors weekly programs on different aspects of divorce and separation for the general public in Framingham at a cost of $10 a program. For information call: 508-668-2514.

5. Written for the general public, *Massachusetts Divorce: A Consumer Guide*, by Wendy Sibbison, is available for $14.95 from Massachusetts Continuing Legal Education, Inc., 10 Winter Place, Boston, MA 02108. MCLE also publishes Attorney Michael Leshin's *1997 Family Law Sourcebook* ($50), which provides statutes, rules, and regulations on family law.

6. Try our web site at "www.DivorceNet.com" which has a section called "FAQ" (Frequently Asked Questions) with information for the public on alimony, child custody, visitation, and

support. Our site also has the electronic version of our newsletter, *The Family Law Advisor,* and an interactive CHILD SUPPORT GUIDELINE WORKSHEET.

SUMMARY

Before filing for divorce, obtain an official copy of your marriage certificate with a raised seal. Then prepare a COMPLAINT FOR DIVORCE (Form 10) or JOINT PETITION FOR DIVORCE UNDER M.G.L. CH. 208, SEC. 1A (Form 1), and a variety of other documents, depending upon the type of your divorce. File your COMPLAINT FOR DIVORCE or JOINT PETITION FOR DIVORCE UNDER M.G.L. CH. 208, SEC. 1A with the official copy of your marriage certificate in the appropriate county Probate and Family Court, depending on where you and your spouse last lived together and where you now live. If you file a COMPLAINT FOR DIVORCE, the court issues the official Summons which you are responsible for "serving" on your spouse, as described in chapter 6. If you file a JOINT PETITION FOR DIVORCE UNDER M.G.L. CH. 208, SEC. 1A, you do not need the Summons.

Now that you know about the basic documents, you face critical choices on whether to mediate, negotiate, or litigate. The next three chapters describe these alternatives.

Settling Your Case

If you and your spouse do not have an agreement, we recommend mediation or negotiation unless litigation is unavoidable. This chapter describes the mediation and negotiation process.

From time to time you hear lawyers and judges referring to the agreement as a *separation agreement* even in the context of divorce, because, under Massachusetts law, you may agree to live separately, but cannot agree to divorce. Only courts grant divorces, although the key document, by any name, is the agreement. In chapter 2 we advised hiring a lawyer to review the agreement before you sign and file it, but if you follow most or all of the following steps we outline, you may save money.

Physicians commonly rate divorce as one of the most stressful events in their patients' lives, along with the death of a spouse and major illness. Some observers note that incidents of heart attack and stroke dramatically increase during divorce. In many instances people engage in self-destructive behavior such as alcohol and drug abuse, poor driving, bad eating habits, lack of exercise, and failure to utilize health care services.

Throughout history, courts and lawmakers have struggled with policies relating to marriage and divorce, trying to minimize the ill effects of divorce on individual families and society.

MEDIATION

During the 1980s, mediation came into fashion among divorcing parties and their lawyers. Professionals hoped that the parties would take control of their own divorces, reducing the overall cost. Over the years, however, people have come away with observations markedly different from those early expectations. Surprisingly, the cost of mediation is sometimes as high or higher than traditional lawyer-negotiated cases, because the parties pay a high hourly rate to a mediator, and each party pays his or her own attorney for outside consultation and final review of the mediation documents.

Another unexpected and disappointing result is that some women do not do well in mediation because of an imbalance of psychological power. A good mediator ought to level the playing field, but some women are still reluctant to enter into divorce discussions without their lawyers, who traditionally stay away from mediation, with occasional exceptions.

Despite the difference between hope and reality, mediation still works for many people. We recommend mediation with trained mediators—usually lawyers with training in mental health—because they are familiar with what courts accept and are sensitive to issues like the imbalance of power. Mediators do not give legal advice, but know when to tell you to see your own lawyer.

Mediators in the Boston area charge between $100 and $250 per hour. Fees are a part of a written mediation agreement which typically requires each spouse to pay one-half of the fees or in proportion to their incomes. Agreements also spell out the mediator's role, often requiring the preparation of a written settlement agreement.

Experienced mediators recommend that you consult with your own lawyer before signing the agreement and welcome your lawyer's comments. The mediator does not go to court and probably will not prepare any of the other court papers. The Massachusetts Council on Family

Mediation, 23 Parker Road, Needham Heights, MA, 02194-2001, telephone number 781-449-4430, maintains a list of members offering services as divorce mediators.

NEGOTIATION

Other people do not need a mediator. They can talk directly with their spouses. The goal of mediation or negotiation is to reach a fair and reasonable settlement acceptable to both spouses and the court. In 1981, Roger Fisher and William Ury wrote the widely acclaimed book on negotiation, *Getting to Yes*. Fisher and Ury believe negotiation leads to a highly desirable win-win situation.

If you and your spouse decide to negotiate, pick a neutral meeting place, such as a coffee shop or restaurant. Do not meet in the marital home or one of the spouse's workplace and under no circumstances should the children be present. Before meeting, you and your spouse should draw up an agenda, focusing first on issues requiring immediate attention such as payment of joint bills and access to the children. In our experience, settlement discussions are more productive if conducted over several sessions. Plan to meet at least an hour or two during each session.

After you reach an agreement on short term issues, develop a list of the remaining issues for the next few sessions. For example, include matters relating to custody and visitation. Then deal with financial issues. Custody and child support discussions may overlap, but try focusing on a single issue such as the importance of your children spending time with each parent. Younger children may need shorter, but more frequent visits with the move-away parent. Older children tend to do better with longer, less frequent visits. Adolescents often want time with friends and school activities away from both parents. When you reach an accord on custody and visitation, then discuss the children's expenses and child support.

Negotiation takes time and patience, so be prepared to meet over several weeks or months. Use the time to try out custodial and visitation schedules, for example, and do not hesitate to fine tune your agreement. Make notes during your meetings, especially on key points of agreement. Share your notes with your spouse. You may be able to reinforce points of agreement or find out whether you still have any differences.

Settlement Checklist and Sample Agreement

Form H in appendix B contains a checklist of possible topics for consideration, as well as a completed sample Settlement/Separation Agreement to familiarize you with the form and language often used by lawyers and judges. A blank Settlement/Separation Agreement (Form 8) may be found in appendix C, which you may use "as is," or to develop your own agreement.

5 Uncontested Divorce

An uncontested divorce may be based on either no-fault or fault grounds. The fault ground is usually *cruel and abusive treatment*. The advantage to a fault divorce ground is timing. It is faster than a no-fault divorce. The disadvantage is you need to tell the judge about your spouse's cruel and abusive treatment. The no-fault procedure takes longer, but you may prefer delay over talking about your problems in court. In this chapter we first discuss the uncontested no-fault divorce, then explain the differences involved in a fault divorce.

Uncontested No-Fault Divorce

Preparing Documents

For an uncontested no-fault divorce (commonly known as a "One-A" divorce, as it is based on provisions found in section 1A of Chapter 208 of the Massachusetts General Laws), you need the following documents:

- ❑ Certified copy of your marriage certificate with a raised seal.
- ❑ Joint Petition for Divorce Under M.G.L. Ch. 208, Sec. 1A (Form 1), signed by you and your spouse or your attorneys.
- ❑ Joint Affidavit Under M.G.L. Ch. 208, Sec. 1A (Form 2), signed by both parties and notarized.

- ❑ Your FINANCIAL STATEMENT (Form 5 or Form 6), sometimes called "Form 401," currently dated and signed by you. Use Form 5 (the short form) printed on pink paper if you make less than $75,000 per year. If you make $75,000 or more, use Form 6 (the long form) printed on purple paper.
- ❑ Your spouse's FINANCIAL STATEMENT, also on the pink or purple Form 401, currently dated and signed by your spouse.
- ❑ Affidavit Disclosing Care or Custody Proceedings, if you have children under eighteen, signed by you or your spouse. Obtain this form from the court clerk.
- ❑ CHILD SUPPORT GUIDELINES WORKSHEET (Form 4), if you have dependent children under the age of twenty-three, on blue paper.
- ❑ SETTLEMENT/SEPARATION AGREEMENT (Form 8), signed by you and your spouse, in the presence of a notary.
- ❑ INCOME ASSIGNMENT WORKSHEET (Form 7).
- ❑ REQUEST FOR TRIAL—PRE-TRIAL ASSIGNMENT (Form 9), signed by you, your spouse, or your attorney.
- ❑ CERTIFICATE OF ABSOLUTE DIVORCE OR ANNULMENT (Form 25).
- ❑ Bank check or money order in the amount of $110 (no personal checks), made payable to the Register of the appropriate county Probate and Family Court (for example: "Register of Essex County Probate and Family Court"). If you cannot pay the filing fee, see chapter 3.

Sample completed forms and instructions are provided in appendix B. Blank forms are provided in appendix C. Many are standard forms, which means they can also be obtained from the court at no cost.

FILING DOCUMENTS

Upon completion of the required documents, file papers in person or by mail at the appropriate county divorce court. See the section on "Filing

Your Forms" in chapter 3 for more information about how and where to file papers.

After you file all of the papers, including your REQUEST FOR TRIAL—PRE-TRIAL ASSIGNMENT (Form 9), the court schedules your case for a hearing within four to eight weeks, depending on the county. You and your spouse will receive written notice approximately two weeks before the hearing, telling you the time, date, and place of your hearing.

YOUR COURT APPEARANCE

Both you and your spouse should appear for the court hearing. Behave courteously to everyone, including your spouse, and dress in a businesslike manner. For more information on courtroom etiquette, see "Tips for the Courtroom" in chapter 6.

If, one spouse is unavailable because of work or illness, and the court may excuse the presence of that party. The more prudent practice is for both parties to appear or to send an attorney for the absent party. The attorney, however, cannot testify or agree to any last minute changes to the SETTLEMENT/SEPARATION AGREEMENT (Form 8) the court may want.

Many people are astonished to learn that occasionally a court comes across an agreement it will not accept. For example, if the husband gives the house to the wife in exchange for her agreement not to pursue him for child support, the court may refuse to accept the agreement. Children are entitled to support from both parents and neither parent has the right to bargain away the children's support rights.

The judge usually reviews all of your divorce papers in the courtroom while you and your spouse stand in front of him or her. If the wife has a lawyer, judges usually request the wife's lawyer to *examine* the witness under oath, that is, to pose questions to the wife about the marriage, all of which may be answered by referring to the information in the first four paragraphs of the JOINT PETITION UNDER M.G.L. CH. 208, SEC. 1A (Form 1). Some judges insist that the party whose name appears first on the petition answer the basic questions.

The oral examination of the wife or husband is conducted by one party's attorney (unless you both appear pro se, in which case the judge asks all of the questions), and is based on the information that appears on your joint petition. The following are typical questions:

- ☛ "Please state your name."
- ☛ "State your address."
- ☛ "Are you married to the co-petitioner John/Jane Doe?"
- ☛ "Does John/Jane Doe reside at _____________?"
- ☛ "When were you married to John/Jane Doe?"
- ☛ "Where were you married?"
- ☛ "When did you last live together?"
- ☛ "Where did you last live together?"
- ☛ "Are there any minor children?"
- ☛ "What are the children's names and dates of birth?"
- ☛ "Do you believe your marriage is irretrievably broken?"
- ☛ "Is there no chance of reconciliation?"
- ☛ "Have you entered into a settlement agreement?"

If a lawyer is asking these questions, some judges take over the questioning and ask both parties the following types of questions:

- ☛ "Have you executed a separation agreement?"
- ☛ "Have you read it?"
- ☛ "Do you understand it?"
- ☛ "Do you believe that it is fair and reasonable?"
- ☛ "Did you sign it voluntarily?"

- "Did you give your spouse complete and accurate information on your financial statement?"
- "Do you believe your spouse gave you complete and accurate information on his/her financial statement?"
- "Did you have a chance to review the agreement with a lawyer?" (**Note:** this does not ask you if you actually did have a lawyer review it, but only whether you could have had a lawyer review it if you so desired.)

The judge may also ask the attorney to summarize the terms of the agreement. If both parties appear without an attorney, the judge may ask you or your spouse questions about your marriage, and questions such as:

- "Did you divide the property?"
- "Who gets the house?"
- "How much child support and/or alimony is to be paid?"
- "Who provides medical insurance?"
- "What are the child custody arrangements?"
- "Does the agreement survive or merge with the judgment?" (This is a highly technical way of asking whether your agreement is more or less difficult to modify by future court order. Surviving agreements are more difficult to change by court order than merging agreements. Courts sometimes allow certain parts of the agreement to survive and other parts to merge. Generally speaking, property divisions survive. Child-related issues should merge. You may decide, however, whether alimony provisions survive or merge. An illustrative reply: "Our agreement survives, except for child related issues, your Honor." Alternatively, "The entire agreement merges" or "The entire agreement survives." The distinction between

surviving and merging agreements is irrelevant, if you and your former spouse agree on future changes.)

The judge asks women whether they wish to resume use of their maiden or former married name, since divorce judges have the authority to allow resumption of the former name as part of the divorce proceedings. If you did not check off the box on your divorce petition requesting use of a former name, file a MOTION TO AMEND COMPLAINT (Form 13) to change your name officially, if you want to do so on the day of the hearing.

To complete the MOTION TO AMEND COMPLAINT (Form 13): Fill in the case caption according to the instructions in chapter 3, check the first box after the paragraph beginning "Now comes the plaintiff...;" check the first box after the paragraph beginning "Wherefore" and type in the full name you want. Then complete the date, signature, name, address, and telephone information at the bottom of the form. By custom you are allowed to use any name you want without a court order, so long as you do not intend to defraud a creditor, but to avoid problems, obtain copies of the order from the court for various agencies such as the Social Security Administration.

At the hearing, the court enters a written order, approves your settlement agreement, and finds there is an "irretrievable breakdown" of your marriage. The court sends you or your lawyer a copy of the order and findings—but you are not divorced yet.

WAITING FOR YOUR FINAL DIVORCE JUDGMENT

As previously explained, you must wait 120 days for a final divorce judgment in an uncontested no-fault case (ninety days in all other cases). You are not required to return to court or take any further action to obtain a final judgment. It happens automatically on the 121st day (assuming it is a business day) following your divorce hearing. The court does not send a copy of the final judgment unless you send a letter to the "Copy Department" of the county Probate and Family Court, along with a bank check or money order in the amount of $10 made payable to the Register of the appropriate county Probate and Family Court.

Enclose a self-addressed stamped envelope and refer to your case by its official name (e.g., "Mary Doe and John Doe"), and docket number. Massachusetts, like most states, does not require a written divorce judgment upon application for a marriage certificate, but most people want copies in their possession for future reference.

Uncontested Fault Divorce

If you decided to use a fault ground for divorce, you need to prepare the following documents:

- ❑ Certified copy of your marriage certificate with raised seal.
- ❑ Complaint for Divorce (Form 10), signed by you or your attorney.
- ❑ Domestic Relations Summons, with your spouse's acceptance of service or sheriff's return of service. Obtain this form from the court clerk.
- ❑ Answer and Counterclaim (Form 14) (optional), signed by your spouse.
- ❑ Your Financial Statement (Form 5 or Form 6), sometimes called "Form 401," currently dated and signed by you. Use Form 5 (the short form) printed on pink paper if you make less than $75,000 per year. If you make $75,000 or more, use Form 6 (the long form) printed on purple paper.
- ❑ Your spouse's Financial Statement, also on the pink or purple Form 401, currently dated and signed by your spouse.
- ❑ An Affidavit Disclosing Care or Custody Proceedings, if you have children under eighteen, signed by you or your spouse. Obtain this form from the court clerk.

- ❑ SETTLEMENT/SEPARATION AGREEMENT (Form 8), signed by you and your spouse before a notary.
- ❑ CHILD SUPPORT GUIDELINES WORKSHEET (Form 4),on blue paper, if you have dependent children under the age of 23.
- ❑ INCOME ASSIGNMENT WORKSHEET (Form 7).
- ❑ REQUEST FOR TRIAL—PRE-TRIAL ASSIGNMENT (Form 9), signed by you, your spouse, or your attorney.
- ❑ CERTIFICATE OF ABSOLUTE DIVORCE OR ANNULMENT (Form 25).
- ❑ Bank check or money order in the amount of $111, made payable to the Register of the appropriate county Probate and Family Court (the additional $1 is for the Domestic Relations Summons). If you cannot pay the fees, see chapter 3.

At the hearing, the court expects testimony from the plaintiff (the spouse who signed and filed the complaint for divorce). In almost every aspect, the testimony follows the format outlined under the no-fault divorce section above with the exception of your reason or ground for divorce. After the preliminary questions about the parties, children, the date of the marriage, and when and where you last lived together the next question and response are:

Question: Directing your attention to the date you last lived together, please tell the court what happened to cause the break-up of the marriage.

Answer: We argued. My spouse came home at 2:00 a.m. I had no idea where my spouse was. For weeks before the separation my spouse continued staying out late and would return home screaming, throwing things at me, and hitting me. I couldn't sleep and lost twenty pounds over a three week period just before we separated. I felt so bad I couldn't go to work or do my errands.

The court or a lawyer for one of the parties then resumes asking questions about the agreement as outlined in the preceding no-fault divorce section.

SUMMARY

Uncontested divorces by definition leave nothing for the judge to resolve because you and your spouse have reached an agreement on all of the issues relating to your marriage and divorce. The judge's role is to determine the fairness of the agreement and whether you have stated a case for divorce. If the agreement is acceptable and you present sufficient facts to warrant a finding of divorce, the court enters the appropriate orders and judgment dissolving your marriage.

When you cannot agree, you may need judicial help and guidance in dealing with such matters as custody, visitation and finances as outlined in the next chapter on contested divorces, i.e., any divorce action without a signed settlement agreement.

Contested Divorce 6

At least eighty percent of all divorces settle without a trial, but until you reach a settlement prepare your case as if you were going to trial. Keep negotiating, but get ready for trial.

Getting Started

File your fault or no-fault COMPLAINT FOR DIVORCE (Form 10) in person or by mail at the Probate and Family Court in the appropriate county. See the section on "Filing Your Forms" in chapter 3 on how and where to file. File the following documents:

- ❑ Certified copy of your marriage certificate with a raised seal.
- ❑ COMPLAINT FOR DIVORCE (Form 10), signed by you or your attorney.
- ❑ Your FINANCIAL STATEMENT (Form 5 or Form 6), sometimes called "Form 401," currently dated and signed by you, if you need immediate temporary orders relating to finances. Use Form 5 (the short form) printed on pink paper if you make less than $75,000 per year. If you make $75,000 or more, use Form 6 (the long form) printed on purple paper.

- ❑ An Affidavit Disclosing Care or Custody Proceedings, if you have children under eighteen, with your signature. Obtain this form from the court clerk.
- ❑ Bank check or money order in the amount of $111 (no personal checks), made payable to the Register of the appropriate county Probate and Family Court (for example: "Register of Essex County Probate and Family Court").

Whether you file papers in person or by mail, the court issues a Domestic Relations Summons with the county's raised seal (obtain from the court clerk). We suggest filing papers in person to find out whether your forms are completed properly or what you need to do.

SERVING PAPERS

PERSONAL SERVICE

Personal service is having your divorce papers personally delivered to your spouse by a deputy sheriff. After you receive the Domestic Relations Summons:

1. Fill in the names of the parties, docket number, and other information (see sample completed Form F in appendix B).
2. Mail or deliver the official Domestic Relations Summons and a copy of your COMPLAINT FOR DIVORCE (Form 10) to the deputy sheriff's office in the county where your spouse lives.

Within forty-five days after the delivery of the Summons each party must send the other party a copy of his or her FINANCIAL STATEMENT (Form 5 or Form 6), and file the original with the court.

ALTERNATE SERVICE

The procedure for serving papers is different if you do not know where your spouse lives, or if your spouse lives outside Massachusetts. In these situations you must use the following procedure:

1. File a MOTION FOR ALTERNATE SERVICE (Form 16). To complete Form 16, first complete the case caption according to the

instructions in chapter 3. In paragraph 1, type in the names of the city or town, county, and state where you were married; and the street address, city or town, and county where you and your spouse last lived together in Massachusetts. At the bottom of the page, type in the date, sign on the line marked "Signature of Party or Attorney," and type in your name, address, and telephone number below the signature line.

2. After the hearing, get a Domestic Relations Summons from the clerk, and a legal notice from the court for publication.
3. Send the legal notice to the newspaper designated by the judge. Remit payment to the newspaper. Fees vary, depending on the newspaper. The Boston Globe charges several hundred dollars, whereas the Newton Tab charges $150.00. Instruct the newspaper to publish the notice once a week for three weeks. Ask for clippings of the published notice to be sent to you.
4. On receipt of the clippings, return the summons and clippings to the court, by mail or in person. Keep photocopies of all of the papers sent to the court.
5. Send a copy of your COMPLAINT FOR DIVORCE (Form 10) and Domestic Relations Summons to your spouse's last known address by certified mail, return receipt requested.
6. File the original green return receipt card with the court. Be sure to keep a photocopy for your file. If your spouse does not claim the item, let the court know on the original Domestic Relations Summons by stating under the Return of Service section that you mailed copies by certified mail, but the copies were returned unclaimed.

Financial Disclosure

Both parties must provide certain financial information to each other within forty-five days after the Summons has been served. Each party must prepare a FINANCIAL STATEMENT (Form 5 or Form 6) within forty-five days of receiving the Summons. Send a copy to your spouse and file the original with the court. Keep a copy for your file.

In addition to the FINANCIAL STATEMENT, each party is required by to deliver the following documents to the other within forty-five days of service of the Summons:

- The parties' federal and state income tax returns and schedules for the past three years, and any non-public, limited partnership, and privately held corporate tax returns for any entity in which either party has an interest, together with all supporting documentation for tax returns, including but not limited to W-2s, 1099s, 1098s, K-1, Schedule C, and Schedule E.
- Statements, for the past three years, for all bank accounts held in the name of either party, individually or jointly, or in the name of another person for the benefit of either party, or held by either party for the benefit of the parties' minor children.
- The four most recent paystubs from each employer for whom you worked.
- Documentation regarding the cost and nature of available health insurance.
- Statements, for the past three years, for any securities, stocks, bonds, notes, and obligations, certificates of deposit owned or held by either party or held by either party for the benefit of the parties' minor children, 401Ks, IRAs, and pension plans listed on the FINANCIAL STATEMENT.

- Copies of any loan or mortgage applications made, prepared, or submitted by either party within the three years prior to the filing of the Complaint for Divorce.
- Copies of any financial statement, or statement of assets and liabilities, prepared by either party within the three years prior to the filing of the Complaint for Divorce.

Under certain circumstances, you may deviate from these requirements. For example, if you need additional time, or do not need all of the documents listed above, you and your spouse can enter into a written agreement to extend the forty-five day deadline, or eliminate providing certain documents. If your spouse will not agree to an extension, you may file a sworn statement with the court (be sure to send a copy to your spouse), stating that you do not have the required document and cannot obtain the document within forty-five days. You must identify the specific documents you cannot produce, the reasons they are unavailable, and what steps you have taken to try to obtain them. As more information becomes available, you must provide it to your spouse.

You may *not* ask the court for any further assistance with discovery if you have not complied with these requirements.

RESPONDING TO A COMPLAINT FOR DIVORCE

If you are the defendant in the divorce proceeding, meaning your spouse filed first, file a written ANSWER AND COUNTERCLAIM (Form 14) within twenty days of receiving the Summons and COMPLAINT FOR DIVORCE. Only an "Answer" is required, but you may want to file counterclaims for divorce too.

Regardless of whether you file an Answer, you will not be defaulted. Nevertheless, we advise filing an Answer, and a Counterclaim, to protect your rights. In addition to the ANSWER AND COUNTERCLAIM, the court often requires a defendant without a lawyer (called a *pro se defendant*) to file a NOTICE OF APPEARANCE (Form 15). This form lets the court know you are representing yourself, and your address and phone number. (See sample completed forms in appendix B.) Under court rules, you must prepare a FINANCIAL STATEMENT (Form 5 or Form 6) within forty-five days of receiving the Summons. Send a copy to your spouse and file the original with the court. Keep a copy for your file.

In addition to exchanging the FINANCIAL STATEMENT within you also need to comply with the disclosure requirements listed above in the section on "Financial Disclosure."

TEMPORARY ORDERS: THE MOTION SESSION

All of the Probate and Family Courts in Massachusetts have a waiting list for divorce trials, but most people cannot wait for support, custody, or visitation, so courts allow parties to obtain interim or temporary orders before trial. These requests are referred to as *motions for temporary orders*, and the court proceedings as *motion sessions*, although they are also known as *ex parte sessions*.

Motion sessions are typically used for court orders for:

- Temporary support (Form 20).
- Temporary visitation or custody (Form 20).
- Abuse prevention (Form 27).
- Restraining orders on marital assets (Form 22).
- Maintenance of insurance benefits (Form 20).

The first court appearance is at a motion session many months before trial. You will need to sign up or ask the motions clerk, sometimes called the *ex parte clerk*, to schedule a hearing date. You will be notified of the hearing date by mail or telephone, depending upon your county.

After you receive your hearing date, notify your spouse about the date [see the certificate of service section on the MOTION FOR TEMPORARY ORDERS OF CUSTODY, SUPPORT, AND MAINTENANCE OF INSURANCE BENEFITS (Form 20)] and provide your spouse with a copy of your motion. Generally you may "give notice" by using first class mail to your spouse's home address. Do not use a private mail service such as FedEx or Airborne Express because courts do not recognize the validity of such notice. Give at least ten days' prior notice by mail, or seven days' prior notice if a deputy sheriff or constable delivers the papers to your spouse. Make sure you follow these rules. If not, your spouse may choose not to attend the hearing with impunity, since the judge may refuse to hear your motion, because you failed to follow the rules.

A sample MOTION FOR TEMPORARY ORDERS OF CUSTODY, SUPPORT, AND MAINTENANCE OF INSURANCE BENEFITS (Form 20) and AFFIDAVIT IN SUPPORT OF MOTION FOR TEMPORARY ORDERS OF CUSTODY, SUPPORT, AND MAINTENANCE OF INSURANCE BENEFITS (Form 21) are included as Form K and Form L in appendix B. Blank versions of these forms are included in appendix C.

If your spouse does not file a FINANCIAL STATEMENT (Form 5 or Form 6), prepare a DEMAND FOR FINANCIAL STATEMENT UNDER SUPPLEMENTAL RULE 401 (Form 3). To complete Form 3: Fill in the case caption according to the instructions in chapter 3. On the first line in the first paragraph, type in the name of the county where you filed your COMPLAINT FOR DIVORCE. On the other lines, type in your mailing address. Complete the date, signature and other information required at the bottom of the page, and sign the form.

Mail the DEMAND FOR FINANCIAL STATEMENT UNDER SUPPLEMENTAL RULE 401 (Form 3) to your spouse and keep a copy for your files. Under court rules, your spouse is required to send a financial statement on the court's form within ten days. If you do not receive a copy, file a MOTION

TO COMPEL PRODUCTION AND ORDER FOR SANCTIONS (Form 26). Schedule a hearing with the clerk, as outlined above, and send your spouse a copy of the motion (be sure to fill in the certificate of service section with the time, date, and place of the court hearing. Advance notice is required as with other motions, meaning at least ten days' prior notice by mail, or seven days if delivered by sheriff or constable.

Some of the most common requests for temporary orders involve abuse prevention orders, sometimes referred to as *temporary restraining orders* because one party is restrained from abusing the other. Other temporary restraining orders prohibit or restrain your spouse from selling marital assets or depleting bank accounts (see Form 22). You or your spouse may also ask for temporary orders of custody, visitation, support, and a wide range of other relief on a temporary basis, including maintenance of medical and life insurance coverage. Courts do not order the sale of marital homes at this early stage.

Document Checklist for Temporary Orders

Nonemergency Cases with Notice to Your Spouse:

Tip: Call the motions clerk of the county probate and family court where you file your papers (depending on where you and your spouse last lived together and where you now live). Ask whether you request a hearing in writing or by telephone.

- ❑ Certified copy of civil marriage certificate.
- ❑ Complaint for Divorce (Form 10).
- ❑ Filing Fee of $111 or Motion to Proceed in Forma Pauperis (Form 17) and Affidavit of Indigency and Request for Waiver, Substitution or State Payment of Fees and Costs (Form 18), and possibly a Supplement to Affidavit of Indigency (Form 19).
- ❑ Domestic Relations Summons with spouse's acceptance of service or sheriff's return of service. Obtain this form from the court clerk.
- ❑ Husband's Financial Statement (Form 5 or Form 6). Form 5 on pink paper if income less than $75,000 per year. Form 6 on purple paper if income is $75,000 or more.
- ❑ Wife's Financial Statement (Form 5 or Form 6). On appropriate form and color (see above).
- ❑ Affidavit Disclosing Care or Custody Proceedings. Obtain this form from the court clerk.
- ❑ Child Support Guidelines Worksheet (Form 4), printed two-sided on blue paper (this can also be obtained from the register).
- ❑ Motion for Temporary Orders of Custody, Support, and Maintenance of Insurance Benefits (Form 20).
- ❑ Affidavit in Support of Motion for Temporary Orders of Custody, Support, and Maintenance of Insurance Benefits (Form 21).
- ❑ Request for Hearing (this is simply your letter asking the court to schedule a hearing on the first available date).

Emergency Cases without Notice to Your Spouse:

Tip: In an emergency (such as your spouse threatening to withdraw all of the money from a joint checking account), walk into the courthouse and ask an assistant register for a hearing that day in front of the judge.

- ❑ COMPLAINT FOR DIVORCE (Form 10).
- ❑ MOTION TO DELAY FILING OF MARRIAGE CERTIFICATE (Form 11), if you do not have a certified copy that day.
- ❑ MOTION FOR TEMPORARY ORDERS OF CUSTODY, SUPPORT, AND MAINTENANCE OF INSURANCE BENEFITS (Form 20), for custody and medical benefits, but not for alimony or child support.
- ❑ AFFIDAVIT IN SUPPORT OF MOTION FOR TEMPORARY ORDERS OF CUSTODY, SUPPORT, AND MAINTENANCE OF INSURANCE BENEFITS (Form 21).
- ❑ Affidavit Disclosing Care or Custody Proceedings. Obtain from the register.
- ❑ Filing fee of $111. If you cannot pay the filing fee, prepare a MOTION TO PROCEED IN FORMA PAUPERIS (Form 17) and an AFFIDAVIT OF INDIGENCY AND REQUEST FOR WAIVER, SUBSTITUTION OR STATE PAYMENT OF FEES AND COSTS (Form 18), and possibly a SUPPLEMENT TO AFFIDAVIT OF INDIGENCY (Form 19).
- ❑ COMPLAINT FOR PROTECTION FROM ABUSE (Form 27), in case of physical abuse, and the supporting AFFIDAVIT (Form 28).
- ❑ MOTION TO PRESERVE MARITAL ASSETS WITHOUT NOTICE TO SPOUSE (Form 22).
- ❑ AFFIDAVIT IN SUPPORT OF MOTION TO PRESERVE MARITAL ASSETS (Form 23).

If custody and visitation are contested, the court often appoints a guardian *ad litem* for the children. The guardian *ad litem* is usually a lawyer or mental health professional responsible for interviewing the parents, children, and other interested people, and for reporting to the court. If the court determines that you or your spouse can pay the guardian *ad litem*, the court orders you or your spouse to pay the fees. If neither of you can pay, the state assumes responsibility.

Courtroom Demeanor and Dress

You are now ready to make your first court appearance at the motion session. Dress in a business-like manner. Women should keep make-up to a minimum and men should wear a tie and jacket. Your appointed time is the same as all of the other cases; typically everyone is expected to be in the courtroom by 9:30 a.m., although many courts start as early as 8:30 a.m., so check with the clerk's office, or follow the special instructions on any court notices you receive.

Courthouse Mediation: Family Services

Arrive on time, go to the courtroom, and check in with the clerk. As soon as your spouse arrives and checks in, the clerk sends both of you to the family service office for *mediation*. Some courts order you directly to family services, bypassing the check-in with the clerk.

If you and your spouse are represented by lawyers, the family service officer usually speaks with the lawyers first, and then speaks with the parties without counsel. If neither party has a lawyer and the family service officer helps you and your spouse reach an agreement, the family service office writes a *stipulation* for your signatures. If you have a lawyer, your lawyer prepares the stipulation. The judge reviews the signed stipulation, and if approved, the stipulation is turned into a temporary court order.

The Hearing

If you cannot resolve your differences with the family service officer, you return to the courtroom. You and your spouse wait until your case is called by the clerk. The judge listens to you, your spouse, and the family service officer, who usually makes a recommendation. The judge does not listen to sworn *testimony*, but listens to each party's opinion and reasons for or against the request for temporary orders. If you and your spouse are represented by counsel, the judge listens to the lawyers' arguments, and may ask you and your spouse to speak. If you have something to say, but are not invited to speak, ask the judge for permission—"Your Honor, may I please say something?"

When appearing before a judge or family service officer, follow these rules:

- Do not interrupt.

- Ask the judge/family service officer for permission to speak.
- Speak respectfully to everyone, including your spouse.
- Address the judge as "Your Honor," "Judge," or "the Court," and never as "you."

You may be tempted to interrupt when your spouse makes an inflammatory or false statement. You make a better impression if you wait until the judge invites you to respond. Write yourself a note while your spouse speaks, so you remember each of the contested points.

Often judges do not want to announce their decisions from the bench. They say they "will take the matter under advisement" and notify you by mail. The clerk usually sends copies of the judge's order within a few days. These orders are temporary in nature. After trial, the court enters "final orders," although no orders relating to children or spousal support are truly final (as we will discuss in chapter 7).

If you fail to obey a temporary order, you may be found in contempt of court. Chapter 7 discusses contempt proceedings in more detail.

Trial Preparation

The two major areas of disagreement during divorce are money and children, so trial preparation requires the collection and assessment of financial information and assessment of custody and visitation. Husbands and wives are required to make full and complete financial disclosure to each other.

Discovery. Court rules allow husbands and wives to look into, or *discover*, various aspects of each other's finances. There are primarily three ways to do this:

1. *Interrogatories*. Written questions to be answered in writing under oath.

2. *Request for Production of Documents.* A written demand for your spouse to give certain documents to you.

3. *Depositions.* Questions answered orally under oath (conducting a deposition is rather complicated, and is probably best left to an attorney).

Subpoenas may also be issued for documents in a party's possession or in the possession of a bank, employer, or other person or business. A standard set of INTERROGATORIES (Form 29) and a REQUEST FOR PRODUCTION OF DOCUMENTS (Form 30) are found in appendix C. Both of these forms are fairly simple to fill out. Complete the case caption according to the instructions in chapter 3, fill in the appropriate dates, names, etc., on the blank lines, and fill in the date, signature, and certificate of service sections at the end of the form. Mail a copy to your spouse. Your spouse is required to send you answers to the INTERROGATORIES in the time-frames stated on the form; and to appear at the time and place indicated to provide the documents in the REQUEST FOR PRODUCTION OF DOCUMENTS. If your spouse fails to do so, prepare a MOTION TO COMPEL PRODUCTION AND ORDER FOR SANCTIONS (Form 26).

Sometimes assets are hard to value or a spouse is hiding income. For example, if a woman owns a restaurant and does not report all of her income to the IRS, her husband may have a hard time finding out what she earns. If the husband owns antiques inherited from his grandparents, he may have no idea what they are worth. A cash business and hard-to-value property raise complex questions, so you may be wise to retain an attorney.

EXPERT WITNESSES

If you and your spouse own a house or have a pension, hire experts to appraise these assets. People often believe the present value of their pension is listed on an annual statement. Pensions must be valued by an actuary after reviewing annual statements, plan descriptions, and other relevant information. Pensions may be divided by the court using a *Qualified Domestic Relations Order* (or QDRO) under federal law.

Other expert witnesses, such as psychologists, may be asked to testify about your children. Sometimes a party may need a medical doctor to testify about a family member's medical needs, or an educator to present evidence on a child's special education needs.

Both parties should cooperate in the appraisal of the marital home. If not, the discovery process allows you to enter property for an inspection. Courts may impose sanctions on the uncooperative spouse, ranging from an assessment of fines to prohibiting him or her from challenging the spouse's valuation of the house.

Courts encourage parties to reach agreement on the value of assets, but few of us have the ability to value pensions, so consider hiring one actuary and sharing the cost for the pension appraisal. In some instances the expert also has the expertise to prepare the QDRO to meet all of the technical requirements of federal law.

Guardian ad Litem: The Children's Representative

The financial aspects of a case are troublesome, but nothing is more bitter than a difficult custody and visitation case. When confronted with hotly contested child-related issues, courts appoint lawyers and guardians *ad litem* for the children. A guardian *ad litem* may be a divorce lawyer or a mental health professional who speaks to the children, the parents, and other people such as teachers and pediatricians. Based on those interviews, the guardian *ad litem* writes a report and makes recommendations to the court on custody and visitation. The court gives considerable weight to these reports and recommendations, but in the final analysis the court makes the decision after all of the evidence is presented at trial.

Pre-Trial Conference and Pre-Trial Memorandum

If you have not reached a settlement by this time, ask the court to schedule a *pre-trial conference* (see Form 9), which is a mandatory meeting of you, your spouse, your lawyers (if any), and the judge.

Before your court date you must meet in person with your spouse and lawyers, if any. The meeting (sometimes called a "four-way" because the two parties and two lawyers meet) gives you a chance to settle the case before going to court. If you do not settle your case at this meeting, each party must file a written pre-trial memorandum on all of the issues for trial, along with a short outline of your proposed testimony, witnesses, and list of documents to be submitted as exhibits. See Form 30.

The following is an explanation of the pre-trial hearing and PRE-TRIAL MEMORANDUM (Form 31) process, reproduced here with the permission of the authors:

A *PRO SE* LITIGANT GUIDE TO DIVORCE PRE-TRIAL HEARINGS IN THE PROBATE AND FAMILY COURT

Honorable Nancy M. Gould, Associate Justice
Probate and Family Court

Peter F. Zupcofska, Esquire
Bingham, Dana & Gould, LLP

BASIC INFORMATION

You are a *pro se* litigant representing yourself without an attorney. A plaintiff or defendant who is *pro se* is representing himself or herself. The term is from the Latin meaning "for your self."

As a *pro se* litigant approaching the pre-trial hearing stage of your divorce, it is necessary to comply with rules of conduct, preparation of pleadings and rules of court to best further your own case. The laws of the Commonwealth require that although some leniency may be appropriate in determining whether a *pro se* through his of her pleading meets the requirements of the rules of court, nonetheless, the rules bind a *pro se* litigant as they bind any other litigant including those represented by counsel. For more detailed analysis of this issue see *Mmoe v. Commonwealth,* 393 Mass. 617 (1985).

PREPARING FOR A PRE-TRIAL

The pre-trial hearing is a very important procedural step in completing the divorce process in the Probate and Family Court. At this hearing you will be meeting with a judge who may provide you with insight into the law that will be applied to your case and the possible outcome of your case. To assess your case properly, the court needs necessary information regarding issues to be addressed in your divorce such as custody, visitation, child support, alimony, and division of assets.

To have this information available, it may be necessary to undertake what is called "Discovery." Discovery is your opportunity to discover facts, research the law and gather evidence to be presented at trial to prove your case. Among the documents you may want to include are hospital records, guardian *ad litem* report, tax returns, pay stubs, appraisals or any other critical personal or financial information regarding your particular needs and circumstances and also your spouse's needs and circumstances.

You have a duty to provide accurate financial information to your spouse and the court. Your divorce may require consideration of financial issues including dividing your property and possibly alimony (support of your spouse) and child support. Both parties in a divorce action need to provide each other with all relevant financial information requested by your spouse or by the court pursuant to the Massachusetts Rules of Domestic Relations Procedure pertaining to discovery, specifically Rules 28 through 45. In addition, you are required under Supplemental Rule 401 of the Probate Court to file a compilation of your financial information in the proscribed form of financial statement.

You will not gain anything by attempting to hide income and property information. Instead, such attempts may cause the judge to determine that you are in violation of court rules, resulting in potential sanctions being imposed or contempt judgments being issued.

EXPERTS, VALUATIONS, AND REPORTS

For the court to assess your case properly, third parties may need to be involved, such as psychologists, psychiatrists, social workers, or medical professionals, regarding issues of custody or domestic violence. Financial experts may be needed to provide information on the fair market value of real estate, valuation of a business, or valuation of retirement plans. All necessary experts should be retained prior to the pre-trial hearing. Further, the court may appoint a guardian *ad litem* or a probation officer to do an investigation. Make sure that report has been completed and filed with the court prior to the pre-trial hearing so that it may be available for the pre-trial hearing.

SETTLEMENT CONFERENCE

Prior to the pre-trial hearing date, you are required to participate in a settlement conference with your spouse and your spouse's counsel, if your spouse is represented. However, note: **IF THERE ARE ISSUES OF DOMESTIC ABUSE, YOU ARE NOT REQUIRED TO PARTICIPATE IN A SETTLEMENT CONFERENCE.**

You have a duty to be courteous to court staff, the judge, your spouse, and your spouse's lawyer. Parties to a divorce are often hurting, both emotionally and financially. Things may be said that upset you because you believe they are unfair or untrue. Court appearances are not an opportunity for venting, but rather an opportunity for a calm and courteous presentation of your important issues. The Court is aware that the statements made are only allegations that may not be true. The judge determines what are the facts. A calm, courteous, and respectful presentation of your case best furthers your interests before the court. Therefore, do not vent your frustrations on the court staff and do not interrupt your spouse, you spouse's lawyer, the judge or court designee when they are speaking in court. The judge will ensure that you have an opportunity to speak to the extent necessary.

THE PRE-TRIAL MEMORANDUM

To comply with the Probate Court's order regarding a pre-trial hearing, you must provide to the court and exchange with your spouse a Pre-Trial Memorandum detailing the present status of the case. Issues to be addressed in the [Pre-Trial] Memorandum include: discovery which may be necessary, exhibits you intend to introduce at trial, including financial information, information regarding custody and visitation that may be at issue, and a description of the events in your marriage. This information will provide the court with the information needed to make findings under Massachusetts General Laws, Chapter 208, Section 34 to determine any award of alimony and division of property. Available for your use is [a PRE-TRIAL MEMORANDUM (Form 31)].

Be mindful of the need to exchange the Pre-Trial Memorandum with your spouse and your spouse's counsel before the pre-trial hearing. In addition, you will be required to file an updated financial statement pursuant to Supplemental Rule 401. Arrive promptly for your pre-trial hearing.

You should be able to complete the PRE-TRIAL MEMORANDUM (Form 31) by following the instructions on the form itself. Some of the sections will not apply to your case. In those instances, simply fill in the words "Not applicable." When filling in Form 31, you do not need to write at great length. The judge needs one or two examples in each category. You do not win an argument be submitting a memorandum of greater length than your spouse.

The court may order an immediate trial on the day of the pre-trial conference if:

1. You and your spouse are the only witnesses; or
2. One party is not present; or
3. Trial is necessary in the judge's discretion "to accomplish justice."

In our experience, few judges order the parties to start trial on the day of the pre-trial conference. Most judges try to resolve the parties' differences and if there is no agreement at the end of the conference (sometimes lasting a few minutes or all day), then the judge sends you to the clerk to get a trial date.

In Middlesex County, however, Judge Ginsburg is well known for starting trial on the same day, so be prepared to try your case. Have all of your documents (including copies for your spouse) ready to offer as exhibits, know what you plan on saying when you are on the witness stand, and what questions you want to ask your spouse when your spouse is on the stand. We suggest calling the assistant register as soon as you get your pre-trial assignment to find out what your judge expects on the day of the pre-trial conference.

Not surprisingly, many cases settle just before or during the pre-trial conference. If you and your spouse go through the process of meeting and then drafting a pre-trial memorandum, you may discover your differences are not insurmountable, or you may begin to see the strengths of your spouse's arguments. Judges are also helpful in pointing out what you and your spouse may realistically expect at the end of a trial.

You should also bring a MOTION TO AMEND COMPLAINT (Form 13), and a proposed SETTLEMENT/SEPARATION AGREEMENT (Form 8), to use for any final settlement you may reach at the end of the conference. If you do reach an agreement, fill out the MOTION TO AMEND COMPLAINT (Form 13) by completing the case caption, checking the second box after the paragraph beginning "Now come the plaintiff...," checking the second box after the paragraph beginning "Wherefore," and filling in the date, name, address, and telephone information. This form will be filed along with the SETTLEMENT/SEPARATION AGREEMENT (Form 8). You may then complete your case according to the instructions in chapter 5 for the uncontested no-fault divorce, by filing a JOINT PETITION UNDER M.G.L. Ch. 208, Sec. 1A (Form 1), along with any other forms outlined in chapter 5.

TIPS FOR THE COURTROOM

Most people are familiar with courtrooms as shown on television and in movies. In reality, you find few divorce cases are neatly encapsulated in a few key lines of testimony as in the film *Kramer v. Kramer*. You are more likely to encounter the "buzz and mumble," as one lawyer describes typical courtroom exchanges.

You speak to a judge, not a jury. All divorce proceedings are tape recorded, but the sound quality of audio tapes is poor, hence, some parties prefer the services of a private court reporter hired at their own expense. Court reporters charge approximately $125 a day for court appearances and charge by the page for the transcript they produce. Expect to pay several hundred dollars or more for each day's transcript. Parties order transcripts for appeals—expensive, lengthy proceedings.

When testifying in court, speak audibly and clearly for the judge and court reporter. Never nod when answering a question. Answer verbally. Do not use "mm-hm" and "mm-mm" for "yes" and "no." The court reporter will need to stop the proceedings to ask whether you mean "yes" or "no." Do not interrupt another speaker, not only for civility's sake, but for the court reporter who cannot transcribe more than one speaker at a time.

Divorce trials may take an hour or many weeks. A typical divorce trial takes approximately two to three days. If your case is scheduled for trial, we recommend retaining an attorney as soon as possible, although by law you are entitled to represent yourself.

The following is a checklist of documents you should have on file, in addition to those listed earlier in this chapter. Some documents should be updated periodically, such as the FINANCIAL STATEMENTS which cannot be dated more than thirty days' prior to your trial and the CHILD SUPPORT GUIDELINE WORKSHEET which should be updated to reflect information on the most current financial statements.

- ❑ REQUEST FOR TRIAL—PRE-TRIAL ASSIGNMENT (Form 9). At this stage, ask for a trial.
- ❑ INCOME ASSIGNMENT WORKSHEET (Form 7)
- ❑ MOTION TO AMEND COMPLAINT (Form 13) (optional)
- ❑ Updated FINANCIAL STATEMENTS (Form 5 or Form 6)
- ❑ Updated CHILD SUPPORT GUIDELINES WORKSHEET (Form 4)

The following is an overview of the divorce trial, without the rules of evidence and procedure. Your divorce will be heard by a probate court judge who hears the witnesses, decides who is telling the truth, and applies the divorce laws to your case. There are no juries in divorce cases.

Most divorces involve few witnesses. Usually the husband and wife testify on the fifteen factors in the Massachusetts divorce law, Chapter 208, Section 34 of the Massachusetts General Laws, which are:

1. length of the marriage.
2. standard of living or station in life.

3. conduct of the parties during the marriage.
4. occupation.
5. age.
6. amount and sources of income.
7. health.
8. vocational skills and education.
9. employability.
10. assets (sometimes called your *marital estate*).
11. liabilities and needs.
12. opportunity to acquire future assets and income.
13. contributions to acquisition, preservation, and appreciation of assets.
14. homemaker contributions.
15. unmet needs of the dependent children.

If custody and visitation are contested, prepare testimony on your observations as to the children's behavior when they are with you (good physical and emotional health, good academic performance, friendly, energetic, well behaved) and after they have been with your spouse (perhaps upset, unable to sleep, acting out with siblings, a decline in academic performance, etc.).

You may be fairly creative in presenting evidence concerning the children, because the courts are willing to hear any evidence so long as it relates to the best interest of the children. For example, you may want to testify about a typical day with the children, starting with your waking them, having breakfast, arriving at school on time, meeting them after school or describing childcare provisions, attending soccer, doing errands, making dinner, supervising homework, and getting ready for bed.

The court probably appointed a guardian *ad litem* to investigate and make recommendations on custody and visitation. If the recommendations favor your side, then call the guardian *ad litem* as your witness. If you contest the recommendations, hire your own expert witness such as a child psychologist.

Child support is determined by the calculations you do on the CHILD SUPPORT GUIDELINES WORKSHEET (Form 4). Courts generally do not deviate from the calculations, but you have room to argue for more money where you believe the children have special and costly needs or if you believe your spouse is underreporting income. You have the burden of proof, meaning you must present solid evidence about the children's needs or your spouse's real income.

If the children's needs are an issue, you may want an expert witness. If hidden or underreported income is an issue, present copies of your spouse's credit card statements and canceled checks, showing your spouse's spending far exceeds stated income. If not bankrupt, your spouse has more money available than disclosed on court documents.

If there are questions about the value of pensions and real estate, each party may hire actuaries and real estate appraisers as expert witnesses. Other experts testify about tax matters, the economic value of a homemaker, medical issues, and any other matter important to your case. If the parties also contest custody, the guardian *ad litem* may testify, in addition to psychological experts hired by each party. After the judge hears all of the evidence, the usual case is taken under advisement; that is, the judge ends the trial, but takes time to sift through the material before writing a judgment, orders, and miscellaneous supporting documents.

The written judgment and orders will be sent by mail to the parties or their attorneys. By law you have thirty days from the date of the judgment to file an appeal. Few people appeal divorce judgments because the cost of an appeal can add at least $15,000 in fees and expenses. Furthermore, few divorce judgments are overturned.

As an alternative to the costly, uncertain appeal process, some people wait for a significant change in their lives, then file a complaint for modification, asking the divorce court to alter or modify the original judgment because of the material change.

Summary

Divorce is not necessarily an end. It can become the starting point for new disagreements and court battles for parties, leading to contempt of court actions, motions for reconsideration, and requests to remove the minor children from Massachusetts. The next chapter discusses these proceedings in more detail.

7 Special Circumstances

While your case is pending, you may have *temporary orders*. If these orders are violated, the aggrieved party may bring a *complaint for contempt* which asks the court to compel compliance with the order. If you disagree with any temporary orders, you may bring a *motion for reconsideration* before the same judge who issued the original order, asking the judge to reconsider his or her decision. Finally, if you want to move out of state with minor children, you must request permission from the court.

Contempts

A common area of disagreement is child support. Failure to pay sometimes happens after the court issues temporary orders, but before the parties are divorced, so contempt actions are appropriate while your divorce is pending. The contempt procedure allows the aggrieved party, the plaintiff, to file a complaint for contempt to collect the arrearages and attorneys fees. There is no filing fee for contempt actions. The court issues a summons with a preassigned trial date. The plaintiff is responsible for hiring a deputy sheriff or constable to serve the original summons and copy of the complaint. The deputy mails the summons to the plaintiff along with *return of service*, a sworn statement that the papers were served, and the plaintiff is responsible for filing the summons and return of service with the court.

The accused, usually referred to as the *defendant*, may contend that he cannot pay the support under the temporary order because he lost his job or suffered a decline in income. The defendant files a written answer to the complaint for contempt, and must mail a copy to the plaintiff. The answer is a legal document following certain formalities, but essentially denies the allegations or provides a legally sufficient excuse for non-compliance.

If you file a contempt action, you will want a speedy hearing, and under current practice, your case will be scheduled for trial within a matter of four to five weeks. Courts acknowledge the need for a quick hearing when a woman claims she is not receiving her court ordered support or a father reports that he is denied visitation.

If a party is found in contempt, the judge may order payment of the winning party's attorneys fees and costs. Often the court allows the party in contempt to make installment payments on the arrearages, or orders immediate access to children in visitation disputes. In cases of repeated and willful noncompliance, the defendant may face incarceration.

If you are presenting a contempt for nonpayment of support, sometimes described as *prosecuting a contempt action*, you must prove all of the following facts:

1. The payor knew the support order was issued, usually because payor was present when the court entered the order, or because the order was sent to the payor.
2. The payor had the income available to pay.
3. The payor did not pay.
4. You kept records of what you were owed under the order, and what you received.

If you are defending yourself against contempt charges for nonpayment, you may be able to avoid being held in contempt if you can satisfy the judge that:

1. You did not receive a copy of the court order, or
2. Even if you received a copy of the order, you did not have the financial ability to comply with the order then or now, or
3. You paid in full, and your spouse's records are inaccurate.

Presumably, if you are asking the court to award attorneys fees, you have an attorney who knows how to file the appropriate paperwork. Courts do not award attorneys fees to pro se litigants—that is, people who represent themselves, even if they are attorneys.

Motions for Reconsideration

If you disagree with any temporary order, you can file a *motion for reconsideration* asking the same judge who entered the order to reconsider his or her prior decision. Many lawyers advise clients defending against a contempt action to seek a change in the original order, claiming that compliance is impossible or that unanticipated problems make compliance overly burdensome. Often the defendant argues: "Judge, please excuse me from doing what you told me to do in the first place, because something terrible happened to me, making it impossible for me to obey your order. Please write a new order I can obey."

If you are defending against a contempt action before divorce, file a motion for reconsideration of the existing orders. As with other motions, you must give your spouse at least ten days prior notice by mail in a nonemergency case, or seven days notice, if delivered by sheriff or constable.

If you believe the temporary orders should be changed, file a motion for reconsideration as soon as possible. For example, if you know you are about to lose your job, file a motion immediately. Too often parties wait until they have violated orders for many weeks or months before seeking a change in orders. Sometimes they rely on the other party's verbal agreement to reduce payments, only to discover that the agreement is unenforceable. Agreements to modify existing orders must be in proper written contractual language and form before a court will give them any weight.

After divorce, you file a complaint to modify the existing divorce judgment and final orders, but unlike contempt actions, the court will not act quickly on post-divorce modification actions.

Moving Out of State

While your divorce is pending, you may not permanently remove minor children from Massachusetts without the other parent's consent or prior court approval. After your divorce, or as part of your divorce trial, you must file a *request for removal*. Courts now apply a *clear advantage* standard to these cases by weighing all of the evidence presented, and then deciding whether there is a clear advantage to the custodial parent in moving out of state. If so, the reasoning flows, the children will benefit from the move. In the balance are the rights of the noncustodial parent to participate in the children's lives in a meaningful way. These are difficult cases, and often involve a guardian *ad litem* for the children.

Tip: If you plan on moving, ask your spouse's written permission first. If your spouse refuses, file the complaint to remove minor children from Massachusetts. Do so as soon as possible, because the court appoints a guardian *ad litem* to investigate and make recommendations to the court. The investigations can take many months. The court gives great weight to the recommendations, but the judge alone decides where the children live.

If the children live with your spouse, and you believe your spouse plans to move out of state with the children, before or after the divorce, and without your approval or the permission of the court, file a PETITION FOR WRIT OF HABEUS CORPUS (Form 24) immediately. The usual notice requirements are waived in an emergency, meaning that the court excuses you from giving prior notice to your spouse. Typical emergency cases involve situations where one parent threatens to put the children on the next plane for a one-way trip to California, or takes the children "on vacation" to Florida and refuses to return them to Massachusetts. The court may grant an order prohibiting your spouse from removing the children from Massachusetts, and if appropriate, may grant you custody of the children. Your spouse, however, remains free to move from Massachusetts without the children, and the court still has the power to grant a divorce and orders relating to the care and custody of the children.

If the children live with you, but your spouse is threatening to take them out of state, you can file a MOTION FOR TEMPORARY ORDERS OF CUSTODY, SUPPORT, AND MAINTENANCE OF INSURANCE BENEFITS (Form 20). Compete Form 20 according to the instructions on page 117. In paragraph 6 on the first page of Form 20, type in an explanation of why you believe your spouse intends to leave with the children (for example: "The defendant has threatened to permanently remove the children from Massachusetts."). In paragraph 6 on the second page of Form 20, type in: "That the defendant be restrained from removing the minor children from Massachusetts without prior permission of the court." You also need to complete the AFFIDAVIT IS SUPPORT OF MOTION FOR TEMPORARY ORDERS OF CUSTODY, SUPPORT, AND MAINTENANCE OF INSURANCE BENEFITS (Form 21). Complete this form according to the instructions on page 119. In paragraph 8 type in the same statement you used in paragraph 6 on the first page of Form 20.

If your spouse tries to start a custody battle in the new state, that state will honor the Massachusetts court's orders and will return the children and the case to Massachusetts. The same is true if your spouse enters Massachusetts from another state with minor children. The other state, called the *home* state, is the appropriate state to decide custody matters.

There are exceptions. For example, if an abused mother flees San Francisco with her two minor children and returns to her parents' home in Boston, the Massachusetts court may decide to *take jurisdiction*, and accept the custody case to protect the mother and children from an abusive situation.

Absent abuse or another emergency, such as a child in need of medical services, courts generally refuse to accept a custody case unless and until the minor children have lived in the new state for at least six months.

Summary

Divorce is an arduous process. Having survived divorce, you now live under new, sometimes unpleasant and unexpected circumstances. Not surprisingly, parties sometimes find themselves embroiled in controversy after divorce.

As a divorced person, you are often told to "move on with your life" by lawyers, judges, mental health professionals, friends, and relatives. Yet you are not free to move out of state with children unless your spouse or the court gives you permission, forcing you to revisit old battlegrounds. Some people look back in humor and detachment; other people rekindle old hostilities.

Lawyers and judges are always in search of a "final resolution," to avoid post-divorce litigation. The public should recognize that courts cannot mandate peace and tranquillity. People should work on rebuilding trust and cooperation after divorce for the sake of the children and their own satisfaction in life.

If court intervention is called for, then expect contempt actions to be filed by the party seeking the benefit of the divorce judgment as written, and requests for reconsideration or complaints for modification by the party seeking a change in the status quo. The full array of post-divorce problems and remedies are not covered here. This book is only intended to take you through the divorce process itself. We hope, however, that the experience and insight gained from divorce provide you and your spouse with the communication skills and and motivation to stay away from court after divorce.

Appendix A
General Laws of Massachusetts

This appendix contains portions of Chapter 208 of the General Laws of Massachusetts. As this appendix may not contain all of the information you need for your case, it is strongly recommended that you go to a public library or law library and review Chapter 208, and the rules of court, in their entirety.

General Laws of Massachusetts
Chapter 208

§ 1. General provisions

A divorce from the bond of matrimony may be adjudged for adultery, impotency, utter desertion continued for one year next prior to the filing of the complaint, gross and confirmed habits of intoxication caused by voluntary and excessive use of intoxicating liquor, opium, or other drugs, cruel and abusive treatment, or, if a spouse being of sufficient ability, grossly or wantonly and cruelly refuses or neglects to provide suitable support and maintenance for the other spouse, or for an irretrievable breakdown of the marriage as provided in sections one A and B; provided, however, that a divorce shall be adjudged although both parties have cause, and no defense upon recrimination shall be entertained by the court.

§ 1A. Irretrievable breakdown of marriage; commencement of action; complaint accompanied by statement and dissolution agreement; procedure

An action for divorce on the ground of an irretrievable breakdown of the marriage may be commenced with the filing of: (a) a petition signed by both joint petitioners or their attorneys; (b) a sworn affidavit that is either jointly or separately executed by the petitioners that an irretrievable breakdown of the marriage exists; and (c) a notarized separation agreement executed by the parties except as hereinafter set forth and no summons or answer shall be required. After a hearing on a separation agreement which has been presented to the court, the court shall, within thirty days of said hearing, make a finding as to whether or not an irretrievable breakdown of the marriage exists and whether or not the agreement has made proper provisions for custody, for support and maintenance, for alimony and for the disposition of marital property, where applicable. In making its finding, the court shall apply the provisions of section thirty-four, except that the court shall make no inquiry into, nor consider any evidence of the individual marital fault of the parties. In the event the notarized separation agreement has not been filed at the time of the commencement of the action, it shall in any event be filed with the court within ninety days following the commencement of said action.

If the finding is in the affirmative, the court shall approve the agreement and enter a judgment of divorce nisi. The agreement either shall be incorporated and merged into said judgment or by agreement of the parties, it shall be incorporated and not merged, but shall survive and remain as an independent contract. In the event that the court does not approve the agreement as executed, or modified by agreement of the parties, said agreement shall become null and void and of no further effect between the parties; and the action shall be treated as dismissed, but without prejudice. Following approval of an agreement by the court but prior to the entry of judgment nisi, said agreement may be modified in accordance with the foregoing provisions at any time by agreement of the parties and with the approval of the court, or by the court upon the petition of one of the parties after a showing of a substantial change of circumstances; and the agreement, as modified, shall continue as the order of the court.

Thirty days from the time that the court has given its initial approval to a dissolution agreement of the parties which makes proper provisions for custody, support and maintenance, alimony, and for the disposition of marital property where applicable, notwithstanding subsequent modification of said agreement a judgment of divorce nisi shall be entered without further action by the parties.

Nothing in the foregoing shall prevent the court, at any time prior to the approval of the agreement by the court, from making temporary orders for custody, support and maintenance, or such other temporary orders as it deems appropriate, including referral of the parties and the children, if any, for marriage or family counseling.

Prior to the entry of judgment under this section, the petition may be withdrawn by mutual agreement of the parties.

An action commenced under this section shall be placed by the register of probate for the county in which the action is so commenced on a hearing list separate from that for all other actions for divorce brought under this chapter, and shall be given a speedy hearing on the dissolution agreement insofar as that is consistent with the wishes of the parties.

§ 1B. Irretrievable breakdown of marriage; commencement of action; waiting period; unaccompanied complaint; procedure

An action for divorce on the ground of an irretrievable breakdown of the marriage may be commenced by the filing of the complaint unaccompanied by the signed statement and dissolution agreement of the parties required in section one A.

No earlier than six months after the filing of the complaint, there shall be a hearing and the court may enter a judgment of divorce nisi if the court finds that there has existed, for the period following the filing of the complaint and up to the date of the hearing, a continuing irretrievable breakdown of the marriage.

Notwithstanding the foregoing, at the election of the court hereunder, the aforesaid six month period may be waived to allow the consolidation for the purposes of hearing a complaint commenced under this section with a complaint for divorce commenced by the opposing party under section one.

The filing of a complaint for divorce under this section shall not affect the ability of the defendant to obtain a hearing on a complaint for divorce filed under section one, even if the aforesaid six month period has not yet expired.

Said six month period shall be determined from the filing of a complaint for divorce. In the event that a complaint for divorce is commenced in accordance with the provisions of section one A or is for a cause set forth under section one, and said complaint is later amended to set forth the ground established in this section, the six month period herein set forth shall be computed from the date of the filing of said complaint.

As part of the entry of the judgment of divorce nisi, appropriate orders shall be made by the court with respect to custody, support and maintenance of children and, in accordance with the provisions of section thirty-four, for alimony and for the disposition of marital property.

Nothing in the foregoing shall prevent the court, at any time prior to judgment, from making temporary orders for custody, support and maintenance or such other temporary orders as it deems appropriate, including referral of the parties and the children, if any, for marriage or family counseling.

Prior to the entry of judgment under this section, in the event that the parties file the statement and dissolution agreement as required under section one A hereinabove, then said action for divorce shall proceed under said section one A.

§ 2. Confinement for crime

A divorce may also be adjudged if either party has been sentenced to confinement for life or for five years or more in a federal penal institution or in a penal or reformatory institution in this or any other state; and, after a divorce for such cause, no pardon granted to the party so sentenced shall restore such party to his or her conjugal rights.

§ 5. Exceptions

If the plaintiff has lived in this commonwealth for one year last preceding the commencement of the action if the cause occurred without the commonwealth, or if the plaintiff is domiciled within the commonwealth at the time of the commencement of the action and the cause occurred within the commonwealth, a divorce may be adjudged for any cause allowed by law, unless it appears that the plaintiff has removed into this commonwealth for the purpose of obtaining a divorce.

§ 6. Venue

Actions for divorce shall be filed, heard and determined in the probate court, held for the county where one of the parties lives, except that if either party still resides in the county where the parties last lived together, the action shall be heard and determined in a court for that county. In the event of hardship or inconvenience to either party, the court having jurisdiction may transfer such action for hearing to a court in a county in which such party resides.

§ 23. Resumption of former name by woman

The court granting a divorce may allow a woman to resume her maiden name or that of a former husband.

§ 28. Children; care and custody; modification of orders; provisions for education and health insurance; preexisting orders for maintenance

Upon a judgment for divorce, the court may make such judgment as it considers expedient relative to the care, custody and maintenance of the minor children of the parties and may determine with which of the parents the children or any of them shall remain or may award their custody to some third person if it seems expedient or for the benefit of the children. Upon a complaint after a divorce, filed by either parent or by a next friend on behalf of the children after notice to both parents, the court may make a judgment modifying its earlier judgment as to the care and custody of the minor children of the parties provided that the court finds that a material and substantial change in the circumstances of the parties has occurred and the judgment of modification is necessary in the best interests of the children. In furtherance of the public policy that dependent children shall be maintained as completely as possible from the resources of their parents and upon a complaint filed after a judgment of divorce, orders of maintenance and for support of minor children shall be modified if there is an inconsistency between the amount of the existing order and the amount that would result from application of the child support guidelines promulgated by the chief justice for administration and management or if there is a need to provide for the health care coverage of the child. A modification to provide for the health care coverage of the child shall be entered whether or not a modification in the amount of child support is necessary. There shall be a rebuttable presumption that the amount of the order which would result from the application of the guidelines is the appropriate amount of child support to be ordered. If, after taking into consideration the best interests of the child, the court determines that a party has overcome such presumption, the court shall make specific written findings indicating the amount of the order that-would result from application of the guidelines; that the guidelines amount would be unjust or inappropriate under the circumstances; the specific facts of the case which justify departure from the guidelines; and that such departure is consistent with the best interests of the child. The order shall be modified accordingly unless the inconsistency between the amount of the existing order and the amount of the order that would result from application of the guidelines is due to the fact that the amount of the existing order resulted from a rebuttal of the guidelines and that there has been no change in the circumstances which resulted in such rebuttal; provided, however, that even if the specific facts that justified departure from the guidelines upon entry of the existing order remain in effect, the order shall be modified in accordance with the guidelines unless the court finds that the guidelines amount would be unjust or inappropriate under the circumstances and that the existing order is consistent with the best interests of the child. A modification of child support may enter notwithstanding an agreement of the parents that has independent legal significance. The court may make appropriate orders of maintenance, support and education of any child who has attained age eighteen but who has not attained age twenty-one and who is domiciled in the home of a parent, and is principally dependent upon said parent for maintenance. The court may make appropriate orders of maintenance, support and education for any child who has attained age twenty-one but who has not attained age twenty-three, if such child is domiciled in the home of a parent, and is principally dependent upon said parent for maintenance due to the enrollment of such child in an educational program, excluding educational costs beyond an undergraduate degree. When the court makes an order for maintenance or support of a child, said court shall determine whether the obligor under such order has health insurance or other health coverage on a group plan available to him through an employer or organization or has health insurance or other health coverage available to him at a reasonable cost that may be extended to cover the child for whom support is ordered. When said court has determined that the obligor has such insurance or coverage available to him, said court shall include in the support order a requirement that the obligor exercise the option of additional coverage in favor of the child or obtain coverage for the child.

When a court makes an order for maintenance or support, the court shall determine whether the obligor under such order is responsible for the maintenance or support of any other children of the obligor, even if a court order for such maintenance or support does not exist, or whether the obligor under such order is under a preexisting order for the maintenance or support of any other children from a previous marriage, or whether the obligor under such order is under a preexisting order for the maintenance or support of any other. children born out of wedlock. If the court determines that such responsibility does, in fact, exist and that such obligor is fulfilling such responsibility such court shall take into consideration such responsibility in setting the amount to paid under the current order for maintenance or support.

§ 34. Alimony or assignment of estate; determination of amount; health insurance

Upon divorce or upon a complaint in an action brought at any time after a divorce, whether such a divorce has been adjudged in this commonwealth or another jurisdiction, the court of the commonwealth, provided there is personal jurisdiction over both parties, may make a judgment for either of the parties to pay alimony to the other. In addition to or in lieu of a judgment to pay alimony, the court may assign to either husband or wife all or any part of the estate of the other, including but not limited to, all vested and nonvested benefits, rights and funds accrued during the marriage and which shall include, but not be limited to, retirement benefits, military retirement benefits if qualified under and to the extent provided by federal law, pension, profit-sharing, annuity, deferred compensation and insurance. In determining the amount of alimony, if any, to be paid, or in fixing the nature and value of the property, if any, to be so assigned, the court, after hearing the witnesses, if any, of each party, shall consider the length of the marriage, the conduct of the parties during the marriage, the age, health, station, occupation, amount and sources of income, vocational skills, employability, estate, liabilities and needs of each of the parties and the opportunity of each for future acquisition of capital assets and income. In fixing the nature and value of the property to be so assigned, the court shall also consider the present and future needs of the dependent children of the marriage. The court may also consider the contribution of each of the parties in the acquisition, preservation or appreciation in value of their respective estates and the contribution of each of the parties as a homemaker to the family unit. When the court makes an order for alimony on behalf of a spouse, said court shall determine whether the obligor under such order has health insurance or other health coverage available to him through an employer or organization or has health insurance or other health coverage available to him at reasonable cost that may be extended to cover the spouse for whom support is ordered. When said court has determined that the obligor has such insurance or coverage available to him, said court shall include in the support order a requirement that the obligor do one of the following: exercise the option of additional coverage in favor of the spouse, obtain coverage for the spouse, or reimburse the spouse for the cost of health insurance. In no event shall the order for alimony be reduced as a result of the obligor's cost for health insurance coverage for the spouse.

Appendix B
Sample Completed Forms with Instructions

This appendix contains instructions on how to complete forms, as well as samples of completed forms from a fictional case. For forms not included in this appendix you will find instructions in the main text of this book or on the blank forms themselves in appendix C. Some forms require you to cross out an optional word or phrase, such as "husband/wife," or "plaintiff/defendant." Cross out the word that does not apply by drawing a line through. For example: "~~husband~~/wife" or "plaintiff/~~defendant.~~" See the sample completed forms in this appendix.

List of Forms

On the following two pages is a list of the forms included in this appendix, along with the page number where the instructions for each form begins. The forms have been given a letter designation, rather than a number, so as to distinguish them from the blank forms in appendix C. Wherever we indicate that a form is "**Standard**," you must use the form in appendix C or from the court. For the Affidavit Disclosing Care or Custody Proceedings and the Domestic Relations Summons, you may only use the form from the court. The corresponding number for each form in appendix C is noted in brackets. For example, Form A in this appendix corresponds to Form 1 in appendix C.

Tip: Many forms are not marked **Standard** because the court does not supply these forms. You are free to use those we provide in appendix C or to make up your own forms, but whatever you do, follow the instructions in chapter 3 for setting up the case caption.

* No separate instructions are provided for these forms, as they are simple forms easily understood by reviewing the sample.

** The CHILD SUPPORT GUIDELINES WORKSHEET (Form 4) must be copied on blue paper, with the second page copied on the reverse side of the first page (i.e., so you are only submitting a single sheet of paper).

*** The example uses the FINANCIAL STATEMENT (SHORT FORM) (Form 5), which would be copied on pink paper. This form is used when the person's annual income is less that $75,000. If annual income is $75,000 or more, the FINANCIAL STATEMENT (LONG FORM) (Form 6) would be copied on purple paper and filled in, instead of Form 5.

Form A. Joint Petition for Divorce under M.G.L. Ch. 208, Sec. 1A (Uncontested No-Fault Divorce)

1. Complete the case caption portion according to the instructions in chapter 3. The Petitioner section requires you to fill in your name and residential address, and your spouse's name and residential address. In this type of case both parties are called "Petitioner."

2. In paragraph 2, after the words "The parties were lawfully married at," fill in the city, county, and state where you were married and the month, day, and year of the marriage. After the words "last lived together at," fill in the residential address, including the street, city, county, and state where you and your spouse last lived together, followed by the month, day, and year when you separated. An approximate date is acceptable if you indicate it is approximate.

3. In paragraph 3, fill in the full names and dates of birth of any children under the age of 18 years. If you have any children over the age of 18 who are full time students and financially dependent on you and your spouse, cross off the word "minor" and write in the word "unemancipated." For any such child over the age of 18 years, insert "a full time student dependent upon the parties" after their date of birth.

4. In paragraph 4, fill in the county and docket number of any other action for divorce, annulment, affirmation of marriage, separate support or custody. If there are no other actions cross off the last printed word "except" and place a period after the word "other."

5. In paragraph 5, fill in the month, day, and year of the irretrievable breakdown. You may use the date you last lived together.

6. In paragraph 6, check off the appropriate boxes:
   a. "grant a divorce on the ground of irretrievable breakdown" must be checked off.
   b. "approve the separation agreement executed by the parties" must be checked off.
   c. "incorporate and merge said agreement in the divorce judgment." Read your separation agreement to determine whether you and your spouse agree to making your agreement subject to modification upon a material change in circumstances.
   d. "incorporate but not merge said agreement, which shall survive and remain as an independent contract," meaning something more than a material change must occur before the agreement will be changed by a court.
   e. "allow Wife to resume her former name of" check off if the wife wishes to resume her maiden name or former married name and fill in the full name, including first, middle, and last name.

7. Fill in the date on which you and your spouse sign the joint petition.

8. Fill in the mailing addresses and telephone numbers for you and your spouse, and sign your names, on the lines indicated. [Note: "B.B.O.#" is for attorneys only.] If you have a lawyer, the lawyer's name, address, telephone number, and signature are required.

9. On the second (reverse) side, fill in the names and addresses of attorneys, if any, or names and addresses of the wife and the husband under "For Wife" and "For Husband." Fill in the assigned docket number in the upper right hand corner. Do not fill in or check off any other item.

Form A

Commonwealth of Massachusetts
The Trial Court

Barnstable Division **Probate and Family Court Department** Docket No. 96D-0789-D1

Joint Petition for Divorce Under M.G.L. Ch. 208, Sec. 1A

Eva Frances Lee Rivers, Petitioner, of 123 Cedar Street (Street and No.), Hyannis (City or Town), MA (State), 02601 (Zip)

and

Louis Rivers, Petitioner, of 45 Maple Avenue (Street and No.), Falmouth (City or Town), MA (State), 02540 (Zip)

1. Now come the Husband and Wife in a joint petition for divorce pursuant to Massachusetts General Laws, Chapter 208, Sec. 1A.

2. The parties were lawfully married at Boston, Suffolk County, MA on July 7, 1980 and last lived together at 123 Cedar Street, Hyannis, Barnstable County, MA on October 11, 19 95.

3. The minor child(ren) of this marriage and date(s) of birth is/are:

   Alan Rivers — April 3, 1982
   Elizabeth Rivers — April 21, 1985

4. The parties certify that no previous action for divorce, annulment, affirmation of marriage, separate support, desertion, living apart for justifiable cause, or custody of child(ren) has been brought by either party against the other ~~except~~ ____________

5. On or about October 11, 19 95, an irretrievable breakdown of the marriage under M.G.L. Ch. 208, Sec. 1A occurred and continues to exist.

6. Wherefore, the parties pray that the Court:

- ☒ grant a divorce on the ground of irretrievable breakdown
- ☒ approve the separation agreement executed by the parties
- ☒ incorporate and merge said agreement in the divorce judgment
- ☐ incorporate but not merge said agreement, which shall survive and remain as an independent contract
- ☒ allow Wife to resume her former name of Eva Frances Lee
- ☐ ____________

Date: July 9, 1996

Eva Frances Lee Rivers
SIGNATURE OF WIFE OR ATTORNEY
Eva Frances Lee Rivers
(Print address if not pro se)
123 Cedar Street
Hyannis, MA 02601
Tel. No. (508) 555-2698
B.B.O.# none

Louis Rivers
SIGNATURE OF HUSBAND OR ATTORNEY
Louis Rivers
(Print address if not pro se)
45 Maple Avenue
Falmouth, MA 02540
Tel. No. (508) 666-2997
B.B.O.# none

Joint Petition for Divorce
Under M.G.L. Ch. 208, Sec. 1A

For Wife:
Eva Frances Lee Rivers, Pro Se
Address 123 Cedar Street
Hyannis, MA 02601
Tel No. (508) 555-2698

For Husband:
Louis Rivers, Pro Se
Address 45 Maple Avenue
Falmouth, MA 02540
Tel No. (508) 555-2997

Docket No. 96D-0789-D1
Filed ____________, 19____
Agreement Approved ____________, 19____
Judgment ____________, 19____

Documents filed:
- ☐ Marriage Certificate
- ☐ Wife's Financial Statement
- ☐ Husband's Financial Statement
- ☐ Separation Agreement
- ☐ Affidavit of Irretrievable Breakdown
- ☐ Affidavit Disclosing Care or Custody Proceedings
- ☐ Child Support Guidelines Worksheet

Form B. Joint Affidavit Under M.G.L. Ch. 208, Sec. 1A

1. Complete the case caption according to the instructions in chapter 3. Both spouses are "Petitioners," so fill in the names in any order, although we recommend for consistency's sake that the name of the party listed on the left hand side of your Joint Petition be placed on the first line and the name of the party on the right hand side of the petition be placed on the second line.

2. In paragraph one, fill in the date of your marriage; the town or city, county, and state where you were married; the month, day, and year you last lived together; and the street address, town or city, county, and state where you last lived together.

3. In paragraph 2, check off the appropriate boxes regarding your children, if any. "Minor children" are under 18 years old. "Unemancipated children" are full time undergraduate students over 18 years and under the age of 23 who are financially dependent on the parties.

4. After paragraph 5, fill in the day, month, and year you and your spouse sign the affidavit.

5. You and your spouse need to sign the affidavit in the presence of a notary public. The notary will complete the "Acknowledgment" section of the form. You do not need to be present when your spouse signs, nor do you need to use the same notary. Note that the first notary provision is for the husband (as it uses the word "his") and the second is for the wife (as it uses the word "her").

Form B

Form B

Commonwealth of Massachusetts
The Trial Court
The Probate and Family Court Department

Barnstable **Division** **Docket No.** 96D-0789-D1

Eva Frances Lee Rivers,
Petitioner

and

Louis Rivers,
Petitioner

Joint Affidavit Under
M.G.L. Ch. 208, Sec. 1A

Now come the petitioners in the above-entitled and numbered case and respectfully state as follows:

1. We were married on July 7, 19 80, at Boston, Suffolk County, Massachusetts, and last lived together on October 11, 19 95, at 123 Cedar Street, Hyannis, Barnstable County, Massachusetts.

2. ☒ There are 2 child(ren) of this marriage under the age of 18 years whose names and dates of birth are:

Alan Rivers — April 3, 1982
Elizabeth Rivers — April 21, 1985

☐ There are ____ child(ren) of this marriage over the age of 18 but less than 23 years who are full time undergraduate students, financially dependent upon the petitioners, whose names and dates of birth are:

☐ There are no minor children of this marriage.

3. During the course of our marriage we developed different interests and goals. As we grew apart, we no longer derived any satisfaction from our married life and now believe there is no chance of reconciliation.

4. We believe our marriage is irretrievably broken and we are best served by ending our relationship under the terms of our settlement agreement.

5. We are both satisfied with the terms of the settlement agreement and ask the court to approve the agreement and incorporate it into a judgment of divorce.

Signed under penalties this 9th day of July, 19 96.

Eva Frances Lee Rivers
Petitioner

Louis Rivers
Petitioner

Acknowledgment

Commonwealth of Massachusetts
Barnstable County — July 9, 19 96

Then personally appeared before me Louis Rivers, the petitioner, and acknowledged the foregoing to be his free act and deed for the purposes stated therein.

Notary Public
My commission expires:

Commonwealth of Massachusetts
Barnstable County — July 9, 19 96

Then personally appeared before me Eva Frances Lee Rivers, the petitioner, and acknowledged the foregoing to be her free act and deed for the purposes stated therein.

Notary Public
My commission expires:

Form C. Child Support Guidelines Worksheet

NOTE: This form must be submitted as a two-sided form on blue paper (you can also get it from the register).

Tip: See our interactive worksheet on-line at "www.DivorceNet.com" at no charge.

1. Complete the case caption according to the instructions in chapter 3.
2. After the phrase "Worksheet Completed By" fill in your full name.
3. In the section marked "1. Basic Order":
   - Fill in item (a) with the non-custodial parent's gross weekly income from all sources. If that parent already pays court ordered support for another family, the income may be reduced by the amount of the other support order. Divide monthly wages by 4.3 to get weekly amounts (or multiply by 12, then divide by 52).
   - For item (b), refer to the reverse side (second page) of the worksheet to determine the percentage of gross weekly income subject to a support order. (For our example, we have circled the applicable items on the second page, so it is clear how we arrived at our numbers.)
   - For item (c), multiply the gross weekly income (reduced by any prior support orders for other families) by the percentage selected for line (b). Fill in the answer on line (A) on the far right-hand side of the worksheet.
4. In the section marked "2. Adjustment for Ages of Children":
   - For item (a), fill in the age of the oldest child.
   - For item (b), refer to the chart on the reverse side (second page) of the worksheet, marked "B. Age Differential," and determine whether support should be increased, and if so, by what percentage.
   - For item (c), multiply the basic order on line (A) by the appropriate percentage from chart B and fill in the blank with your answer.
   - For item (d), add the figure on line 2(c) to the basic order on line (A). Fill in your answer on line (B) on the far right-hand side of the worksheet.
5. In the section marked "3. Custodial Parent Income Adjustment":
   - For item (a), fill in the custodial parent's gross income from all sources.
   - Item (b) allows the custodial parent to deduct the first $15,000 from his or her annual income.
   - For item (c), the custodial parent may deduct the annual cost of day care.
   - For item (d), subtract the amounts on lines 3(b) and 3(c) from the gross income on line 3(a), and write in the answer on line 3(d).
   - For item (e), fill in the non-custodial parent's gross annual income from all sources as shown in item 1(a).
   - For item (f), add the amounts on lines 3(d) and 3(e), and write in the total on line 3(f).
   - For item (g), fill in the amounts from lines 3(d) and 3(f).
   - For item (h), divide the amount on line 3(d) by the amount on line 3(f). This will give you a percentage, which should be written on the line in 3(h).
   - For item (i), take the adjusted order from line (B) on the far right-hand side of the worksheet and multiply it by the percentage on line 3(h). [Note that you must move the decimal point two places to the left in order to make this calculation correctly. For example: 6.47 percent needs to be converted to .00647 for the calculation.] Fill in your answer on line (C) on the far right-hand side of the worksheet.
6. In the section marked "4. Calculation of Final Order":
   - for item (a), fill in the amount from line (B).
   - For item (b), fill in the amount from line (C).
   - For item (c), fill in the amount equal to one-half (50%) of the cost of your family's group health insurance, if any, but only if the noncustodial parent pays for the family's insurance.
7. For the item marked "Weekly Support Order (B)-(C)-4(c)," take the amount from line (B) and subtract the amounts from lines (C) and 4(c). Write in this answer. This is the amount of the weekly child support order.

Commonwealth of Massachusetts
The Trial Court

Barnstable **Division** **Probate and Family Court Department** **Docket No.** 98D-0789-D1

Eva Frances Lee Rivers **VS.** Louis Rivers

Worksheet
Child Support Guidelines

Worksheet Completed By ____________ Date Completed ____________

All provisions of the Guidelines (pp. 1-6) should be reviewed prior to the completion of the worksheet. These guidelines will apply (absent a prior agreement acceptable to both parties) in cases where combined gross income of both parties does not exceed $100,000.00 and where the income of the non-custodial parent does not exceed $75,000.00.

1. Basic Order

a) Non-custodial gross weekly income (less prior support orders actually paid, for child/family other than the family seeking this order) $ 1,000.00

b) % of gross/number of children (from chart III A) 30 %

c) Basic order (a) x (b) (A) $ 300.00

2. Adjustment For Ages of Children

a) Age of oldest child 14

b) % of increase for age (from chart III B) 15 %

c) Age add on (2b) x (A) $ 45.00

d) Adjusted order (A) + (2c) (B) $ 345.00

3. Custodial Parent Income Adjustment

a) Custodial parent gross income $ 18,460.00

b) Less $15,000.00 - 15,000.00

c) Less day care cost (annual) - 0.00

d) Custodial adjusted gross $ 3,460.00

e) Non-custodial gross (annual) $ 50,000.00

f) Total available gross 3(d) + 3(e) $ 53,460.00

g) Line 3(d) 3,460.00 Line 3(f) 53,460.00

h) 3(d) divided by 3(f) 6.47 per cent

i) Adjustment for custodial income (line 3h %) x (B) (C) $ 22.33

4. Calculation of Final Order

a) Adjusted order (B) above (B) $ 345.00

b) Less adjustment for income (C) above (C) - 22.33

c) Less 50% weekly cost of family group health insurance [under the provisions of section G(1)] - 30.00

or

Plus 50% weekly cost of obligee's family group health insurance [under the provisions of section G(1)] + ______

Weekly Support Order (B) - (C) ± 4(c) $ 292.67

III Child Support Obligation Schedule

A. Basic Order

The basic child support obligation, based upon the income of the non-custodial parent is as follows.

Gross Weekly Income	Number of Children 1	2 (circled)	3
$0 - $124	Discretion of the Court, but no less than $50.00 per month ($11.55 per week)		
$125 - $200	15% (± 2%)	18% (± 2%)	21% (± 2%)
$201 - $500	25% (± 2%)	28% (± 2%)	31% (± 2%)
$501 - max. (circled)	27% (± 2%)	30% (± 2%) (circled)	33% (± 2%)

Within the discretion of the Court, and in consideration of the totality of the circumstances of the parties, the order may be either increased or decreased by 2 percent. Where the court must set a support order where there are more than three children, the minimum order is to be no less than that contained in this guideline for three children, to be increased within the discretion of the Court depending upon the circumstances of each case.

B. Age Differential

The above orders are to be increased to reflect the costs of raising older children. The following percentages are intended to be applied to the age of the oldest child in the household for whom support is sought under the pending action.

Age of Oldest Child	Percentage Increase
0 - 6	Basic Order Applies
7 - 12	Basic Order + 10% of Basic Order
13 - 18 (circled)	Basic Order + 15% of Basic Order (circled)
Over 18	If statute permits, at discretion of the Court.

C. Custodial Parent Income Adjustment

Where the custodial parent works and earns income in excess of $15,000.00 after consideration of day care expenses, the support order is to be reduced by the percentage that the excess represents in relation to the combined incomes of both parents minus the custodial parent's disregard.

(see other side)

Form D. Financial Statement (Short Form)

Form D is the FINANCIAL STATEMENT (SHORT FORM) (Form 5 from appendix C). The FINANCIAL STATEMENT (LONG FORM) is not shown in this appendix due to its length. The following instructions relate to the FINANCIAL STATEMENT (SHORT FORM), which you will use only if your annual income is *under $75,000.*

1. Copy Form 5 on pink paper, or get the pink version from the register.
2. Complete the case caption according to the instructions in chapter 3. Also read the instructions printed on the form below the case caption. Fill in each line on the form. Do not leave any blanks. Insert the word "none" where appropriate.
3. In paragraph 1, fill in the information required information.
4. Complete paragraph 2 by filling in all of your sources of income on the appropriate lines. Be sure to use weekly amounts. If you are paid monthly, multiply your gross pay by 12 and then divide by 52. If you are paid twice a month, multiply your gross pay by 24 and then divide by 52. If you are paid every two weeks, multiply your gross pay by 26 and then divide by 52. If any item does not apply, write in the word "none." If you are self-employed, complete Schedule A and attach it to your Financial Statement. Refer to your federal and state income tax returns, if your current income is the same; otherwise estimate the current year's income and divide by 52. Add a notation in the margin, along side the amount, indicating it is an "estimate." If your employment is seasonal, make the appropriate adjustments on a month-to-month basis on page two of Schedule A. If you have any rental income, fill in Schedule B and attach it to the Financial Statement. If you receive income from any other source, including alimony and child support, fill in the total on line 2(k). Write in the source, such as "$100 in alimony and $300 in child support." Add income from all sources and fill in the total on line 2(j).
5. For paragraph 3, use your pay stub to determine the amount of your deductions. Determine weekly amounts by using the same arithmetic method outlined above. Include the number of exemptions claimed on lines 3(a) and (b), and fill in the federal and state income tax deductions on a weekly basis. If you are self-employed and using last year's income, use last year's taxes also, and make a notation that the information is based on the prior year's taxes. If you are projecting income for the current year, estimate your taxes and divide by 52. Use a notation to indicate the income is "estimated." In item (c), state the amount withheld for Social Security. In item (d), state the amount withheld, if any, for medical insurance. If you pay for medical insurance directly instead of by a payroll deduction, do not fill in the amount here. Instead, insert the amount in item 8. In item (e), fill in the amount of union dues, if any. Add all of your deductions and fill in the total on line 3(f).

6. For paragraph 4, subtract the amount on line 3(f) from the amount on line 2(l), and fill in the answer.
7. Paragraph 5 deals with "Other Deductions from Salary." If you have funds withheld from your paycheck for your credit union, indicate whether funds are for savings, or loan repayment, or both. If both, indicate the amounts allocated to savings and loan repayment. "Other Deductions" may include life insurance, disability insurance, United Way, MBA passes, parking, etc. Add together all other deductions and fill in the total on line 5(e). Do not duplicate any expense listed in paragraphs 8 or 11.
8. Paragraph 6 deals with "Net Weekly Income." Subtract line 5(e) from paragraph 4. Fill in the answer.
9. Paragraph 7 calls for your "Gross Yearly Income from Prior Year." If you had any income from any source last year, fill in the total amount for the entire *year* on this line. Do not include your spouse's income. Be sure to attach copies of all W-2s and 1099s for the prior year.
10. Paragraph 8 deals with "Weekly Expenses." Not all categories in this section will apply to you. Insert the word "none," on those lines. Be sure to convert to *weekly* amounts, if necessary. See the instructions in paragraph 3 above. If expenses vary monthly, review canceled checks and estimate cash expenditures over the past 12 months to calculate a weekly average. If you do not have canceled checks, estimate weekly expenses. Be sure to make a notation in the margin that expenses are "estimated." If you expect increases in rent, child care, and other weekly expenses, use the higher amounts and disclose effective dates of increases. Do not include expenses already deducted from pay, such as life and medical insurance. If you are living with your spouse, include anticipated expenses for moving, rent, and utilities, along with a notation that these are "anticipated expenses." Add expenses and fill in the weekly total where indicated.
11. Paragraph 9 deals with counsel fees. If you represent yourself, disregard this section. If you have a lawyer, fill in the amount of your retainer on line 9(a), the amount of fees incurred to date against the retainer on line 9(b), and ask your lawyer for an anticipated range of fees and expenses to complete the divorce. Of course, if you have a lawyer, he or she should be helping you complete this form.
12. Paragraph 10 asks for a list of property you own. If necessary, attach a separate sheet of paper. Under the heading "Real Estate," include property address(es); name(s) in which property is held; your estimate of the current fair market value (i.e., the price you would accept today); and any outstanding mortgage. Subtract the mortgage balance from the fair market value, and fill in the answer under "equity." If the fair market value is based on a recent appraisal, make a notation in the margin. Items (b), (c), (d), and (e) are self-explanatory. Under item (f), include the year, make, and model of all vehicles. If you do not know the current balances of any accounts, or the current market value of any asset,

simply indicate "unknown." Assets are subject to appraisal. Fill in the total value of assets on line 10(g).

13. Paragraph 11 deals with "Liabilities." List your debts in this section. Use additional sheets of paper, if necessary. If you listed payments in paragraph 8 for your car, mortgage, and current expenses such as clothing, do not list them again in this section. Be careful to sort out credit card expenses which may be listed under paragraph 8 for clothing, incidentals, toiletries, travel, and entertainment. Fill in the total amount due, as well as the total weekly payments..
14. Paragraph 12 asks for the number of years you have paid into Social Security. You should confirm this with the Social Security Administration.
15. Fill in the date and sign below paragraph 12. If you represent yourself, disregard the **Statement by Attorney** section. If you have a lawyer, then that section must be completed and signed by the lawyer.

Financial Statement (Long Form)

You will use the FINANCIAL STATEMENT (LONG FORM) (Form 6 in appendix C) only if you annual income is *at least $75,000*. The following instructions will help you if you need to use this form.

1. Copy Form 6 on purple paper, or can get the purple version from the register.
2. Refer to the instructions above for the FINANCIAL STATEMENT (LONG FORM). In many ways, the long and short forms are the same. These instructions simply highlight the significant differences.
3. If you are self-employed, complete Schedule A, which is found as the third and fourth pages of Form 5 in appendix A. If you have rental income, complete Schedule B, which is found as the fifth page of Form 5 in appendix A. In other words, Schedule A and Schedule B are used when necessary for both the FINANCIAL STATEMENT (SHORT FORM) (Form 5 from appendix C) and the FINANCIAL STATEMENT (LONG FORM) (Form 6). However, to avoid unnecessary repetition, we have only included these schedules at the end of Form 5.
4. Paragraph II deals with gross weekly income/receipts from all sources, including contributions from household members. On line (p), fill in the amount of cash received from a new spouse, live-in companion, parent, or any other person residing with you. If you do not receive cash, but share expenses, make a note to that effect.
5. Sign the FINANCIAL STATEMENT (LONG FORM) on page 8 of the form, in the presence of a notary public. If you represent yourself, disregard the **Statement by Attorney** section. If you have a lawyer, then that section must be completed and signed by the lawyer.

Commonwealth of Massachusetts
The Trial Court
Probate and Family court Department

Barnstable **Division** **Docket No.** 98D-0789-D1

FINANCIAL STATEMENT
(SHORT FORM)

Eva Frances Lee Rivers v. Louis Rivers
Plaintiff/Petitioner Defendant/Petitioner

INSTRUCTIONS: If your income equals or exceeds $75,000.00, you must complete the LONG FORM financial statement, unless otherwise ordered by the Court. All questions on both sides of this form must be answered in full or word "none" inserted. If additional space is needed for any answer, an attached sheet may be filed in addition to, but not in lieu of, the answer. Information contained herein is confidential and only available to the parties and persons under Probate and Family Court Department Supplemental Rule 401.

1. Your Name: Eva Frances Lee Rivers — Soc. Sec. No. 000-00-0000
   Address: 123 Cedar Street (street and no.), Hyannis (city or town), MA (state), 02601 (zip)
   Age: 43 — Telephone No. 508-555-2698 — No. of Children living with you ______
   Occupation: Bank Manager — Employer: Hyannis Savings Bank
   Employer's Address: 456 Main Street (street and no.), Hyannis (city or town), MA (state), 02601 (zip)
   Employer's Tel. No.: 508-555-1111 — Health Ins. Coverage: Yes
   Health Insurance Provider: through spouse — Cert. No. GRIA-000-07-147

2. **Gross Weekly Income from All Sources**

a).	Base pay from salary, wages	$ 350.00
b).	Self Employment Income **(attach a completed Schedule A)**	$ none
c).	Income from overtime - commissions - tips - bonuses - part-time job	$ none
d).	Dividends - interest	$ 5.00
e).	Income from trusts or annuities	$ none
f).	Pensions and retirement funds	$ none
g).	Social Security	$ none
h).	Disability, unemployment insurance or worker's compensation	$ none
i).	Public Assistance (welfare, A.F.D.C. payments)	$ none
j).	Rental from Income Producing Property **(attach a completed Schedule B)**	$ none
k).	All other sources (including child support, alimony)	$ 355.00
l).	**Total Gross Weekly Income** (a through k)	$

3. **Itemize Deduction from Gross Income**

a).	Federal income tax deductions (claiming 1 exemptions)	$ 39.00
b).	State income tax deductions (claiming 1 exemptions)	$ 16.30
c).	F.I.C.A. / Medicare	$ 25.38
d).	Medical Insurance	$ none
e).	Union Dues	$ none
f).	**Total Deductions** (a through e)	$ 80.68

4. **Adjusted Net Weekly Income**
   2(l) minus 3 (f) — $ 274.32

5. **Other Deductions from Salary**

a).	Credit Union (Loan Repayment or Savings)	$ none
b).	Savings	$ none
c).	Retirement	$ none
d).	Other (specify)	$ none
e).	**Total Deductions** (a through d)	$ none

6. **Net Weekly Income** — 4 minus 5 (e) — $ 274.32

7. **Gross Yearly Income from Prior Year** — $ 18,460.00
   (attach copy of all W-2 and 1099 forms for prior year)

8. **Weekly Expenses** (Do Not Duplicate Weekly Expenses - Strike Inapplicable Words)

a).	Rent - Mortgage (PIT)	$ 125.00	l)	Life Insurance	$ none
b).	Homeowner's / Tenant Insurance	$ 16.00	m)	Medical Insurance	$ none
c).	Maintenance and Repair	$ 25.00	n)	Uninsured Medicals	$ 25.00
d).	Heat (Type ____________)	$ 30.00	o)	Incidentals and Toiletries	$ 25.00
e).	Electricity and/or Gas	$ 30.00			
f).	Telephone	$ 22.00	p)	Motor Vehicle Expenses	$ 40.00
g).	Water / Sewer	$ 10.00	q)	Motor Vehicle Loan Payment	$ none
h).	Food	$ 100.00	r)	Child Care	$ none
i).	House Supplies	$ 10.00	s)	Other (attach additional schedule if necessary)	
j).	Laundry and Cleaning	$ 10.00		____________	$ 30.00
k).	Clothing	$ 25.00		____________	$ 12.00
				Total Weekly Expenses (a through s)	$ 535.00

9. **Counsel Fees**
   a). Retainer amount(s) paid to your attorney(s) ____________ $ none
   b). Legal fees incurred, to date, against retainer(s) ____________ $ none
   c). Anticipated range of total legal expense to prosecute this action ____ $ ____________ to $ none

10. **Assets** (Attach additional schedule for additional real estate and other assets, if necessary) none
    a). Real Estate: Home
    Location: 123 Cedar Street, Hyannis, MA
    Title: Eva Rivers & Louis Rivers
    Fair Market Value 175,000 - Mortgage(s) 75,000 = Equity $ 100,000.00
    b). IRA, Keogh, Pension, Profit Sharing, Other Retirement Plans
    List Financial Institution or Plan Names and Account Numbers
    Savings, Hyannis Savings Bank, #71147 $ 12,000.00
    Checking, Hyannis Savings Bank, #040349 $ unknown
    ____________ $ none
    c). Tax Deferred Annuity Plan(s) ____________ $ none
    d). Life Insurance: Present Cash Value ____________ $ none
    e). Savings & Checking Accounts, Money Market Accounts, & CDs which are held individually, jointly, in the name of another person for your benefit, or held by you for the benefit of your minor child(ren) **List Financial Institution Names and Account Numbers**
    ____________ $ 2,500.00
    ____________ $ 500.00
    ____________ $ none
    f). Motor Vehicles
    Fair Market Value 3,000 - Motor Vehicle Loan none = Equity $ 3,000.00
    Fair Market Value none - Motor Vehicle Loan none = Equity $ none
    g). Other (such as - stocks, bonds, collections)
    Furniture, furnishings (estimate) $ 3,000.00
    Jewelry (estimate) $ 1,000.00
    h). **Total Assets** (a through g) $ 25,000.00

11. **Liabilities (DO NOT list weekly expenses but DO list all liabilities)**

	Creditor	Nature of Debt	Date of Origin	Amount Due	Weekly Payment
a).	Visa	Consumer	varies	1,200.00	25.00
b).	none	none	none	none	none
c).	none	none	none	none	none
d).	none	none	none	none	none
e).	**Total Amount Due and Total Weekly Payment**		none	none	none

11. **Number of Years you have paid into Social Security** 10 years

I certify under penalties of perjury that my income and expenses, assets, and liabilities as stated herein are true to the best of my knowledge and belief. I have carefully read this financial statement and I certify the information is true and complete.

Date July 8, 1998 Signature *Eva Frances Lee Rivers*

STATEMENT BY ATTORNEY

I, the undersigned attorney, am admitted to practice law in the Commonwealth of Massachusetts--am admitted pro hoc vice for the purposes of this case--and am an officer of the court. As the attorney for the party on whose behalf this Financial Statement is submitted, I hereby state to the court that I have no knowledge tha any of the information contained herein is false.

Attorney Signature ____________ Date ____________
Address ____________ Tel. No. ____________
BBO# ____________

Form E. Affidavit Disclosing Care or Custody Proceedings

(**Note:** This is a two-page, carbonless copy form that you will need to obtain from the court clerk. Be sure to read the instructions printed on the back of the form itself.)

1. The case style section of this form is somewhat different than most other forms, but the same basic information is required. Under the heading "TRIAL COURT OF MASSACHUSETTS," the "Name Of Case" calls for the official name of your case. For example, Jane Doe v. John Doe. If you file a joint petition for an uncontested no-fault divorce, the name of the case would be Jane Doe and John Doe. Check the box for "Probate & Family Court," and fill in the name of the county where your case is filed on the line above the word "Division." The following will help you with each of the other sections:
2. Section 1: Type in your name.
3. Section 2: Type in the names of your children under 18 years of age.
4. Section 3: Check the box if you want your address kept confidential, i.e., not disclosed to an abusive spouse. You may check this box if you are living in a shelter for battered persons, or if you believe you or your children are in danger of physical or emotional abuse, or if you are filing a COMPLAINT FOR PROTECTION FROM ABUSE (Form 27). If you check this box, do not complete Sections 4 or 5. Instead, you will complete Sections 10 and 11 on the reverse side of the form.
5. Section 4: Type in your children's current address, and prior addresses going back two years if different.
6. Section 5: Type in your current address.
7. Section 6: Check the appropriate box to indicate that you either "have" or "have not" participated in any other care or custody proceedings involving the named children, and whether you "know" or "do not know" of any other care or custody proceedings in Massachusetts or elsewhere.
8. Section 7: Fill in information on other care or custody proceedings, if any. Look at Section 2 to determine the letters assigned to each child. Using the same letters, fill in Section 7, providing the name of the court under "Court," the case number of the other proceeding under "Docket No.," to whom custody was awarded and date of the award under "Status of Case," and whether custody was awarded to a witness (W) (someone other than you or your spouse who may testify in your divorce case), a party (P) (you or your spouse), other (O) (none of the above) or none (N) (meaning the court has not entered any orders or judgments in the other case.) If there are other cases, you may also need to complete Section 12 on the reverse side of the form.
9. Section 8: Identify, by letter only (from Section 2), the children involved in your divorce case. Under "Name of Party/Claimant" type in the name of your spouse, and under "Current (or last known) Address of Party/Claimant" type in your spouse's current address. Do not list yourself in this section.
10. Section 9: This section applies to adoptions only.
11. Complete the date and signature information at the bottom of the first page of the form.
12. If you checked the box in Section 3, indicating that you want certain addresses to be kept confidential, you will need to complete Section 10 and Section 11 on the reverse side of the first page of this form, which is the same information called for in Sections 4 and 5 (the reverse side of this form is not shown on the next page).
13. If there are other custody cases listed in Section 7, fill in the names of any attorneys or guardian ad litem involved in those cases.

Form E

BEFORE COMPLETING, READ INSTRUCTIONS ON BACK OF PART 2
TYPE OR PRINT WITH A BALLPOINT PEN - - PRESS HARD

AFFIDAVIT DISCLOSING CARE OR CUSTODY PROCEEDINGS Pursuant to Trial Court Rule IV	TRIAL COURT OF MASSACHUSETTS Name Of Case: Eva Frances Lee Rivers v. Louis Rivers	DOCKET NUMBER 96D-0789-D1

☐ Boston Municipal Court	☐ District Court	☐ Juvenile Court	☒ Probate & Family Court	☐ Superior Court
	Division	Division	Barnstable Division	County

Section 1 I, Eva Frances Lee Rivers, hereby declare, to the best of my knowledge, information, and belief that all the information on this form is true and complete:

Section 2 The name(s) of the child(ren) whose care or custody is at issue in this case are:

A. Rivers, Alan (LAST, FIRST) B. Rivers, Elizabeth (LAST, FIRST) C. ______ (LAST, FIRST)

Use only the letter appearing in frnt of the child's name above when referring to that child in completing the remaining sections.

Section 3 The party filing this affidavit may request certain addresses to be kept confidential if the address is a shelter for battered persons and their dependent child(ren), or the party filing this affidavit believes that he/she or the child(ren) are in danger of physical or emotional abuse, or the party is filing an action under G.L.C.c.209A. **If you believe that this provision applies to you, check the box at the right, complete sections 10 and 11 on the reverse side of this page and DO NOT complete sections 4 and 5 below.** ☐

Section 4 The address(es) of the above-named child(ren whose care and custody is at issue in this case are:

	Address(es)	Address(es) During Last 2 Years, If Different
CHILD A.	123 Cedar St., Hyannis, MA	
CHILD B.	123 Cedar St., Hyannis, MA	
CHILD C.		

Section 5 My address is: 123 Cedar St., Hyannis, MA

Section 6 I ☐ **have** ☐ **have not** participated in and I ☐ **know** ☐ **do not know** of other care or custody proceedings involving the above-named child(ren) in Massachusetts or in any other state or country.

Certified copies of any pleadings or determinations in a care or custody proceeding outside of Massachusetts listed in sections 7 and 8 must be filed with this affidavit unless already filed with this court or an extension for filing these documents has been granted by this court.

Section 7 The following is a list of all pending or concluded proceedings I have participated in or know of involving the care or custody of the above-named child(ren):

Letter of Child	Court	Docket No.	Status of Case (Custody awarded to) (Date of award)	[W]itness [P]arty [O]ther [N]one
CHILD ____				[ ]
CHILD ____				[ ]
CHILD ____				[ ]

Section 8 The names and addresses of parties to care or custody proceedings involving any of the above-named child(ren) or those claiming a legal right to these child(ren) during the last two years (not including myself) are:

Letter of Child	Name of Party/Claimant	Current (or last known) Address of Party/Claimant
CHILD A	Louis Rivers	45 Maple Ave., Falmouth, MA
CHILD B	Louis Rivers	45 Maple Ave., Falmouth, MA
CHILD		

Section 9 **If the box at the right is checked, this affidavit discloses the adoption of one or more of the above-named child(ren) and I am requesting the court to impound this affidavit. See instructions.** ☐

This affidavit must be personally signed by the party listed in section 1 above, unless he/she is under 18 years of age or has been adjudged incompetent in which case the attorney of record must sign. A revised affidavit must be filed with the court if new information is discovered subsequent to this filing.

Signed this 9th day of July, 19 96 under the penalties of perjury.

X Eva Frances Lee Rivers — Eva Frances Lee Rivers

SIGNATURE OF PARTY OR ATTORNEY OR RECORD FOR INCOMPETENT/JUVENILE — PRINTIED NAME OF PERSON SIGNING

____

ADDRESS OF ATTORNEY OF RECORD FOR INCOMPETENT/JUVENILE

THE PARTY FILING THIS AFFIDAVIT MUST FURNISH A COPY OF IT TO ALL OTHER PARTIES TO THIS ACTION.

Form F. Domestic Relations Summons

1. Complete the case caption according to the instructions in chapter 3.

2. For "Plaintiff," fill in your full name, including your former name, if you wish to resume that name after divorce. For example, "Jane Marie Johnson Doe."
   For "Defendant," fill in complete name of party being sued.

3. After the phrase "You are hereby summoned and required to serve upon," fill in your name and cross off the words "plaintiff's attorney" (if you are represented by counsel, your lawyer completes the summons with the lawyer's name and address).

4. After the words "whose address is," fill in your mailing address.

5. After the words "a copy of your answer to the complaint for," type in the word "divorce."

6. After the words "file your answer to the complaint in the office of the Register of this Court at," type in the name of the town or city where the main court is located (Cambridge, for example), as opposed to a satellite court location (Concord and Marlborough, for example). If you are unsure about the location of the main court, call the telephone number of your county Probate and Family Court listed in chapter 1 of this book.

7. The clerk usually provides the name of the First Justice (senior judge), which is to be written in on the line in the second paragraph after the word "Witness." Also fill in the name of the county and the date on the appropriate lines. The register will sign on the line marked "Register of Probate."

8. The section marked "ACCEPTANCE OF SERVICE" must be filled in and signed by your spouse in the presence of a notary public. If your spouse refuses to sign, hire a deputy sheriff or constable to serve the Domestic Relations Summons and Complaint for Divorce. The deputy then returns the original Summons to you along with a sworn statement called "Proof of Service" (which is on the reverse side of the Summons form, but not shown on the next page.) If you do not have the court's permission to serve papers without an identifying witness, then the witness accompanies the deputy sheriff when your spouse is served and fills in the required information and signs under the section marked "Affidavit of Identifying Witness (Applicable in Divorce Action Only)."

Form F

Commonwealth of Massachusetts
The Trial Court

Barnstable Division **Probate and Family Court Department** Docket No. 96D-0789-D1

Domestic Relations Summons

Eva Frances Lee Rivers, Plaintiff

v.

Louis Rivers, Defendant

To the above named Defendant:

You are hereby summoned and required to serve upon Eva Frances Lee Rivers plaintiff's ~~attorney~~ whose address is 123 Cedar Street, Hyannis, MA 02601 ____________ a copy of your answer to the complaint for Divorce (type of action) which is herewith served upon you, within 20 days after service of this summons upon you, exclusive of the day of service. If you fail to do so, the Court will proceed to the hearing and adjudication of this action. You are also required to file your answer to the complaint in the office of the Register of this Court at ____________ either before service upon the plaintiff's ~~attorney~~ or within a reasonable time thereafter.

Witness Robert E. Terry Esquire, First Justice of said Court at Barnstable, this eighth day of July, 19 96.

____
Register of Probate

ACCEPTANCE OF SERVICE

I, ____________, the above named Defendant hereby accept service of this summons and understand that judgment may be rendered against me in accordance with the complaint a copy of which I have received this day.

Date ____________

____
Signature of Defendant

NOTARIZATION

____________ ss Date ____________

Then personally appeared the above named ____________

who made oath that the foregoing acceptance was his free act and deed.

Signature of Notary Public ____________

Print Name ____________

My Commission Expires ____________

Form G. Income Assignment Worksheet

1. Complete the case caption according to the instructions in chapter 3. Note that this case caption also calls for the address, telephone number, and social security number for you and your spouse. If you are filing a joint petition for divorce, you may, but are not required to change "Plaintiff" and "Defendant" to "Petitioner."

2. In the section marked "Obligor's Place of Employment," type in the required employment information about the party who will be paying support.

3. Check the box for either "Effective Immediately" or "Suspended," whichever you prefer based upon your circumstances and expectations. This is a choice between an order taking effect immediately or being suspended until further notice. If you are to receive support and the obligor has a history of late payments on a temporary order or in a previous divorce case, or if you believe payments will not be made on a regular basis, an "effective immediately" order makes sense. If you are paying support, you may want to either pay on your own, or have the convenience of a payroll deduction for the support.

4. On the line above the word "Date," type in the month, day, and year on which you file this form.

5. On the line after the words "Obligor to pay $," type in the amount of money and circle "week" or "month." Also, circle either "alimony" or "child support." If the obligor pays both alimony and child support, cross off the word "or."

6. On the line for "Arrearage," fill in the exact amount owed, if any, from a temporary order. On the line for "Current Order," fill in the weekly or monthly amount to be paid. On the line for "Arrears Order," fill in an amount, if the court orders current payment toward arrearage. For example, if defendant owes $500 as arrearage and pays $100 per week under the current order, the court may order an additional $25 per week toward the arrearage of $500 until paid in full. Thus, defendant pays a total of $125 a week.

7. In the section marked "Payment made payable to:," check the appropriate box to determine whether the support check is to be paid to the court's probation department or directly to your spouse. In the section marked "Send to (to reimburse):," check the box marked "Spouse," unless your spouse is receiving welfare benefits, or a third party has custody of your children.

8. In the section marked "Health Insurance:," fill in the name of the insurance company and the policy number.

Form G

INCOME ASSIGNMENT WORKSHEET

Barnstable, SS.

PROBATE AND FAMILY COURT
NO. 96D-0789-D1

PLAINTIFF:	DEFENDANT:
Name Eva Frances Lee Rivers	Name Louis Rivers
Address 123 Cedar Street	Address 45 Maple Avenue
Hyannis, MA 02601	Falmouth, MA 02540
Telephone Number (508) 555-2698	Telephone Number (508) 666-2997
Social Security No. 000-00-0000	Social Security No. 111-00-0000

Obligor's Place of Employment

Employer's Name: Cape and Island Transport

Address: 10 Seagull Lane
Wareham, MA

Telephone Number: (508) 777-1000

Effective Immediately ☒

Suspended ☐

July 26, 1996
Date

Obligor to pay $ 292.67 per week / ~~month~~
as ~~alimony and / or~~ child support.

Arrearage	$ 0
Current Order	$ 292.67
Arrears Order	$ 0

Payment made payable to:
☐ Probation Department
☒ Spouse directly

Send to (to reimburse):
☒ Spouse
☐ DPW-________ office
☐ Other ________

Health Insurance:
Obligor's Insurer HealthCare, Inc.   Policy No. GR 1A-000-07-1147

Form H. Settlement/Separation Agreement

There are so many variables in any divorce case, thus making the creation of a single settlement/separation agreement for all cases difficult. Rather than presenting a form with line-by-line instructions, we provide a checklist for the types of matters that may need to be covered in your agreement. Following the checklist is a sample agreement. In appendix C you will find a blank agreement designed to be used in as many cases as possible. However, if your case involves unusual situations, you may need to create your own agreement, using the checklist and forms in this book as a guideline. For example, the custody provision in Form 7 only covers a joint custody situation. If you and your spouse agree to sole custody or "split" custody (some children will live with you and others with your spouse), you will need to change the form accordingly.

Property Division

Real Estate:

- ❑ Transfer of title between spouses or sale to third party
- ❑ Use and occupancy pending transfer or sale
- ❑ Responsibility for mortgages, collecting rent
- ❑ Responsibility for maintaining and preserving real estate
  - ❑ Maintenance and repairs
  - ❑ Real estate taxes
  - ❑ Utilities
  - ❑ Insurance
  - ❑ Monthly condominium fees
- ❑ Tax consequences
  - ❑ Deductions on income tax returns
  - ❑ Capital gain tax
    - ❑ Allocation
    - ❑ Roll-over
    - ❑ Sale after 55 years of age

Personal Property:

- ❑ Bank accounts
- ❑ Securities
- ❑ Trusts
- ❑ CDs
- ❑ Furniture, fixtures, equipment
- ❑ Antiques, jewelry, art work, china, crystal, oriental rugs
- ❑ Autos, boats, planes, etc.
- ❑ Business interests

Pension plans and qualified domestic relations orders:

- ❑ IRA
- ❑ 401(k)
- ❑ All other retirement benefits

Debt:

- ❑ Consumer debt
- ❑ Car loans
- ❑ Student loans
- ❑ Business loans
- ❑ Tax obligations

Child Custody and Visitation

- ❑ Joint or sole legal custody
- ❑ Primary or shared physical custody
- ❑ Parenting plan
  - ❑ Time sharing or visitation plan
  - ❑ Parental decision-making on religion, education, health care
  - ❑ Parental participation in school activities, social activities
  - ❑ Moving out of state
  - ❑ Cost of children's transportation

Alimony

- ❑ Alimony waivers or duration and amount
- ❑ Social security numbers for husband and wife
- ❑ Contingencies terminating alimony
  - ❑ Death of either or both husband and wife
  - ❑ Remarriage of recipient
  - ❑ Cohabitation of recipient
  - ❑ Retirement of payor
  - ❑ Employment of recipient
  - ❑ Involuntary termination of payor's employment
  - ❑ Disability of payor
- ❑ Increases or decreases

Child Support

- ❑ Amount
- ❑ Dependency exemption and execution of IRS form 8332
- ❑ Termination
  - ❑ Age
  - ❑ Change of child's residence
  - ❑ Child's full time employment
  - ❑ Child's marriage
  - ❑ Child's entry into military service
  - ❑ Child's student status
  - ❑ Child's death
- ❑ Reduction
  - ❑ Assumption of college expenses by payor
  - ❑ Assumption of other extraordinary expenses by payor
  - ❑ Recipient's increase in income
- ❑ Increases
  - ❑ Cost of living adjustment
  - ❑ Other special needs
  - ❑ Payor's increase in income
  - ❑ Payor's increase in income
- ❑ Child support guidelines: ❑ Deviations ❑ Periodic reviews

Medical and Dental Insurance and Expenses

- ❑ Spouse
  - ❑ Payment for coverage
  - ❑ Method of insurance: ❑ Individual ❑ Employer ❑ COBRA
  - ❑ Change in coverage: ❑ Employment ❑ Retirement ❑ Remarriage of either party
  - ❑ Notification of changes
  - ❑ Uninsured medical and dental costs
- ❑ Children
  - ❑ See checklist for spouse above
  - ❑ Coverage through emancipation
  - ❑ Payment of reasonable uninsured medical and dental expenses
  - ❑ Payment of extraordinary uninsured medical and dental expenses
  - ❑ Reimbursement of insured expenses

Life Insurance

- ❑ Whose life is insured and for what amount
- ❑ Beneficiaries
- ❑ How long is insurance maintained and for what amount
- ❑ Who owns policy
- ❑ Who pays premium

Education

- ❑ Decision-making process of choice of school
- ❑ Definition of education expenses: what is covered and what is not
- ❑ Private primary and secondary school expenses
- ❑ College expenses
- ❑ Termination of obligation for child's education expenses
- ❑ Allocation of education expenses between parents and use of scholarships, loans, student's savings, and earnings
- ❑ Relationship, if any, between payment of education expenses and child support

Taxes

- ❑ Allocation of deficiencies and refunds
- ❑ Filing separate or joint returns
- ❑ Choice and payment of tax preparer

Miscellaneous

- ❑ Legal fees
- ❑ Will agreement be modifiable by a court and on what standard: material change in circumstances or some thing more than a material change?

Form H

Commonwealth of Massachusetts
The Trial Court
The Probate and Family Court Department

Barnstable **Division** **Docket No.** 96D-0789-D1

Eva Frances Lee Rivers,
Petitioner/Plaintiff

V. Settlement/Separation Agreement

Louis Rivers,
Petitioner/Defendant

This agreement is made this 9th day of July 19 96, by and between Eva Frances Lee Rivers of Hyannis, Barnstable County, Massachusetts (hereinafter called the "wife"), and Louis Rivers of Falmouth, Barnstable County, Massachusetts (hereinafter called the "husband"). All references to the "parties" shall mean the above-mentioned husband and wife.

Statement of Facts

The husband and wife were married at Boston, Suffolk County, Massachusetts on July 7, 19 80. The husband and wife are now living separate and apart.

☐ There are no minor or unemancipated children.
☒ There is/are 2 unemancipated minor child(ren).
☐ There is/are ___ unemancipated child(ren), over the age of 18 years, but full time undergraduate student(s) under the age of 23 years, dependent upon the parties for financial support.

This agreement is made in order to settle finally and completely and determine:

a. The property rights of each of the parties;
b. What should be paid to the parties for their respective support in consideration of the provisions of Massachusetts General Laws, Chapter 208, Section 34;
c. Whether and to what extent all or any part of the estate of the husband or wife should be assigned to the other in consideration of the provisions of Massachusetts General Laws, Chapter 208, Section 34;
d. All other rights and obligations arising from the marital relationship, including, but not limited to child-related matters;
e. All other matters which should be settled finally and completely in view of the pending divorce action. Notwithstanding the foregoing, the parties acknowledge that any provisions relating to the unemancipated children shall remain subject to modification by the court upon a material change in circumstances of either parent, a child, or if a modification is consistent with the best interests of child.

I. General Understanding and Disclosure. The husband and wife declare and acknowledge that each understands the position, circumstances, income, financial resources, expenses, and prospects represented by the other; and the terms, provisions, and conditions of this agreement, and, based on the information received, believe that its terms, provisions, and conditions are fair, reasonable, and acceptable. The parties further state that they have negotiated the terms of this agreement directly and have had the opportunity to consult with legal counsel of their own choosing, and that after being fully and fairly informed as to all the facts and circumstances herein set forth, and after having read this agreement line by line, they freely and fully accept the terms, conditions, and provisions and enter into this agreement voluntarily and without any coercion whatsoever. The parties further acknowledge and declare that this agreement contains the entire agreement between the parties and that there are no agreements, promises, terms, conditions, or understandings, and no representations or inducements leading to the signing of the agreement, expressed or implied, other than those set forth herein, and that no oral statement or prior written matter extrinsic to this agreement shall have any force or effect. The parties represent and acknowledge that each has fully described his or her assets and liabilities to the other party to the best of his or her knowledge and ability, both orally and otherwise, and by the exchange of copies of current Massachusetts Rules of Domestic Relations Procedure Supplemental Rule 401 Financial Statements, duplicate signed copies of which shall be filed with the court.

II. Separate Status

A. From the date of this agreement, the husband and wife agree to respect the privacy of one another for the rest of their lives, as fully as if sole and unmarried.

B. The husband and wife warrant, represent, and agree that they have not in the past and shall not contract or incur any debt, charge, or liability whatsoever in the name of the other or for which the other, his or her legal representatives or his or her property or estate shall or may become liable hereafter, except as otherwise provided in this agreement. As of the date of this agreement, there are no outstanding bills, debts, charges, or liabilities incurred by the husband or wife for which the other party may be liable other than as provided in this agreement. The husband and wife further covenant at all times to hold the other free, harmless, and indemnified from and against all debts, charges, or liabilities hereafter contracted or incurred by him or her in breach of the provisions of this paragraph, and from any and all reasonable attorneys' fees, costs, and expenses incurred by the other as a result of any such breach.

III. Waiver of Estate Claim

A. Except as provided herein, the husband and wife hereby waive any right at law or in equity to take against any last will made by the other, including all rights of dower or of curtesy, and hereby waive, renounce, and relinquish to the other, their respective heirs, executors, administrators, and assigns forever, each and every interest of any kind or character, which either may now have or may hereafter acquire in or to any real or personal property of the other, whether now owned or hereafter acquired by either, to share in the other party's estate in the event of intestacy, or to act as executor or administrator of the other party's estate.

B. Except as provided herein, the husband and wife shall have the right to dispose of his or her property by will, or otherwise, in such manner as each, in his or her uncontrolled discretion, may deem proper as if no marriage between them ever existed; and neither one shall claim any interest in the estate of the other, except to enforce any obligation imposed by this agreement.

IV. Mutual Release. Except for any cause of action for divorce, or any enforcement of any Probate and Family Court judgment concerning dissolution of the marital relationship, or to enforce the provisions of this agreement in any court, or to enforce any existing abuse prevention case against either party, the husband and wife hereby release and forever discharge the other in connection with matters arising out of the marital relationship from any and all actions, suits, debts, claims, demands, and obligations whatsoever, both in law and at equity, which either of them has ever had, now has, or may hereafter have against the other or any third party, upon or by reason of any matter, cause or thing up to the date of this agreement, as the parties intend that henceforth there shall exist between them only such rights and obligations as are specifically provided in this agreement.

V. Full Satisfaction. The husband and wife agree to accept the provisions set forth in this agreement in full satisfaction and discharge of all claims, past, present, and future, which either party may have against the other, and which in any way arise out of the marital relationship.

VI. Exhibits. There are annexed hereto and hereby made a part hereof Exhibits A, B, C, D & E. The husband and wife agree to be bound by, and to perform and carry out, all of the terms of the exhibits to the same extent as if each of the exhibits were fully set forth in the text of this agreement.

VII. Agreement to Survive/Merge with Judgment of Divorce. At any hearing on the divorce complaint, a copy of this agreement shall be submitted to the court with the request that it be ☐ incorporated but not merged ☒ merged in the judgment of divorce and that it shall ☒ survive ☐ not survive as an independent contract. Notwithstanding the foregoing, any provisions relating to the unemancipated children shall remain modifiable by the court upon a material change in circumstances of a party or a child, or if a modification is consistent with the best interests of a child.

VIII. Strict Performance. The failure of the husband or of the wife to insist in any instance upon the strict performance of any of the terms hereof shall not be construed as a waiver of such terms for the future, and such terms shall nevertheless continue in full force and effect.

IX. Validity. In the event any part of this agreement shall be held invalid, such invalidity shall not invalidate the whole agreement, but the remaining provisions of this agreement shall continue to be valid and binding to the extent that such provisions continue to reflect fairly the intent and understanding of the parties.

X. Documents. Whenever called upon to do so by the other party, each party shall forthwith execute, acknowledge, and deliver to or for the other party, without further consideration, any and all deeds, assignments, bills of sale, or other instruments that may be necessary or convenient to carry out the provisions of this agreement, or that may be required to enable the other party to sell, encumber, hypothecate, or otherwise dispose of the property now or hereafter owned or acquired by such other party.

XI. Governing Law. This agreement shall be construed and governed according to the laws of the Commonwealth of Massachusetts.

XII. Modification. This agreement shall not be altered or modified except by an instrument signed and acknowledged by the husband and wife or by order of a court of competent jurisdiction.

Signed on the day and year first above written and executed in several counterparts.

Eva Frances Lee Rivers ______ Louis Rivers ______
Signature of Wife Signature of Husband

Barnstable ______, ss. July 9 ______, 19 96

Then personally appeared before me the above-named Eva Frances Lee Rivers ______ and acknowledged the foregoing to be her free act and deed,

Before me,

______
Notary Public
My commission expires:

Barnstable ______, ss. July 9 ______, 19 96

Then personally appeared before me the above-named Louis Rivers ______ and acknowledged the foregoing to be his free act and deed,

Before me,

______
Notary Public
My commission expires:

Exhibit A

Child Custody and Visitation

The parties shall have joint legal custody of the 2 minor child(ren) who shall reside primarily with the ~~husband/~~ wife. The other parent shall have reasonable access to the minor child(ren), including overnight visits at all reasonable times and places. The parties also agree to share ~~equitably/~~ equally all holidays, the child(ren)'s birthdays, school and summer vacations, and other special occasions, except that the husband shall be entitled to spend every Father's Day with the child(ren), and the wife shall be entitled to spend every Mother's Day with the child(ren).

Both parents shall have access to the child(ren)'s school and medical records. The party with primary physical custody shall ensure that the other parent has timely notice of school meetings and events.

Both parents shall encourage the child(ren)'s respect and affection for the other parent. Neither shall denigrate the other parent in the presence of the child(ren).

Exhibit B

Alimony, Child Support, and College Expenses

1. Alimony

Both parties waive their rights to seek past, present, and future alimony from the other.

Commencing August 1, 19 96, and on the first day of every month/ ~~week~~ thereafter until the ~~husband's/~~ wife's remarriage, or the death of either party, the husband/ ~~wife~~ shall pay the ~~husband/~~ wife the sum of $ 500.00 as alimony. The parties agree that the husband/ ~~wife~~ shall be/ ~~shall not be~~ entitled to deduct alimony payments made, and the ~~husband/~~ wife shall be taxed/ ~~not taxed~~ on alimony received. The husband's social security number is 111-00-0000 and the wife's is 000-00-0000.

2. Child Support

The husband/ ~~wife~~ shall pay the wife/ ~~husband~~ the sum of $ 292.67 each and every ~~month/~~ week, commencing on July 16, 1996, and continuing each and every Monday until the emancipation of a child. Emancipation (defined below) of a child shall allow the reduction of child support by $146.34 a ~~month/~~ week. Child support is payable ~~monthly/~~ weekly until the last child's emancipation. So long as the husband/ ~~wife~~ pays child support in a timely manner in the amounts required by this exhibit, he/ ~~she~~ shall be entitled to claim the child dependency exemption, and the other party shall release the dependency exemption by signing and delivering IRS Form 8332, upon request.

Child support shall be adjusted annually upon review of the parties' respective incomes from all sources. Adjustments shall be made in keeping with the then current Child Support Guidelines for the Commonwealth of Massachusetts. The parties agree to exchange federal and state tax returns on or before ___June 15___, in order to implement the adjusted rate by ___July 15___ of each year. If the parties wish, they may provide a letter from a certified public accountant as to income from all sources in lieu of supplying tax returns.

3. Children's Education Expenses

The parties shall share ☑ equally ☐ in proportion to income from all sources the unemancipated child(ren)'s college education expenses not covered by scholarships, loans, grants, and the child(ren)'s savings, provided, however, that each party has been consulted as to the child(ren)'s choice of college, and given prior permission which shall not be withheld or delayed unreasonably. Both parents wish to promote the child(ren)'s interest in higher education, and shall cooperate with the other parent and the children in finding the best possible college in keeping with the child's interests and aptitude. The parties agree to cooperate with one another in applying for financial aid, including but not limited to scholarships and loans.

For purposes of this agreement, "emancipation" is defined as the first to happen to a child:

a. attaining the age of 18 unless the child has plans to enroll as a full time student in an accredited post-secondary school program, in which event, emancipation shall occur upon cessation of full time enrollment in an undergraduate program or the age of 23, whichever occurs first.

b. death.

c. marriage.

d. entry into the U.S. military, except that cessation of service shall require emancipation to be determined under the remaining provisions of this definition.

e. full time employment, excluding summer jobs or work during the school year.

f. living permanently away from both parents, excluding time away at summer camp or school.

For purposes of this agreement, "college expenses" is defined to include tuition, room, board, books, laboratory fees, ___2___ round trips from college to a child's home each school year, and all items customarily listed on college bills, and precollege expenses such as preparatory courses, test fees, reasonable travel to and from prospective schools, and application fees.

Exhibit C

Division of Marital Assets

1. **General Provisions.** The parties acknowledge that in entering into this agreement, they have considered the length of their marriage, their ages, health, stations in life, occupations, sources of income, vocational skills employability, assets, conduct, liabilities, financial needs, and the opportunity of each with regard to the future acquisition, preservation, and appreciation in the value of their assets, and the contributions of the parties as homemakers to the family unit.

2. **Personal Property.** The parties agree that they have divided all of their personal property (with the exception of those items on a list, if any, attached hereto), tangible and intangible, to their mutual satisfaction. The property in the name or possession of a party shall be his or hers absolutely, and the other party shall have no further claim.

3. **Real Estate** (select one option and check the appropriate box)

☑ The parties agree that the ~~husband/~~wife may use and occupy the marital domicile at ___123 Cedar Street___, ___Hyannis___, ___Barnstable___ County, Massachusetts, until such time as the house sells on or about ___September 1___, ___2003___, or the ~~husband/~~wife chooses to move, whichever is sooner. In the interim, the ~~husband/~~wife shall pay principal, interest, taxes, insurance, and general maintenance for the property. If the ~~husband/~~wife no longer resides at the marital domicile, the parties shall share the foregoing expenses equally unless the husband ~~/wife~~ uses and occupies the marital domicile, in which event he ~~/she~~ shall be solely liable for those expenses.

The parties agree that the marital domicile shall remain on the market until sold. When sold, the net proceeds shall be divided ☑ equally ☐ with ____ percent to the husband/wife, and the balance to the other spouse.

"Net proceeds" shall be defined as the gross sales price reduced by a broker's commission, if any, and the principal balance of the first mortgage of approximately $___64,000.00___, in addition to reasonable seller's costs, including but not limited to attorneys fees associated with the transaction. Each party represents that there are no other encumbrances, and if either party causes voluntarily or involuntarily any encumbrance to be placed on the marital home, he or she shall use best efforts to remove the encumbrance and shall indemnify and hold harmless the other against any loss or liability in connection with the encumbrance.

Each party shall be liable for capital gain tax, if any, on his and her share of net proceeds received from the sale.

☐ **Alternate** (for parties who agree for one spouse to buy the other spouse's share): The parties agree that the husband/wife shall pay the wife/husband the sum of $________ within ________ months of the date of this agreement, whereupon the wife/husband shall transfer all of her/his right, title, and interest in the marital domicile to the husband/wife, subject to the existing first mortgage. The husband/wife shall indemnify the wife/husband against any loss or liability in connection with the first mortgage, including but not limited to attorneys' fees and costs. The husband/wife shall refinance the existing first mortgage upon becoming the sole owner of the marital domicile.

4. **Liabilities**

Except as otherwise provided herein, the parties acknowledge that they currently have no outstanding joint liabilities incurred during the marriage. The parties agree that any other indebtedness incurred during the marriage by either the husband or the wife shall be the full and sole responsibility of the party incurring the liability.

Exhibit D

Medical and Life Insurance

1. Medical Insurance

The husband ~~/wife~~ presently has medical insurance as a benefit of his ~~/her~~ employment. So long as the husband ~~/wife~~ is eligible for his ~~/her~~ current medical and health insurance policy, or its equivalent, he ~~/she~~ shall maintain and keep in force such policy or its equivalent, for the benefit of the wife ~~/husband~~ until the wife ~~/husband~~ dies, remarries, or ceases to make timely payments, and for any additional cost for ~~his/~~ her coverage, and if the wife ~~/husband~~ is eligible under the policy. The husband ~~/wife~~ also agrees to continue coverage for the benefit of each unemancipated child, so long as a child remains eligible.

Both parties shall have all the rights and benefits set forth in Massachusetts General Laws Chapter 175, Section 110(I).

Each party shall be solely liable for each party's own uninsured health-related expenses, but shall share equally in any uninsured health-related expense of an unemancipated child. For purposes of this exhibit, uninsured health-related expenses shall be defined as any payment, deductible, or co-payment for medical or dental office or emergency room visits, prescription medication, surgery, orthodontia, eyeglasses, contact lenses, and other audiovisual aids, psychotherapy, physical or occupational therapy, and so forth. Neither party shall be liable for a child's uninsured health-related expense unless the party gives prior permission, except in an emergency. Permission shall not be withheld or delayed unreasonably. The parent with physical custody of a child in need of emergency medical or other health-related treatment shall be authorized to obtain such treatment without the other parent's prior permission, but shall notify the other parent as soon as possible.

2. Life Insurance

Both parties acknowledge and agree that each maintains life insurance for the benefit of the other and the unemancipated children with death benefits in the amounts of $ 50,000.00 payable in the event of the husband's death for the wife and $ 100,000.00 for the children; and $ 50,000.00 payable in the event of the wife's death for the husband and $ 100,000.00 for the children.

Each shall maintain insurance in the amount stated above for the benefit of the children, so long as there are any unemancipated children, and the husband ~~/wife~~ shall maintain insurance in the amount stated above for the benefit of the other party, so long as he ~~/she~~ has any alimony obligation.

The parties may use insurance trusts for the benefit of the children, provided, however, that the terms and the trustee(s) shall be subject to the approval of the other party. Approval shall not be withheld or delayed unreasonably.

Exhibit E

Tax Returns and Legal Fees

1. Tax Returns

The husband and wife each hereby represent and warrant to the other that each has paid all income taxes, local, state and federal, on all joint returns filed by the parties; that to their knowledge no interest or penalties are due and owing, no tax deficiency proceeding is pending or threatened, and no audit is pending.

If there is a deficiency assessment in connection with any of the joint returns, the party receiving notice of such deficiency shall notify the other party immediately in writing. The party responsible for the act or omission which caused the deficiency assessment shall be solely liable for any deficiency assessment, penalty, and interest, and shall indemnify and hold the other harmless against any loss or liability in connection therewith. In the event neither party is responsible for the act or omission which caused the deficiency assessment, then the parties shall pay the assessment ☐ equally ☒ in proportion to their income for that tax year.

2. Legal Fees

The husband and wife shall be solely responsible for, and shall pay, his and her own expenses incurred in connection with the negotiation and preparation of this agreement and all related matters, including all court appearances and the prosecution of any complaints for divorce. Each agrees to indemnify and save harmless the other from any and all claims on account of such legal fees and expenses which the other shall be obligated to pay.

3. Legal Fees and Cost of Enforcement

After written notice, if either the husband or the wife is adjudicated in default of his or her obligations under this agreement, the defaulting party shall be required to pay any and all reasonable counsel fees and expenses incurred by the other party in enforcing any of the terms and provisions of this agreement.

Form I. Complaint for Divorce

The COMPLAINT FOR DIVORCE (Form 10) is used in all cases except an uncontested no-fault divorce (which uses Form 1). As Form 10 will be prepared with slight variations in different types of cases, separate instructions are given below for each situation.

Complaint for Contested No-Fault Divorce Under M.G.L. Ch. 208, Sec. 1B

1. Complete the case caption according to the instructions in chapter 3.

2. In Paragraph 1, fill in the complete residential address (not the mailing address if different) of both parties, including the street number, street, town or city, county, and state.

3. In Paragraph 2, fill in the town or city, county, and state where married, followed by the month, day, and year of the marriage. After the words "last lived together," type in the street number, street, town or city, county, and state, followed by the month, day, and year you last lived together (the approximate date is acceptable, if you so indicate).

4. In Paragraph 3, fill in the full names and birth dates of any children under the age of 18 years. Add names and birth dates of children between 18 and 23 years, if they are full time undergraduate students, financially dependent upon you, and legally residing with you (include children who live at school, while maintaining legal residences with you).

5. In Paragraph 4, fill in name of the county and the docket number of any other case involving your marriage or custody of your children. Do not include the names of the parties. If there are no other cases, cross off the word "except" and insert a period following "other."

6. In Paragraph 5, fill in month, day, and year of the breakdown of the marriage. Immediately after the date, cross off the words "the defendant." On the lines following, type in: "there was and continues to be an irretrievable breakdown of the marriage under M.G.L. Ch. 208, Sec. 1B."

7. In Paragraph 6, select the court orders you want by checking off the appropriate boxes, considering the following information and instructions:
   - The provision for "waive the 30 day requirement for filing this complaint" should be ignored. The requirement was abolished, but it appears on old forms still used by courts.
   - Check the provision for "grant a divorce for," and type in "an irretrievable breakdown of the marriage under M.G.L. Ch. 208, Sec. 1B.
   - If you want an abuse prevention order, check the box for "prohibit defendant from imposing any restraint on personal liberty."
   - If you have children under the age of 18 years, check the box for the custody provision. Sometimes plaintiffs delete "custody" (meaning sole custody) and insert a written request for "joint legal custody." See the sample completed form.

- The provision for "order a suitable amount for support of the plaintiff and the minor children" should be revised, if necessary, to reflect your actual request. As written, this provision asks for both alimony and child support. If you do not want alimony, cross off the words "plaintiff and." If you want support for a child over 18 years, delete the word "minor" and insert the term "unemancipated."
- The provision for "order conveyance of the real estate located at…" should be checked off if you and your spouse own any real estate. Fill in the street address, town or city, county and state where the real estate is located. If necessary, attach a separate sheet of paper for other properties. After the words "standing in the name of," fill in the name or names of the owners as they appear on the deed. After the words "as recorded with," fill in name of the county and state (if not Massachusetts) where the deed is recorded. Fill in the book (Bk.) and page (Pg.) numbers (usually stamped on the top margin of the deed) where the deed is recorded.
- If the wife wishes to resume her maiden or a former married name, check the box for "allow plaintiff to resume her former name of," and type in the first, middle, and last name to be resumed.
- Check the last box (to the left of the blank line) and type in: "order an equitable distribution of marital assets under M.G.L. Ch. 208, Sec. 34."

8. Fill in the date on which you file the complaint. Sign the complaint in the lower right hand corner on the line marked "Plaintiff's Signature, if Pro Se," and print your name and address below your signature.

On the second (reverse side) page:

9. Fill in the name of the county on the line before the designation "SS," and the names of you and your spouse on the lines marked "Plaintiff" and "Defendant."

10. Below the words "For Plaintiff:," fill in your name, mailing address, and telephone number. Do not fill in any other information.

Complaint for Contested and Uncontested Fault Divorce

1. Follow instructions 1 through 5 for the contested no-fault divorce above.

2. In Paragraph 5, fill in the month, day, and year of the incident you are using to justify a divorce. After the words "the defendant," type in: "was guilty of cruel and abusive treatment toward the plaintiff as well as on divers other occasions." (Note: the word "divers" is spelled correctly. It is a legal term that means "various.")

3. In Paragraph 6, select the court orders you want by checking off the appropriate boxes. Complete this section according to the instructions for the contested no-fault divorce above, except that when you check the box for "grant a divorce for," type in "cruel and abusive treatment."

4. Do not fill in any other information.

Form I

COMMONWEALTH OF MASSACHUSETTS

Barnstable SS.

PROBATE COURT
No. 96D-0789-D1

Eva Frances Lee Rivers Plaintiff

v.

Complaint for Divorce

Louis Rivers Defendant

1) Plaintiff, who resides at 123 Cedar St., Hyannis, Barnstable County, MA was lawfully married to the defendant, who now resides at 45 Maple Av., Barnstable Co., MA

2) The parties were married at Boston, Suffolk Co., MA on July 7, 1980, and last lived together at 123 Cedar St., Hyannis, Barnstable Co., MA on October 11, 1995.

3) The minor child(ren) of this marriage, and date(s) of birth is/are:

Alan Rivers — April 3, 1982

Elizabeth Rivers — April 21, 1985

4) Plaintiff certifies that no previous action for divorce, annuling or affirming the marriage, separate support, desertion, living apart for justifiable cause, or custody of child(ren) has been brought by either party against the other ~~except~~.

5) On or about October 11, 1995 ~~the defendant~~ there was and continues to be an irretrievable breakdown of the marriage pursuant to G.L.C. 208, s. 1B.

6) Wherefore, plaintiff demands that the court:

- ☐ waive the 30 day requirement for filing this complaint
- ☒ grant a divorce for irretrievable breakdown of the marriage pursuant to G.L.C.208,s.1B
- ☐ prohibit defendant from imposing any restraint on plaintiff's personal liberty
- ☒ grant her Joint legal custody of the above-named child(ren)
- ☒ order a suitable amount for support of the plaintiff and said minor child(ren)
- ☒ order conveyance of the real estate located at 123 Cedar St., Hyannis, Barnstable Co., MA standing in the name of Eva F. Rivers and Louis Rivers as recorded with Barnstable Registry of Deeds, Bk. 0000 Pg. 00000
- ☒ allow plaintiff to resume her former name of Eva Frances Lee
- ☒ order an equitable distribution of marital assets pursuant to M.G.L.Ch. 208, Sec. 34.

Dated: July 8, 1996

Signature of Attorney

Plaintiff's Signature, if Pro Se *Eva Frances Lee Rivers*

Print name and address Eva Frances Lee Rivers
123 Cedar St., Hyannis, MA

COMMONWEALTH OF MASSACHUSETTS

Barnstable SS.

Eva Frances Lee Rivers Plaintiff

V.

Complaint for Divorce

Louis Rivers Defendant

For Plaintiff:

Eva Frances Lee Rivers

Address 123 Cedar Street
Hyannis, MA 02601

Tel No. (508) 555-2698

For Defendant:

Address

Tel No.

Filed ________, 19___

Judgment ________, 19___

Temporary Orders ________, 19___

Documents filed:

- Marriage Certificate ☐
- Plaintiff's Financial Statement ☐
- Defendant's Financial Statement ☐
- Service on Summons ☐

INSTRUCTIONS

Refer to Massachusetts General Laws Chapter 208 and Massachusetts Rules of Domestic Relations Procedure.

1) A certified copy of your civil marriage certificate must be filed with this Complaint.

2) Recite street address, city or town, and county in paragraphs one and two; city or town and county or state in paragraph five.

3) In completing paragraph four, please provide only the docket number and county.

4) The allegations in paragraph five must comply with General Laws Chapter 208, Sections 1 and 2 and Massachusetts Rules of Domestic Relations Procedure Rule 8.

5) All requests for temporary relief must be made by motion, although several prayers may be contained in one. For temporary restraining orders see Mass. R. Dom. Rel. P. Rule 65, affidavit requirement.

6) If attachment or trustee process is desired, a motion with affidavit must be filed. A certificate of insurance is normally not required in domestic relations cases. See Massachusetts Rules of Domestic Relations Procedure Rules 4.1 and 4.2.

7) Plaintiff must sign this Complaint if appearing pro se; otherwise plaintiff's attorney must sign and give his address in the space provided.

Form J. Answer and Counterclaim

1. Fill in the case caption according to the instructions in chapter 3.

2. In paragraph one, indicate which paragraphs of the divorce complaint you accept or admit as true. In most cases, there is no disagreement about the allegations or claims the plaintiff makes in the first four paragraphs of the complaint, as these paragraphs contain basic information about you and your spouse, such as your names, addresses, place and date of the marriage, and names and birth dates of your children. If the complaint incorrectly states any of the foregoing, answer as follows: "Admits the allegations in paragraphs one through 4, except that defendant further answers by stating that [*fill in the correct information*].

3. In paragraph 2, most defendants deny the allegations in paragraph 5 of the complaint. For example, if your spouse claims you are guilty of cruel and abusive treatment, simply answer: "Denies the allegations in paragraph 5." If your spouse claims "There is an irretrievable breakdown of the marriage under M.G.L. Ch. 208, Sec. 1B (contested no-fault divorce) you may agree and simply answer by stating "Admits the allegations in paragraph 5. If you disagree, then deny the allegation.

4. In paragraph 3, you also tell the court whether you believe your spouse is entitled to a divorce or any other relief requested by your spouse in paragraph 6 of the complaint.

5. If you have nothing further to ask of the court by way of a counterclaim, then sign and date the answer. Type in your address and telephone number under your signature and complete a certificate of service, the section following your signature on the answer. Fill in the name of the county where you live and the date on which you mail a copy of the answer to your spouse or your spouse's attorney. That date should be the same as the date you mail the answer to the court. Fill in your spouse's mailing address or the name and address of your spouse's attorney, if your spouse is represented by counsel. Sign the certificate. Send the original to the court, keep a copy for your files, and mail a copy to your spouse or your spouse's lawyer. If you file a counterclaim, do not sign the answer or fill in the certificate at the end of the answer. Instead, complete the section called "Counterclaim" as outlined below, and then sign the "Answer and Counterclaim," before completing the certificate of service. Indicate on the certificate that you are serving the "Answer" or the "Answer and Counterclaim," as the case may be.

   The counterclaim is not an essential ingredient, but many people want to process their own divorce, in addition to responding or defending against their spouses' complaint for divorce.

   Follow the instructions for completing a divorce complaint. The only change is the name of the document, now called a counterclaim for divorce instead of a complaint for divorce. You may choose as your reason for divorce a fault ground or a no-fault ground. In either case, the divorce is contested.

Form J

Commonwealth of Massachusetts
The Trial Court
The Probate and Family Court Department

Barnstable **Division** **Docket No.** 96D-0789-D1

Eva Frances Lee Rivers,
Plaintiff

and Answer and Counterclaim

Louis Rivers,
Defendant

Now comes the defendant in the above-entitled matter and responds to the plaintiff's complaint for divorce as follows:

1. Admits the allegations in paragraph(s) 1, 2, 3, and 4 .
2. Denies the allegations in paragraph(s) 5 .
3. Denies that the plaintiff is entitled to:
   (a) a divorce on the ground of cruel and abusive treatment ;
   (b) or any other relief pursuant to his/~~her~~ complaint for divorce.

Counterclaim

1. Louis Rivers, the above-named defendant and plaintiff in the counterclaim (hereinafter referred to as the "husband"/~~"wife"~~), who resides at 45 Maple Avenue, Falmouth, Barnstable County, Massachusetts was lawfully married to Eva Frances Lee Rivers, the above-named plaintiff and defendant in the counterclaim (hereinafter referred to as the ~~"husband"~~/"wife") who now resides at 123 Cedar Street, Hyannis, Barnstable County, Massachusetts .

2. The parties were married at Boston, Suffolk County, Massachusetts, on July 7, 19 80, and last lived together at 123 Cedar Street, Hyannis, Barnstable County, Massachusetts, on October 11, 19 95 .

3. The minor child(ren) of this marriage, and date(s) of birth ~~is~~/are:

Alan Rivers April 3, 1982
Elizabeth Rivers April 21, 1985

4. The husband/~~wife~~ certifies that no previous action for divorce, annulling or affirming marriage, separate support, desertion, living apart for justifiable cause, or custody of child(ren) has been brought by either arty against the other ~~except:~~

5. On or about October 11, 19 95, ~~the husband/wife~~ there was and continues to be a irretreivable breakdown of the marriage pursuant to M.G.L.Ch. 208, Sec. 1B.

6. Wherefore, the husband/wife requests that this court:

- ☑ grant a divorce for an irretrievable breakdown pursuant to M.G.L.Ch. 208, Sec. 1B
- ☐ prohibit defendant from imposing any restraint on the husband's/wife's personal liberty
- ☑ grant him/her custody of the above-named child(ren)
- ☑ order a suitable amount for support of the husband/wife and the said minor child(ren)
- ☑ order conveyance of the real estate located standing in the names of Eva F. Rivers and Louis Rivers as recorded with Barnstable Registry of Deeds, Book 0000, Page 00000
- ☐ allow the wife to resume her former name of
- ☑ order an equitable distribution of marital assets under MGL ch. 208, sec. 34, and such other relief as this court deems just.

Dated: July 29, 1996

Louis Rivers
Signature of Party or Attorney Louis Rivers

Address: 45 Maple Avenue
Falmouth, MA 02540

Telephone no.: (508) 666-2997

Certificate of Service

Barnstable County July 29, 19 96

I, Louis Rivers, certify that I served the foregoing answer and counterclaim on my spouse/~~spouse's attorney~~, by mailing a copy, first class mail, postage prepaid to my spouse's residence ~~or attorney's office~~ at 123 Cedar St., Hyannis, MA 02601 .

Signed under penalties of perjury.

Signature of Party or Attorney Louis Rivers

Form K. Motion for Temporary Orders of Custody, Support, and Maintenance of Insurance Benefits

1. Complete the case caption according to the directions in chapter 3.
2. In paragraph one, fill in the number of years you were married and the street address, town or city and county where you last lived together.
3. In paragraph 2, check off the appropriate box and fill in the names and dates of birth of any children who are under the age of 18 years or any children over 18 years who are full time undergraduate students under the age of 23.
4. In paragraph 3, check off the appropriate boxes. You may ask for alimony and child support or just alimony or child support.
5. In paragraph 4, if you do not have your own medical insurance, circle plaintiff (if you are the plaintiff) or defendant (if you are the defendant). If you have your own insurance, cross off paragraph 4.
6. In paragraph 5, if your spouse has life insurance and you want the court to order your spouse to maintain insurance during the pendency of the divorce, circle plaintiff (if your spouse is the plaintiff) or defendant (if your spouse is the defendant) and fill in the name of the insurance company and number of the policy, along with the dollar amount of the benefits payable on death. If your spouse has a whole life insurance policy, your spouse may be able to cash in or borrow against the policy. Consider asking the court to prohibit your spouse from taking any action diminishing the value of the death benefits. See motion to preserve marital assets (Form M).

After the "Wherefore" clause following paragraph 5, fill in your requests as follows:

7. In paragraph one, circle the appropriate party responsible for paying alimony and fill in the amount of weekly alimony you want. If you prefer, ask for a monthly amount. Be sure to fill in the date alimony should commence.
8. In paragraph 2, change the request if you want sole legal custody or a different visitation schedule. "Reasonable time" is the most flexible, but also the most dangerous when parents cannot agree on the time and place of visitation.
9. In paragraph 3, circle the appropriate party responsible for paying child support and fill in the amount of weekly child support, usually determined by completing the Child Support Guideline Worksheet (Form 4). If you prefer, ask for a monthly amount. To convert the weekly child support order from the worksheet, simply multiply the weekly amount by 52 and divide by 12. *Do not* multiply the weekly amount by 4. Be sure to fill in the information regarding the start-up date for child support and when payments should be made thereafter.
10. In paragraph 4, circle the appropriate party to be ordered to maintain medical insurance and fill in the name of the party responsible for the cost.
11. In paragraph 5, circle the party responsible for maintaining life insurance and provide the court with the information on the policy. Circle the appropriate party to be named as beneficiary of the policy. If you have children, you may include them as beneficiaries. If not, delete "unemancipated children."
12. Fill in the date, sign the motion, and print your name, address and telephone number below the signature line. Then complete the certificate of service with the appropriate information. Call your county Probate and Family Court for the first available court date. Mail the original motion to the court; keep a copy for your files and mail one to your spouse or your spouse's lawyer. Send your spouse a copy of the motion on the same day as you mail the original to the court. Be sure you provide at least ten days prior notice by mail. For example, if you mail a copy to your spouse on October 1, you cannot schedule your hearing before October 11.

[Note: If you are using this form to keep your spouse from removing the children from the state, see the additional instructions under the heading "Responding to a Complaint for Divorce" in chapter 6.]

Form K

Commonwealth of Massachusetts
The Trial Court
The Probate and Family Court Department

Barnstable **Division** **Docket No.** 96D-0789-D1

Eva Frances Lee Rivers,
Plaintiff

and

Louis Rivers,
Defendant

Motion for Temporary Orders of Custody, Support, and Maintenance of Insurance Benefits

Now comes the plaintiff ~~/defendant~~ in the above-entitled matter and respectfully states as follows:

1. The parties have been married for 16 years, and last lived together at 123 Cedar St., Hyannis, Barnstable County, Massachusetts.

2. ❑ There are no minor children.

   ☑ There is/are 2 unemancipated child(ren) of the marriage, namely:

Name	Date of Birth
Alan Rivers	April 3, 1982
Elizabeth Rivers	April 21, 1985

3. ☑ The plaintiff ~~/defendant~~ is without adequate means of support for ~~himself~~/herself, and thus requires alimony.

   ☑ The plaintiff ~~/defendant is~~ living with the unemancipated children, and is requires child support.

4. The plaintiff ~~/defendant~~ does not have ~~his~~/her own medical insurance.

5. The ~~plaintiff/~~ defendant has a life insurance policy with Cape Cod Life Assurance Company, Policy No. XX1098765, with a face amount of $ 150,000.00.

Wherefore, the plaintiff/defendant requests that this court enter the following orders for the foregoing reasons and those more fully outlined in a supporting affidavit filed with this motion:

1. That plaintiff's ~~/defendant's~~ spouse be ordered to pay alimony of $ 100.00 per week, commencing on forthwith, 19____, and continuing thereafter each and every Monday.

2. That the parties be given joint legal custody of the child(ren) with primary physical custody to plaintiff ~~/defendant,~~ and reasonable time with the other parent, including overnight visits at all reasonable times and places.

3. That ~~plaintiff/~~ defendant's spouse be ordered to pay child support of $ 300.00 per week, commencing ~~on~~ forthwith, ~~19~~____, and continuing thereafter each and every Monday.

4. That plaintiff's ~~/defendant's~~ spouse obtain/maintain medical insurance for the benefit of the family at the sole cost of the defendant, and that the parties share equally all uninsured medical and dental expenses of the unemancipated child(ren).

5. That plaintiff's ~~/defendant's~~ spouse obtain/maintain life insurance on his ~~/her~~ life with Cape Cod Life Assurance Company, Policy No. XX1098765, with a face amount of $ 150,000.00, for the benefit of the plaintiff ~~/defendant/ unemancipated child(ren)~~.

6. Such other orders as the court deems just.

Dated: July 8, 1996

Eva Frances Lee Rivers
Signature of Pro Se Party or Attorney

Print name: Eva Frances Lee Rivers

Address: 123 Cedar Street
Hyannis, MA 02601

Telephone No.: (508) 555-2698

Certificate of Service

Barnstable, ss. July 8, 19 96

I, Eva Frances Lee Rivers, certify that I served the foregoing motion and supporting affidavit on the ~~plaintiff/~~ defendant by mailing a copy, first class mail, postage prepaid, to the ~~plaintiff/~~ defendant ~~or opposing counsel~~ at 45 Maple Avenue Falmouth, MA 02540, together with notice that I scheduled a hearing on the motion on July 29, 19 96, at 8:30 a.m. at the Barnstable County Probate and Family Court at __________.

____
Signature of Pro Se Party or Attorney

Form L. Affidavit in Support of Motion for Temporary Orders of Custody, Support, and Maintenance of Insurance Benefits

1. Fill in the case caption according to the instructions in chapter 3.

2. In the first, unnumbered paragraph, cross out the word "defendant." (This assumes that you are the plaintiff. If your spouse filed for divorce and you are the defendant, cross out the word "plaintiff.")

3. The first three numbered paragraphs require basic information about you, your spouse, the marriage, and the children, if any. Take the information from your complaint for divorce. Cross out the word "plaintiff" or "defendant," whoever the children do not live with.

4. In paragraph 4, if you have minor children and want custody, cross out the word "defendant" (if you are the plaintiff) or the word "plaintiff" (if you are the defendant).

5. In paragraph 5, cross out the word "plaintiff" or the word "defendant," whichever applies to your spouse. Check off the appropriate box or boxes to indicate the type of support you are requesting, then cross out the word "plaintiff's" or the word "defendant's," whichever does not apply to you.

6. In paragraphs 6 and 7, cross out the word "plaintiff" or the word "defendant," whichever applies to your spouse.

7. Feel free to add information to the affidavit. You are signing under penalties of perjury, so be careful to make statements you believe to be true. Fill in the date above your signature. Sign the affidavit.

8. Fill in the certificate of service by including the name of the county where you live and the date on which you mail the affidavit to your spouse just below the title "Certificate of Service." Fill in your name on the line after the word "I." If your spouse does not have an attorney, cross out the word "attorney," and fill in your spouse's address on the line after the word "to." If your spouse does have an attorney, cross out the word "party," and fill in the attorney's name and address on the line. Cross out "delivering" if you mail the copy or "mailing" if you hand deliver it. Sign the certificate of service. File the original affidavit and certificate with the court; as with all other court documents, keep a copy for your files and one copy for your spouse.

Note: If you are using this form to keep your spouse from removing the children from the state, see the additional instructions under the heading "Responding to a Complaint for Divorce" on page in chapter 6.

Form L

Commonwealth of Massachusetts
The Trial Court
The Probate and Family Court Department

Barnstable **Division** | **Docket No.** 96D-0789-D1

Eva Frances Lee Rivers,
Plaintiff

and

Louis Rivers,
Defendant

Affidavit in Support of Motion for Temporary Orders of Custody, Support, and Maintenance of Insurance Benefits

Now comes the plaintiff/~~defendant~~ in the above-entitled matter, under oath, and deposes as follows:

1. The parties were married at Boston, Suffolk County, Massachusetts, on July 7, 19 80, and last lived together at 123 Cedar St., Hyannis, Barnstable County, Massachusetts, on October 11, 19 95.

2. Plaintiff now resides at 123 Cedar Street, Hyannis, Barnstable County, Massachusetts, and the defendant resides at 45 Maple Avenue, Falmouth, Barnstable County, Massachusetts.

3. ❑ There are no minor children of the marriage.

☑ The 2 unemancipated child(ren) of the marriage, namely:

Name	Date of Birth
Alan Rivers	April 3, 1982
Elizabeth Rivers	April 21, 1985

☑ reside with the plaintiff/~~defendant~~.

4. During the marriage, the plaintiff/~~defendant~~ was the primary caretaker of the child(ren), and continues in that roll. The child(ren) ~~is~~/ are doing well as a result of plaintiff's/~~defendant's~~ child care.

5. The plaintiff/~~defendant~~ is without adequate means to provide support for the family, and requires:

❑ alimony
☑ alimony and child support
❑ child support

from the plaintiff's/~~defendant's~~ spouse.

6. On information and belief, the plaintiff's/~~defendant's~~ spouse is employed full time, and has sufficient means to provide for the spouse's own support and the support of the family.

7. On information and belief, the plaintiff's/~~defendant's~~ spouse has medical and life insurance as a benefit of employment, and can maintain benefits at reasonable cost for the family.

Signed under penalties of perjury this 8th day of July, 19 96.

Eva Frances Lee Rivers
Signature of Party Eva Frances Lee Rivers

Certificate of Service

Barnstable, ss July 8, 19 96

I, Eva Frances Lee Rivers, certify that I served the foregoing affidavit on the opposing party/~~attorney~~, by ~~delivering~~/mailing a copy, first class mail, postage prepaid, to 45 Maple Avenue, Falmouth, MA 02540.

Signed under penalties of perjury.

Signature of Party or Attorney
Eva Frances Lee Rivers

Form M. Motion to Preserve Marital Assets Without Notice to Spouse

1. Fill in the case caption according to the instructions in chapter 3. Where appropriate, cross out the word "plaintiff" or "defendant," and "him" or "her," whichever does not apply.
2. In paragraph one, fill in the basic information about when you were married and when and where you last lived together. If you are living together as you complete the form, indicate that you have not separated and live at the same address.
3. In paragraph 2, fill in the reason you are seeking a divorce from your spouse. See paragraph 5 of your complaint for divorce. The court only wants the legal basis, not all of the details causing the break-up of your marriage.
4. In paragraph 3, fill in the name of your spouse's employer, if any.
5. In paragraph 5, indicate which bank accounts, automobiles, checking accounts, stock brokerage accounts, certificates of deposit, mutual funds, etc. should be preserved and whether you want your spouse to maintain certain benefits for you, such as life insurance and death benefits, retirement account, etc. Cross off any sub-parts of paragraph 4, which do not apply to you.
6. Date and sign the motion, adding your address and telephone number below your signature.
7. You do not serve a copy of this motion on your spouse, (and hence do not need a certificate of service) because you are appearing in court without advance notice. If the court decides in your favor, the judge will enter an order and may give your spouse a chance to come to court on another date to argue against the order to preserve assets. Generally, courts allow these orders to remain in place, so long as the parties have the ability to pay ordinary living expenses.

Form N. Affidavit in Support of Motion to Preserve Assets

1. Complete the case caption according to the instructions in chapter 3. Where appropriate, cross out the word "plaintiff" or "defendant," whichever does not apply.
2. In paragraph 1, circle the appropriate parties, identifying the party in need of financial support.
3. In paragraph 2, tell the court about one or two recent incidents which lead you to believe your spouse may hide, sell, transfer, or borrow against marital assets without your prior knowledge or permission. For example, your spouse may have closed a joint checking account from which you usually pay bills and did not give you any money to pay the mortgage.
4. In paragraph 3, fill in the names of any child who should also have medical insurance or life insurance benefits.
5. Date and sign the affidavit.

Form M

Commonwealth of Massachusetts
The Trial Court
The Probate and Family Court Department

Barnstable **Division** **Docket No.** 96D-0789-D1

Eva Frances Lee Rivers,
Plaintiff

and

Louis Rivers,
Defendant

Motion to Preserve Marital Assets Without Notice to Spouse

Now comes the plaintiff/~~defendant~~ in the above-entitled case and respectfully states as follows:

1. The parties have been married since July 7, 19 80, and last lived together at 123 Cedar Street, Hyannis, Barnstable County, Massachusetts, on October 11, 19 95.
2. On or about July 1, 19 96, the ~~plaintiff/~~defendant closed the parties' joint checking account with no notice to the plaintiff.
3. The ~~plaintiff/~~defendant is an employee of Cape and Island Transport, and has employment benefits such as health, dental, disability, and life insurance, in addition to various retirement benefits.
4. The plaintiff/~~defendant~~ will suffer irreparable harm without an immediate order being entered for the preservation of marital assets and the maintenance of benefits for ~~him~~/her through the ~~plaintiff's~~/defendant's employment, including but not limited to:
   a. the following specific assets:
      (1) Cape's Best Bank, checking account no. 54
      (2) Cape's Best Bank, CD no. 88
      (3) Mass. Bay Savings, account no. 1010
      (4) 1996 Buick Century
   b. such other assets not specifically named herein, but which may be subject to an equitable division between the parties.
   c. maintenance of all health-related benefits.
   d. maintenance of any and all past, present and future benefits of the ~~plaintiff's~~/defendant's employment for third parties, including but not limited to any death benefits of life insurance and retirement plans.

Dated: July 8, 1996

Eva Frances Lee Rivers
Signature of Party or Attorney for Party

Address: 123 Cedar Street
Hyannis, MA 02601

Telephone no.: (508) 555-2698

Form N

Commonwealth of Massachusetts
The Trial Court
The Probate and Family Court Department

Barnstable **Division** **Docket No.** 96D-0789-D1

Eva Frances Lee Rivers,
Plaintiff

and

Louis Rivers,
Defendant

Affidavit in Support of Motion to PreserveMarital Assets

Now comes the plaintiff/~~defendant~~ in the above-entitled matter, under oath, and deposes as follows:

1. Throughout the marriage the plaintiff/~~defendant~~ has been dependent upon the ~~plaintiff/~~defendant for financial support, as the ~~plaintiff/~~defendant has been the stay-at-home parent of the parties' 2 minor child(ren).
2. On information and belief, the ~~plaintiff/~~defendant:
   (a) closed the parties' joint checking account with no notice to the plaintiff, thereby denying her access to approximately $2,500.00.
   (b) removing the parties' 1996 Buick Century automobile from the marital home and placing it at a location unknown to the plaintiff.
   (c) threatens to remove all of the parties' liquid assets from accounts now known to plaintiff and conceal assets.
   (d) threatens to remove plaintiff's name from the defendant's medical insurance.
3. On information and belief, the plaintiff/~~defendant~~ will suffer irreparable harm without an immediate order being entered for the preservation of marital assets and maintenance of benefits, in that the ~~plaintiff/~~defendant will have an opportunity to conceal assets, and possibly terminate medical coverage for plaintiff/~~defendant, and~~.

Signed under penalties of perjury this 8th day of July, 19 96.

Eva Frances Lee Rivers
Signature of plaintiff/~~defendant~~

Form O. Petition for Writ of Habeas Corpus

1. Complete the case caption according to the instructions in chapter 3.
2. Fill in your street address, town or city, and name of county in the blank space just below the case caption.
3. In paragraph one, fill in the town or city and name of the county and state where you were married; the street address, town or city, name of the county and state where you and your spouse last lived together in Massachusetts; and the number of children under the age of 18 years. Provide the names and birth dates of each child.
4. In paragraph 2, fill in the date you last lived together: Indicate where the children presently reside in Massachusetts by providing the street address, town or city, and name of county.
5. In paragraph 3, fill in the number of children under 18 years.
6. In paragraph 4, fill in the basic facts causing you to seek court intervention. For example, you may have recently discovered your former spouse plans to move out of state with the minor children without your permission or the court's. In other cases, some parents remove children by stealth from Massachusetts. The parent remaining in Massachusetts searches for the children and upon finding them, needs orders to compel the move-away parent to release the children to Massachusetts authorities.
7. In paragraph 5, indicate the name of the state or country where your spouse is planning to move or has moved already.
8. After the paragraph beginning with the word "Wherefore," fill in the names of the children on the line in paragraph 1, and the number of minor children on the line in paragraph 2.
9. Fill in the date, then sign the petition in the presence of a notary public, and print your name, address, and telephone number below your signature.

Form P. Certificate of Absolute Divorce or Annulment

1. In the section marked "HUSBAND," fill in the husband's full name, usual residence, including county, his date of birth, and number of this marriage.
2. In the section marked "WIFE," fill in the wife's full name, maiden name, usual residence, including county, her date of birth, and number of this marriage.
3. On the bottom line of the top portion of the form:
   - Under "DATE OF THIS MARRIAGE," fill in the month, day, and year of marriage.
   - Under "NUMBER OF CHILDREN BORN ALIVE OF THIS MARRIAGE," fill in the number of all children born alive, regardless of whether the children are over the age of 18 years at the time of the divorce.
   - Under "NUMBER OF CHILDREN UNDER AGE 18 IN THIS FAMILY," fill in the number of children under the age of 18 at the time of the divorce.
4. Do not fill in the bottom portion of the form (this is the portion surrounded by the heavier line, which is marked FOR COURT USE ONLY).

Form O

Commonwealth of Massachusetts
The Trial Court
The Probate and Family Court Department

Barnstable Division　　　　Docket No. 96D-0789-D1

Eva Frances Lee Rivers ,
Plaintiff　　　　Petition for Writ of Habeas Corpus
and
Louis Rivers ,
Defendant

Now comes the plaintiff/defendant, of 45 Maple Avenue, Falmouth, Barnstable County, Massachusetts, in the above-entitled matter and respectfully represents that:

1. The parties were married at Boston , Suffolk County, Massachusetts , and last lived together at 123 Cedar Street , Hyannis , Barnstable County, Massachusetts, with the 2 minor child(ren) of the marriage, namely:

Name	Date of Birth
Alan Rivers	April 3, 1982
Elizabeth Rivers	April 21, 1985

2. On or about October 4 , 19 95 the parties separated. The plaintiff/defendant and 2 minor child(ren) continue to reside at 123 Cedar Street , Hyannis , Barnstable County, Massachusetts.

3. From date of separation until the present, the plaintiff/defendant spends significant time with the 2 minor child(ren), and has a close loving relationship with the child(ren).

5. The plaintiff/defendant recently discovered that the plaintiff/defendant plans to move to Illinois with the two minor children .

6. Plaintiff/defendant would be compelled to commence litigation in Illinois for the return of the children, causing unnecessary expense, confusion, delay, and irreparable harm to the plaintiff/defendant.

Wherefore, the plaintiff/defendant asks under M.G.L. Ch. 208, Sec. 32 that this court:

1. Issue an order directing the Sheriff and the Sheriff's deputies to have before this court the minor child(ren), Alan Rivers and Elizabeth Rivers , and to summon the plaintiff/defendant to appear and show cause why the child(ren) is/are imprisoned and restrained by the plaintiff/defendant.

2. Enter such other orders as this court deems just and consistent with the best interests of the minor child(ren), including but not limited to granting plaintiff/defendant a temporary order of custody of the 2 minor child(ren).

Dated: January 3, 1997

Louis Rivers [signature]
~~Plaintiff's~~/Defendant's signature
Print name: Louis Rivers
Address: 45 Maple Avenue
Falmouth, MA 02540
Telephone no.: (508) 666-2997

Commonwealth of Massachusetts
Barnstable County　　　　Date: January 3, 1997

Then personally appeared the above-named Louis Rivers and acknowledged that the foregoing statements are true.

Notary Public
My commission expires:

Form P

The Commonwealth of Massachusetts
DEPARTMENT OF PUBLIC HEALTH
REGISTRY OF VITAL RECORDS AND STATISTICS
CERTIFICATE OF ABSOLUTE
DIVORCE OR ANNULMENT
(Chap. 208, Sec. 46 G.L.)
R-408

HUSBAND

1. HUSBAND NAME — FIRST	MIDDLE	LAST	
Louis		Rivers	
2a. USUAL RESIDENCE - STREET ADDRESS		2b. CITY, TOWN OR LOCATION	
45 Maple Avenue		Falmouth	
2c. COUNTY	2d. STATE	3. DATE OF BIRTH (Mo., Day, Yr.)	4. NUMBER OF THIS MARRIAGE (1st, 2, Specify)
Barnstable	MA	4/3/49	First

WIFE

5a. WIFE - NAME — FIRST	MIDDLE	LAST	5b. MAIDEN NAME
Eva	Frances Lee	Rivers	Lee
6a. USUAL RESIDENCE - STREET ADDRESS		6b. CITY, TOWN OR LOCATION	
123 Cedar Street		Hyannis	
6c. COUNTY	6d. STATE	7. DATE OF BIRTH (Mo., Day, Yr.)	8. NUMBER OF THIS MARRIAGE (1st, 2nd, Specify)
Barnstable	MA	10/11/53	First

9. DATE OF THIS MARRIAGE (Mo., Day, Yr.)	10a. NUMBER OF CHILDREN BORN ALIVE OF THIS MARRIAGE	10b. NUMBER OF CHILDREN UNDER AGE 18 IN THIS FAMILY
7/7/80	Two	Two

JUDGMENT — *FOR COURT USE ONLY*

11. COUNTY OF JUDGMENT		11b. TITLE OF COURT
12. DATE OF JUDGMENT NISI (Mo., Day, Yr.)	13. TYPE OF JUDGMENT - DIVORCE OR ANNULMENT (Specify)	14. DATE OF JUDGMENT
15. DOCKET NUMBER	16. NAME OF PLAINTIFF	17. CAUSE FOR WHICH GRANTED
18a. SIGNATURE OF CERTIFYING OFFICAL		18b. TITLE OF OFFICIAL

Form Q

THE TRIAL COURT
THE PROBATE AND FAMILY COURT DEPARTMENT

Barnstable DIVISION   DOCKET NO. 96D-0789-D1

REQUEST FOR TRIAL — ~~PRE-TRIAL~~ ASSIGNMENT
THE FORM SHOULD NOT BE USED FOR MARK-UP OF TEMPORARY ORDERS AND MOTIONS
Please print or type

Please assign for hearing: Eva Frances Lee Rivers
Plaintiff

v.

Louis Rivers
Defendant

TYPE OF CASE Divorce   TIME REQUIRED 5 minutes   HEARING AT Barnstable

(✔) Uncontested
( ) Contested

( ) Merits
( ) Custody
( ) Support
( ) Visitation
( ) 208, §34
( ) Other ______

The following papers must be on file before cases can be assigned for hearing:

( ) Summons or Return of Service
( ) Marriage Certificate
( ) Statistical Form R408
( ) Financial Statement (Supp. Rule 401)
( ) Affidavits of Both Parties (1A Divorces)
( ) Notarized Agreement (1A Divorces)
( ) ______

Has Discovery Been Completed (✔) Yes ( ) No

Has This Case Been Pre-Tried ( ) Yes (✔) No

I hereby certify that, in my opinion, this case is ready for trial.

Requested by:
Eva Frances Lee Rivers — Name
123 Cedar St., Hyannis, MA 02601 — Address, Zip
(508) 555-2693 — Phone No.

Opposing Counsel/Defendant
Louis Rivers
45 Maple Ave., Falmouth, MA02540
(508) 666-2997

FOR REGISTER'S USE ONLY
ACTION

The above-entitled matter has been assigned for

______ (Trial) ______ (Pre-Trial Conterence)

at ______ on ______, 19____, at ______ A.M.

______. Returned without action. Data Incomplete. See Above.

Register of Probate   Clerk's Initials

Form R

Commonwealth of Massachusetts
The Trial Court
The Probate and Family Court Department

Barnstable Division   Docket No. 96D-0789-D1

Eva Frances Lee Rivers,
Plaintiff

and

Louis Rivers,
Defendant

Affidavit in Support of Motion to Delay Filing of Marriage Certificate

Now comes the plaintiff in the above-entitled matter and under oath states as follows:

1. Plaintiff and defendant were married on July 7, 19 80, and last lived together at 123 Cedar St., Hyannis, Barnstable County, MA, on October 11, 19 95.

2. They are the parents of the 2 minor child(ren), whose name(s) and date(s) of birth ~~is~~/are:

Alan Rivers   April 3, 1982
Elizabeth Rivers   April 21, 1985

3. The child(ren) presently reside(s) with plaintiff at 123 Cedar Street, Hyannis, Barnstable County, Massachusetts.

4. The plaintiff requires immediate temporary orders concerning the care and custody of the minor child(ren), including but not limited to temporary orders of support and maintenance of medical insurance for the benefit of the family.

5. The plaintiff used due diligence to locate and obtain a copy of the parties' marriage certificate from the state of Masssachusetts where the parties were married.

6. The plaintiff has been informed that the request for a certified copy of the marriage certificate will take approximately three weeks to fulfull.

7. The plaintiff will file the certificate upon receipt.

Signed under penalties of perjury this 8th day of July, 19 96.

Eva Frances Lee Rivers
Signature of Plaintiff

Form S

Commonwealth of Massachusetts
The Trial Court
The Probate and Family Court Department

Barnstable **Division** **Docket No.** 96D-0789-D1

Eva Frances Lee Rivers,
Plaintiff

V. Notice of Appearance

Louis Rivers,
Defendant

To the Register of the above-named court:

Please enter my appearance (pro se) as attorney for Louis Rivers in the above named case.

Dated: July 14, 1996

Louis Rivers
Signature of Pro Se Party or Attorney

Address: 45 Maple Avenue
Falmouth, MA 02540

Telephone No.: (508) 555-2997

Certificate of Service

Barnstable County July 14, 19 96

I, Louis Rivers, certify that I served the foregoing Notice of Appearance on my spouse ~~/spouse's attorney~~, by mailing a copy, first class mail, postage prepaid to my spouse's residence or attorney's office at 123 Cedar Street, Hyannis, MA 02601.

Signed under penalties of perjury.

Louis Rivers
Signature of Party or Attorney

Form T

Commonwealth of Massachusetts
The Trial Court
The Probate and Family Court Department

Barnstable **Division** **Docket No.** 96D-0789-D1

Eva Frances Lee Rivers,
Plaintiff

V.

Louis Rivers,
Defendant

Affidavit of Indigency and Request for Waiver, Substitution or State Payment of Fees and Costs

Pursuant to M.G.L. Ch. 261, Sections 27A-G, the applicant, Eva Frances Lee Rivers, swears (or affirms) as follows:

1. Applicant is indigent in that he/she is a person [check only one]:
   - ☐ (a) who receives public assistance under the Massachusetts Aid to Families with Dependent Children, General Relief, or Veteran's Benefits programs, or receives assistance under Title XVI of the Social Security Act, or the Medicaid Program, 42 USC 1396, et seq., or
   - ☐ (b) whose income, after taxes, is 125% or less of the current poverty threshhold annually established by the Community Services Administration pursuant to Section 625 of the Economic Opportunity Act, as amended, or
   - ☒ (c) who is unable to pay the fees and costs of the proceeding in which ~~he/~~she is involved, or is unable to do so without depriving ~~him/~~herself or ~~his/~~her dependents of the necessities of life, including food, shelter, and clothing. [Note: If the applicant checks (c), he/she should fill in the information called for in the "Supplement to Affidavit of Indigency."]
2. Applicant requests that the following normal fees and costs (e.g., filing fee, service of process costs, etc.) either be waived, substituted, or paid by the state.
   [Note: In filling in blanks in this paragraph and paragraph 3, be as specific as possible as to fees and costs known at time of filing this request. A supplementary request may be filed at a later time, if necessary.]
   Filing fee
   Service of process costs
3. Applicant requests that the following extra fees and costs (e.g., cost of transcribing a deposition, expert assistance, etc.) either be waived, substituted, or paid by the state.
   None at this time.

Signed under the penalties of perjury.

Date: July 8, 1996

Eva Frances Lee Rivers
Signature of applicant

Printed name: Eva Frances Lee Rivers

Address: 123 Cedar Street
Hyannis, MA 02601

Telephone No.: (508) 555-2698

Form U

Commonwealth of Massachusetts
The Trial Court
The Probate and Family Court Department

Barnstable **Division** **Docket No.** 96D-0789-D1

Eva Frances Lee Rivers,
Plaintiff

and

Supplement to
Affidavit of Indigency

Louis Rivers,
Defendant

If the applicant checks (c) on the affidavit of indigency, he/she should fill in the information called for on this supplementary form.

Note: Pursuant to General Laws Ch. 261, Sections 27A-G, the applicant, Eva Frances Lee Rivers, swears (or affirms) as follows:

(a) Date of birth: 10/11/53
(b) Highest grade attained in school: 12
(c) Special training: none
(d) List any physical or mental disabilities: none

(e) Number of dependents: two
(f) Income, expense, asset & liability information:
Gross Income (specify whether monthly or weekly):
$ 708.00 per month
If from employment, list your occupation and your employer's name and address: Cashier at Pets 'N Vets Supplies
One Washington Street
Boston, MA 02200
Source of income, if not from employment: Not applicable

If applicant's spouse is employed, list occupation and name and address of his/her employer: Not applicable

Applicant's gross annual income for preceding year: $ none
Deductions: per month
Federal tax: 70.80
State tax: 50.00
Social Security: 25.00
Health insurance: none
Pension: none

Other: none
Total: 145.80
Net Income (specify whether monthly or weekly):
$ 562.20 per month
Expenses (specify whether monthly or weekly): monthly
Rent: $400.00
Food: $216.66
Clothing: $ 43.33
Utilities: $ 50.00
Other expenses: none
Net income minus expenses (specify whether monthly or weekly):
$ -147.79 per month
Assets
Own car? No year and make Not applicable
Market value: none
Balance due: none
Bank accounts: 100.00
Other property: 500.00 - furniture & furnishings
Liabilities
Sears $2,000
Landlord 800

(g) Other facts which may be relevant to applicant's ability to pay fees and costs?
my aunt cannot babysit for me after Thanksgiving, so I may not be able to work as many hours.

Dated: July 9, 1996

Signed under penalties of perjury.

Eva Frances Lee Rivers
Signature of applicant

Print name: Eva Frances Lee Rivers

Address: 123 Cedar Street
Hyannis, MA 02601

Telephone No.: (508) 555-2698

Form V

Commonwealth of Massachusetts

Eva Frances Lee Rivers v. Louis Rivers

Docket No. 96D-0789-D1

Barnstable, SS. Report of Louis Rivers

To: the keeper of the Payroll Records at Hyannis Savings Bank, located at 456 Main Street, Hyannis, MA,

greeting.

You are hereby commanded, in the name of the Commonwealth of Massachusetts, to appear before the Barnstable County Probate and Family Court at Barnstable, Massachusetts, within and for the county of Barnstable on the sixth day of January, 19 97, at 9:00 a.m., and from day to day thereafter, until the action hereinafter named is heard by the court, to give evidence of what you know relating to an action of divorce then and there to be heard and tried between Eva Frances Lee Rivers and Louis Rivers. You are further required to bring with you: all records of wages, bonuses, commissions, salary, employment contracts, deferred compensation and all other earnings paid and any other records relating to Eva Frances Lee River's employment with your company.

Hereof fail not, as you will answer your default under the pains and penalties of the law in that behalf made and provided.

Dated at Falmouth on the tenth day of December, 19 96.

____
Notary Public
My commission expires:

I this day summoned the within named Keeper of the Payroll Records of Hyannis Savings Bank to appear and give evidence at court as within directed by delivering to the Keeper in hand at 456 Main Street, Hyannis, MA, an attested copy of the subpoena together with fees for attendance and travel.

____
Constable or Deputy Sheriff

Service and Travel	$_______
Copies	$_______
Witness Fee	$_______
Motor Vehicle	$_______

It being necessary I actually used a motor vehicle the distance of _______ miles in the service of this process.

____
Constable or Deputy Sheriff

Subscribed and sworn to before me this _______ day of _______, 19___.

____
Notary Public
My commission expires:

Form W

Commonwealth of Massachusetts
The Trial Court
The Probate and Family Court Department

Barnstable **Division** **Docket No.** 96D-0789-D1

Eva Frances Lee Rivers,
Plaintiff

V.

Motion to Compel Production and Order for Sanctions

_______________,
Defendant

Now comes the plaintiff in the above-entitled matter and states as follows:

1. On or about September 16, 199 6, the plaintiff served a Request for Production of Documents, Request for Financial Statement, and Interrogatories on defendant, requiring defendant to file and serve a response on or before October 16, 199 6.

2. As of the date of this motion, defendant refuses or fails to respond.

3. Plaintiff cannot adequately negotiate or prepare for trial without the response(s).

Wherefore, plaintiff requests that this court order defendant to respond within 5 days or be subject to such sanctions as this court deems just, including but not limited to prohibiting the defendant from raising any issues concerning child support & custody, alimony, and division of assets which is the subject of the discovery plaintiff seeks.

Dated: October 23, 1996

Eva Frances Lee Rivers
Plaintiff's signature
Print name: Eva Frances Lee Rivers
Address: 123 Cedar Street
Hyannis, MA 02601
Telephone No.: (508) 555-2698

Certificate of Service

Barnstable, ss. October 23, 19 96

I, Eva Frances Lee Rivers, certify that I served the foregoing Motion to Compel Production and Order for Sanctions on defendant by mailing a copy, first class mail, postage prepaid, to: Louis Rivers, 45 Maple Ave., Falmouth, MA 02540, together with notice that the motion has been scheduled for hearing at the Barnstable County Probate and Family Court on Wednesday, November 6, 19 96 at 8:30 a.m.

____
Eva Frances Lee Rivers

Form X

COMPLAINT FOR PROTECTION FROM ABUSE (G.L. c. 209A) | FOR COURT USE ONLY | DOCKET NO. 96D-0789-D1 | TRIAL COURT OF MASSACHUSETTS

PART 1
[ ] BOSTON MUNICIPAL COURT
[ ] DISTRICT COURT ______ DIVISION
[X] PROBATE & FAMILY COURT Barnstable DIVISION
[ ] SUPERIOR COURT ______ COUNTY

PART 2
NAME OF PLAINTIFF (the person seeking protection)
Eva Frances Lee Rivers

PART 3
3A Write your address here if you are NOT asking the Court to keep it confidential
123 Cedar St.
Hyannis, MA 02601
Daytime Phone No. (508) 555-1111

3B Write your address here only if you are asking the Court to keep it CONFIDENTIAL (that is, impounded)

Daytime Phone No. ( )

PART 4
If you left a former residence to avoid abuse, write that address here:

PART 5
Your attorney (if any)
Name
Address

PART 6
I [ ] am [X] am not under the age of eighteen.
The defendant [ ] is [X] is not under the age of eighteen.

PART 7
NAME & ADDRESS OF DEFENDANT (the person causing abuse)
Louis Rivers
45 Maple Ave.
Falmouth, MA 02540
Daytime Phone No. (508) 777-1000
Date of Birth (if known) 10/26/59

PART 8
CHECK AS MANY AS APPLY: The defendant and I:
[X] are currently married to each other.
[ ] were formerly married to each other.
[ ] are not married but we are related to each other by blood or marriage; specifically, the defendant is my
[X] are the parents of one or more children.
[ ] are not related but we now live in the same household.
[ ] are or were in a dating or engagement relationship of the following nature:
Date relationship began:
Nature of relationship:
Frequency of contact during relationship:
If it has ended, date relationship ended:

PART 9
Are there any prior or pending court actions in any state or country involving you and the defendant for divorce, annulment, paternity, child custody or support, guardianship, separate support, legal separation, or abuse prevention?
[X] No [ ] Yes If Yes, give court, type of case, date and *(if available)* docket number:

PART 10
On or about (dates) July 12, 1996 I suffered abuse when the defendant:
[X] attempted to cause me physical harm.
[X] placed me in fear of imminent serious physical harm.
[X] caused me physical harm.
[ ] caused me unwillingly to engage in sexual relations by force, threat of force, or duress.

Therefore:
[X] 1. I ask the Court to order the defendant to stop abusing me.
[X] 2. I ask the Court to order the defendant not to contact me, or any child(ren) listed below, unless authorized by the Court.
[X] 3. I ask the Court to order the defendant to leave and remain away from my residence which is located at:
123 Cedar St., Hyannis, MA
If this is an apartment building or other multiple family dwelling, check here. [ ]
[ ] 4. I ask the Court to impound my address to prevent its disclosure to the defentant, the defendant's attorney, or the public.
Do not check item 4 if you wrote your address in Part 3A above.
[X] 5. I ask the Court to order the defendant to leave and remain away from my workplace which is located at:
456 Main St., Hyannis, MA
[X] 6. I ask the Court to award me temporary custody of the following children under 18

NAME	DATE OF BIRTH
Alan Rivers	4/3/82
Elizabeth Rivers	4/21/85

You may not obtain an Order from the Boston Municipal Court or a District or Superior Court covering items (6) or (7) in Part 10 if there is a prior or pending Order for custody or support from the Probate and Family Court.

[X] 7. I ask the Court to order the defendant, who has a legal obligation to do so, to pay temporary support [ ] for me [X] for any child(ren) in my custody [ ] for both
[X] 8. I ask the Court to order the defendant to pay me $ 765.43 in compensation for the following losses suffered as a direct result of the abuse emergency room fees and prescription drugs for fractured jaw
[ ] 9. I ask the Court to order the following
10. I ask the Court to order the relief I have requested above, except for items (7) and (8), without advance notice to the defendant because ther is a substantial likelihood of immediate danger of abuse. I understand that if the Court issues such a temporary Order, the Court will schedule a hearing within 10 court business days to determine whether such a temporary Order shoud be continued, and that I must appear in court on that day if I wish the Order to be continued.

PLAINTIFF'S SIGNATURE Eva Frances Lee Rivers

Form Y

AFFIDAVIT

Describe in detail the most recent incidents of abuse. State what happened, the dates, who did what to whom, and describe any injuries. Also describe any history of abuse.

On or about July 12, 1996, the defendant hit the plaintiff in the jaw with a closed fist, causing swelling and a broken tooth. He also threw a heavy crystal ashtray, hitting the plaintiff in the forehead, causing her to pass out. The defendant is often under the influence of alcohol, and prone to sudden fits of rage directed against the plaintiff. There are numerous other incidents of physical violence throughout the marriage, often in the presence of the parties' minor children.

The defendant has threatened the plaintiff with further bodily harm. The plaintiff also believes the minor children will suffer emotional harm as a result of the defendant's behavior in their presence.

If more space is needed, attach additional pages and check this box: [ ]

I declare under penalty of perjury that all statements of fact made above, or in any additional pages attached, are true.

DATE SIGNED	PLAINTIFF'S SIGNATURE	
July 14, 1996	x Eva Frances Lee Rivers	
WITNESSED BY	**PRINTED NAME OF WITNESS**	**TITLE/RANK OF WITNESS**
C. U. Sine	C. U. Sine	Deputy Register

Appendix C
Blank Forms

Wherever we indicate a form is **Standard**, you must use a copy available from the court or the one supplied in this appendix. Many forms are not marked **Standard** because the court does not provide a preprinted version. Thus, you must use your own version or those provided here. Do not request any form except the **Standard** forms from the court. The following forms are in this appendix:

* From *A Pro se Litigant Guide to Preparing a Divorce Pre-Trial Memorandum for the Probate and Family Court,* by Hon. Nancy M. Gould and Peter F. Zupcofska; reprinted with permission of the authors.

Commonwealth of Massachusetts

The Trial Court

_______________ Division **Probate and Family Court Department** Docket No.______________

Joint Petition for Divorce Under M.G.L. Ch. 208, Sec. 1A

_________________________________ and _________________________________

Petitioner   Petitioner

of _______________________________ of _______________________________

(Street and No.)   (Street and No.)

_________________________________ _________________________________

(City or Town) (State) (Zip)   (City or Town) (State) (Zip)

1. Now come the Husband and Wife in a joint petition for divorce pursuant to Massachusetts General Laws, Chapter 208, sec. 1A.
2. The parties were lawfully married at ____
on ___________________________ and last lived together at ____________________________
on _________________________________, __________.
3. The minor child(ren) of this marriage and date(s) of birth is/are:

_________________________________ _________________________________

_________________________________ _________________________________

4. The parties certify that no previous action for divorce, annulment, affirmation of marriage, separate support, desertion, living apart for justifiable cause, or custody of child(ren) has been brought by either party against the other except ____
____
5. On or about ______________________________, ________, an irretrievable breakdown of the marriage under M.G.L. Ch. 208, sec. 1A occurred and continues to exist.
6. Wherefore, the parties pray that the Court:
   - ❑ grant a divorce on the ground of irretrievable breakdown
   - ❑ approve the separation agreement executed by the parties
   - ❑ incorporate and merge said agreement in the divorce judgment
   - ❑ incorporate but not merge said agreement, which shall survive and remain as an independent contract
   - ❑ allow Wife to resume her former name of ____
   - ❑ ____

Date: ________________________________

_________________________________ _________________________________

SIGNATURE OF WIFE OR ATTORNEY   SIGNATURE OF HUSBAND OR ATTORNEY

_________________________________ _________________________________

(Print address if not pro se)   (Print address if not pro se)

_________________________________ _________________________________

Tel. No. ___________________________ Tel. No. ___________________________

B.B.O.# ___________________________ B.B.O.# ___________________________

Joint Petition for Divorce
Under M.G.L. Ch. 208, Sec. 1A

For Wife:

____

Address ______________________________

____

Tel No. ______________________________

For Husband:

____

Address ______________________________

____

Tel No. ______________________________

Docket No. ______________________________

Filed ______________________, ________

Agreement Approved ________________, ________

Judgment ____________________, ________

Documents filed:

- Marriage Certificate ❑
- Wife's Financial Statement ❑
- Husband's Financial Statement ❑
- Separation Agreement ❑
- Affidavit of Irretrievable Breakdown ❑
- Affidavit Disclosing Care or Custody Proceedings ❑
- Child Support Guidelines Worksheet ❑

Commonwealth of Massachusetts
The Trial Court
The Probate and Family Court Department

______________________ **Division** **Docket No.** ___________________

__________________________________,
Petitioner

Joint Affidavit Under
M.G.L. Ch. 208, Sec. 1A

and

__________________________________,
Petitioner

Now come the petitioners in the above-entitled and numbered case and respectfully state as follows:

1. We were married on ______________________________________, ______, at __________________________________, ______________________________ County, _________________________________, and last lived together on _________________, ________, at ____, __________________________________, ______________________________County, __________________________________.

2. ❑ There are _____ child(ren) of this marriage under the age of 18 years whose names and dates of birth are:

❑ There are _____ child(ren) of this marriage over the age of 18 but less than 23 years who are full time undergraduate students, financially dependent upon the petitioners, whose names and dates of birth are:

❑ There are no minor children of this marriage.

3. During the course of our marriage we developed different interests and goals. As we grew apart, we no longer derived any satisfaction from our married life and now believe there is no chance of reconciliation.

4. We believe our marriage is irretrievably broken and we are best served by ending our relationship under the terms of our settlement agreement.

5. We are both satisfied with the terms of the settlement agreement and ask the court to approve the agreement and incorporate it into a judgment of divorce.

Signed under penalties this ______ day of ________________________, _______.

____
Petitioner

____
Petitioner

Acknowledgment

Commonwealth of Massachusetts
______________________ County   _________________________, _______

Then personally appeared before me ____________________________________, the petitioner, and acknowledged the foregoing to be his free act and deed for the purposes stated therein.

____
Notary Public
My commission expires:

Commonwealth of Massachusetts
______________________ County   _________________________, _______

Then personally appeared before me ____________________________________, the petitioner, and acknowledged the foregoing to be her free act and deed for the purposes stated therein.

____
Notary Public
My commission expires:

Commonwealth of Massachusetts
The Trial Court
The Probate and Family Court Department

______________________ **Division** **Docket No.** ____________________

___________________________________,
Plaintiff

V.

___________________________________,
Defendant

Demand for Financial
Statement Under
Supplemental Rule 401

You are hereby requested to file with the __________________________________ County Probate and Family Court your signed financial statement, and to provide a signed copy to me at the following address:____
____.

Under Rule 401 the filing and serving of the copy shall be completed within 48 hours.

Dated:___________________________

____
Signature of Party

Print name:______________________________

Address:__________________________________
____

Telephone No.:____________________________

Commonwealth of Massachusetts

The Trial Court

_____________**Division** **Probate and Family Court Department** **Docket No.** ___________

_________________________________ **VS.** _________________________________

Worksheet
Child Support Guidelines

Worksheet Completed By _________________________________Date Completed___________________

All provisions of the Guidelines (pp. 1-6) should be reviewed prior to the completion of the worksheet. These guidelines will apply (absent a prior agreement acceptable to both parties) in cases where combined gross income of both parties does not exceed $100,000.00 and where the income of the non-custodial parent does not exceed $75,000.00.

1. Basic Order

a) Non-custodial gross weekly income (less prior support orders actually paid, for child/family other than the family seeking this order) $____________

b) % of gross/number of children (from chart III A) ____________%

c) Basic order (a) x (b) (A) $____________

2. Adjustment For Ages of Children

a) Age of oldest child ____________

b) % of increase for age (from chart III B) ____________%

c) Age add on (2b) x (A) $____________

d) Adjusted order (A) + (2c) (B) $____________

3. Custodial Parent Income Adjustment

a) Custodial parent gross income $____________

b) Less $15,000.00 - 15,000.00

c) Less day care cost (annual) -____________

d) Custodial adjusted gross $____________

e) Non-custodial gross (annual) $____________

f) Total available gross 3(d) + 3(e) $____________

g) Line 3(d)___________ Line 3(f)___________

h) 3(d) divided by 3(f) __________ per cent

i) Adjustment for custodial income (line 3h %) x (B) (C) $____________

4. Calculation of Final Order

a) Adjusted order (B) above (B) $____________

b) Less adjustment for income (C) above (C) -____________

c) Less 50% weekly cost of family group health insurance [under the provisions of section G(1)] - ____________

or

Plus 50% weekly cost of obligee's family group health insurance [under the provisions of section G(1)] + ____________

Weekly Support Order (B) - (C) ± 4(c) $____________

CJ-D 304 (1/98)

III Child Support Obligation Schedule

A. Basic Order

The basic child support obligation, based upon the income of the non-custodial parent is as follows.

Gross Weekly Income	Number of Children		
	1	2	3
$0 - $124	Discretion of the Court, but no less than $50.00 per month ($11.55 per week)		
$125 - $200	15% (± 2%)	18% (± 2%)	21% (± 2%)
$201 - $500	25% (± 2%)	28% (± 2%)	31% (± 2%)
$501 - max.	27% (± 2%)	30% (± 2%)	33% (± 2%)

Within the discretion of the Court, and in consideration of the totality of the circumstances of the parties, the order may be either increased or decreased by 2 percent. Where the court must set a support order where there are more than three children, the minimum order is to be no less than that contained in this guideline for three children, to be increased within the discretion of the Court depending upon the circumstances of each case.

B. Age Differential

The above orders are to be increased to reflect the costs of raising older children. The following percentages are intended to be applied to the age of the oldest child in the household for whom support is sought under the pending action.

Age of Oldest Child	Percentage Increase
0 - 6	Basic Order Applies
7 - 12	Basic Order + 10% of Basic Order
13 - 18	Basic Order + 15% of Basic Order
Over 18	If statute permits, at discretion of the Court.

C. Custodial Parent Income Adjustment

Where the custodial parent works and earns income in excess of $15,000.00 after consideration of day care expenses, the support order is to be reduced by the percentage that the excess represents in relation to the combined incomes of both parents minus the custodial parent's disregard.

(see other side)

Commonwealth of Massachusetts

The Trial Court
Probate and Family court Department

_______________**Division** **Docket No.** _____________

FINANCIAL STATEMENT (SHORT FORM)

_________________________________ v. _________________________________

Plaintiff/Petitioner Defendant/Petitioner

INSTRUCTIONS: If your income equals or exceeds $75,000.00, you must complete the LONG FORM financial statement, unless otherwise ordered by the Court. All questions on both sides of this form must be answered in full or word "none" inserted. If additional space is needed for any answer, an attached sheet may be filed in addition to, but not in lieu of, the answer. Information contained herein is confidential and only available to the parties and persons under Probate and Family Court Department Supplemental Rule 401.

1. Your Name ______________________________ Soc. Sec. No. ________________
   Address ____
   (street and no.) (city or town) (state) (zip)
   Age ________ Telephone No. ______________ No. of Children living with you ________
   Occupation ________________ Employer ________________________________
   Employer's Address ____
   (street and no.) (city or town) (state) (zip)
   Employer's Tel. No. ____________________ Health Ins. Coverage________________
   Health Insurance Provider ____________________ Cert. No. ________________

2. **Gross Weekly Income from All Sources**
   a). Base pay from salary, wages ______________________ $__________
   b). Self Employment Income **(attach a completed Schedule A)**__________ $__________
   c). Income from overtime - commissions - tips - bonuses - part-time job ________ $__________
   d). Dividends - interest ______________________ $__________
   e). Income from trusts or annuities ______________________ $__________
   f). Pensions and retirement funds ______________________ $__________
   g). Social Security ______________________ $__________
   h). Disability, unemployment insurance or worker's compensation __________ $__________
   i). Public Assistance (welfare, A.F.D.C. payments) __________ $__________
   j). Rental from Income Producing Property **(attach a completed Schedule B)**___ $__________
   k). All other sources (including child support, alimony) __________ $__________

   l). **Total Gross Weekly Income** (a through k) $__________

3. **Itemize Deduction from Gross Income**
   a). Federal income tax deductions (claiming ________ exemptions) ____ $__________
   b). State income tax deductions (claiming ________ exemptions) ____ $__________
   c). F.I.C.A. / Medicare______________________ $__________
   d). Medical Insurance ______________________ $__________
   e). Union Dues ______________________ $__________

   f). **Total Deductions** (a through e) $__________

4. **Adjusted Net Weekly Income**
   2(l) minus 3 (f) ______________________ $__________

5. **Other Deductions from Salary**
   a). Credit Union (Loan Repayment or Savings) __________ $__________
   b). Savings ______________________ $__________
   c). Retirement ______________________ $__________
   d). Other (specify) ______________________ $__________

   e). **Total Deductions** (a through d) $__________

6. **Net Weekly Income** 4 minus 5 (e) $__________

7. **Gross Yearly Income from Prior Year** ______________________ $__________
   (attach copy of all W-2 and 1099 forms for prior year)

CJ-D301 (11/97)

8. **Weekly Expenses** (Do Not Duplicate Weekly Expenses - Strike Inapplicable Words)

a). Rent - Mortgage (PIT) $______________
b). Homeowner's / Tenant Insurance $______________
c). Maintenance and Repair $______________
d). Heat (Type_____________) $______________
e). Electricity and/or Gas $______________
f). Telephone $______________
g). Water / Sewer $______________
h). Food $______________
i). House Supplies $______________
j). Laundry and Cleaning $______________
k). Clothing $______________
l) Life Insurance $______________
m) Medical Insurance $______________
n) Uninsured Medicals $______________
o) Incidentals and Toiletries $______________
p) Motor Vehicle Expenses $______________
q) Motor Vehicle Loan Payment $______________
r) Child Care $______________
s) Other (attach additional schedule if necessary)
______________ $______________
______________ $______________

Total Weekly Expenses (a through s) $______________

9. **Counsel Fees**

a). Retainer amount(s) paid to your attorney(s)____________________ $______________
b). Legal fees incurred, to date, against retainer(s)____________________ $______________
c). Anticipated range of total legal expense to prosecute this action____ $______________ to $______________

10. **Assets** (Attach additional schedule for additional real estate and other assets, if necessary)

a). Real Estate ____________________________
Location ____________________________
Title ____________________________
Fair Market Value ____________ - Mortgage(s) ____________ = Equity $______________

b). IRA, Keogh, Pension, Profit Sharing, Other Retirement Plans
List Financial Institution or Plan Names and Account Numbers
____________________________ $______________
____________________________ $______________
____________________________ $______________

c). Tax Deferred Annuity Plan(s) ____________________ $______________
d). Life Insurance: Present Cash Value ____________________ $______________
e). Savings & Checking Accounts, Money Market Accounts, & CDs which are held individually, jointly, in the name of another person for your benefit, or held by you for the benefit of your minor child(ren) **List Financial Institution Names and Account Numbers**
____________________________ $______________
____________________________ $______________
____________________________ $______________

f). Motor Vehicles
Fair Market Value __________ - Motor Vehicle Loan __________ = Equity $______________
Fair Market Value __________ - Motor Vehicle Loan __________ = Equity $______________

g). Other (such as - stocks, bonds, collections)
____________________________ $______________
____________________________ $______________

h). **Total Assets** (a through g) $______________

11. **Liabilities (DO NOT list weekly expenses but DO list all liabilities)**

	Creditor	Nature of Debt	Date of Origin	Amount Due	Weekly Payment
a).					
b).					
c).					
d).					

e). **Total Amount Due and Total Weekly Payment** ____________________

11. **Number of Years you have paid into Social Security** ______________ years

I certify under penalties of perjury that my income and expenses, assets, and liabilities as stated herein are true to the best of my knowledge and belief. I have carefully read this financial statement and I certify the information is true and complete.

Date __________________ Signature ____________________________

STATEMENT BY ATTORNEY

I, the undersigned attorney, am admitted to practice law in the Commonwealth of Massachusetts--am admitted pro hoc vice for the purposes of this case--and am an officer of the court. As the attorney for the party on whose behalf this Financial Statement is submitted, I hereby state to the court that I have no knowledge that any of the information contained herein is false.

Attorney Signature ____________________________ Date__________________
Address ____________________________ Tel. No. __________________
BBO# ____________________________

FINANCIAL STATEMENT SCHEDULE A

Name: ______________________ Docket No. ______________________

MONTHLY SELF-EMPLOYMENT OR BUSINESS INCOME

GROSS MONTHLY RECEIPTS $ [   ]

Monthly Business Expenses

Cost of goods sold	$ ______
Advertising	$ ______
Bad debts	$ ______
Auto:	
Gas	$ ______
Insurance	$ ______
Maintenance	$ ______
Registration	$ ______
Commissions	$ ______
Depletion	$ ______
Dues and publications	$ ______
Employee Benefit Programs	$ ______
Freight	$ ______
Insurance (other than health), please specify type:	
______________________	$ ______
______________________	$ ______
Interest on mortgage to banks	$ ______
Interest on loans	$ ______
Legal and professional services	$ ______
Office expenses	$ ______
Laundry and cleaning	$ ______
Pension and profit sharing	$ ______
Rent on leased equipment	$ ______
Machinery/Equipment	$ ______
Other business property	$ ______
Repairs	$ ______
Supplies	$ ______
Taxes	$ ______
Travel	$ ______
Meals and entertainment	$ ______
Utilities and phone	$ ______
Wages	$ ______
Other expenses (specify)	
______________________	$ ______
______________________	$ ______

TOTAL MONTHLY EXPENSES $ [   ]

WEEKLY BUSINESS INCOME (Gross monthly receipts less total monthly expenses divided by 4.3) Enter this amount in Section II, line (d) of CJ-D 301-L or Section 2(b). of CJ-D 301-S. $ [   ]

FINANCIAL STATEMENT SCHEDULE A - Continued

NATURE OF SELF-EMPLOYMENT OR BUSINESS

. Is this business seasonal in nature? ____________

. If a seasonal business, please specify percentage of income received and expenses incurred for each month of the year.

MONTH	PERCENTAGE OF INCOME RECEIVED	EXPENSES INCURRED
January		
February		
March		
April		
May		
June		
July		
August		
September		
October		
November		
December		

3. State whether your business accounts on a calendar year basis or fiscal year basis. ____________

4. If your business accounts on a fiscal year basis, give the starting and ending dates of your chosen fiscal year.

____________ Starting

____________ Ending

5. State your gross receipts, year to date (note whether calendar or fiscal year). $ [ ]

____

6. State your gross expenses year to date (note whether calendar or fiscal year). $ [ ]

____

FINANCIAL STATEMENT SCHEDULE B

Name: ______________________ Docket No. ______________________

RENT FROM INCOME PRODUCING PROPERTY

ANNUAL RENT RECEIVED $ [ ]

ANNUAL RENTAL EXPENSES

Advertising	$ ________
Auto and travel	$ ________
Insurance	$ ________
Cleaning and maintenance	$ ________
Commissions	$ ________
Interest on mortgage to bank	$ ________
Other interest (specify)	
______________________	$ ________
______________________	$ ________
Legal and professional services	$ ________
Repairs	$ ________
Supplies	$ ________
Taxes	$ ________
Utilities	$ ________
Wages	$ ________
Other expenses (specify)	
______________________	$ ________
______________________	$ ________

TOTAL ANNUAL EXPENSES $ [ ]

TOTAL WEEKLY RENTAL INCOME (Gross rent received less expenses, divided by 52). Enter this amount in Section II, line (n) of CJ-D 301-L or Section 2(j) of CJ-D 301-S. $ [ ]

Commonwealth of Massachusetts

The Trial Court
Probate and Family court Department

_______________**Division** **Docket No.** ____________

FINANCIAL STATEMENT
(LONG FORM)

________________________________ v. ________________________________

Plaintiff/Petitioner Defendant/Petitioner

INSTRUCTIONS: This financial statement should be completed if your income equals or exceeds $75,000.00 or if ordered by the court. All items on both sides of this form must be addressed either with the appropriate amount or the word "none" inserted for items that are not applicable to your personal situation. Additional sheets may be attached to supplement any item. You must complete and attach Schedule A if you are self-employed or have other business income, and/or Schedule B if you own rental property.

1. PERSONAL INFORMATION

Your Name ____________________________ Social Security Number ________________

Address ____
(street and no.) (city or town) (state) (zip)

Telephone Number ________________ Date of Birth ______________ Age________

Occupation ____

Employer ____________________________ Employer's Tel. Number ___________

Employer's Address ____
(street and no.) (city or town) (state) (zip)

Do you have health ins. coverage __________ If **yes**, name of health insurance provider ____________

Do you have any natural, adopted, stepchild(ren), foster child(ren) or children of partners who are living in your household half time or more? __________ If so, how many child(ren)? _____

II. GROSS WEEKLY INCOME / RECEIPTS FROM ALL SOURCES (strike inapplicable words)

a). Base pay, salary, wages $______________

b). Overtime $______________

c). Part-time job $______________

d). Self-employment **(attach a completed Schedule A)** $______________

e). Tips $______________

f). Commissions - Bonuses $______________

g). Dividends - interest $______________

h). Income from trusts and annuities $______________

i). Pensions and retirement funds $______________

j). Social Security $______________

k). Disability, unemployment or worker's compensation $______________

l). Public Assistance (welfare, A.F.D.C. payments) $______________

m). Child Support - Alimony (actually received) $______________

n). Rental income **(attach a completed Schedule B)** $______________

o). Royalties and other rights $______________

p). Contributions from household member(s) $______________

q). Other (specify) ____ $______________

TOTAL GROSS WEEKLY INCOME / RECEIPTS (Add items a-q) $______________

III. WEEKLY DEDUCTIONS FROM GROSS INCOME

TAX WITHHOLDING

a) Federal tax withholding / estimated payments $________

Number of withholding allowances claimed ________

b) State tax withholding / estimated payments $________

Number of withholding allowances claimed ________

OTHER DEDUCTIONS

c) F.I.C.A. $________
d) Medicare $________
e) Medical Insurance $________
f) Union Dues $________
g) Child Support $________
h) Spousal Support $________
i) Retirement $________
j) Savings $________
k) Deferred Compensation $________
l) Credit Union (Loan) $________
m) Credit Union (Savings) $________
n) Charitable Contributions $________
o) Life Insurance $________
p) Other (specify) ________ $________
q) Other (specify) ________ $________
r) Other (specify) ________ $________

TOTAL WEEKLY DEDUCTIONS FROM PAY (Add items a-r) $________

IV. NET WEEKLY INCOME

a) Enter total gross weekly income / receipts $________
b) Enter total weekly deductions from pay $________

NET WEEKLY INCOME (Subtract IV(b) from IV(a)) $________

V. GROSS INCOME FROM PRIOR YEAR $________

(attach copy of all W-2 and 1099 forms from prior year and Schedule A, if self-employed)

Number of years you have paid into Social Security ________

VI. COUNSEL FEES

Retainer amount(s) paid to your attorney(s) $________

Legal fees incurred, to date, against the retainer(s) $________

Anticipated range of total legal expense to prosecute this action $________ to $________

VII. WEEKLY EXPENSES NOT DEDUCTED FROM PAY

INSTRUCTIONS: All expense figures must be listed by their WEEKLY total. DO NOT list expenses by their MONTHLY total. In order to compute the weekly expense, divide the monthly expense by 4.3. For example, if your rent in $500.00 per month, divide 500 by 4.3. This will give you a weekly expense of $116.28. Do not duplicate weekly expenses. Strike inapplicable words.

Rent	$______________
Mortgage (P & I, Taxes / Insurance, if escrowed)	$______________
Property taxes and assessment	$______________
Homeowner's Insurance	$______________
Tenant's Insurance	$______________
Maintenance Fees - Condominium Fees	$______________
Maintenance / Repairs	$______________
Heat (Type) ______________	$______________
Electricity	$______________
Propane / Natural Gas	$______________
Telephone	$______________
Water / Sewer	$______________
Food	$______________
House Supplies	$______________
Laundry	$______________
Dry cleaning	$______________
Clothing	$______________
Life insurance	$______________
Medical insurance	$______________
Uninsured medical - dental expenses	$______________
Incidentals / toiletries	$______________
Motor vehicle expenses	
Fuel	$______________
Insurance	$______________
Maintenance	$______________
Loan payment(s)	$______________
Entertainment	$______________
Vacation	$______________
Cable TV	$______________
Child Support (attach a copy of the order, if issued by a different court)	$______________
Child(ren)'s Day Care Expense	$______________
Child(ren)"s Education	$______________
Education (self)	$______________
Employment related expenses (which are not reimbursed)	
Uniforms	$______________
Travel	$______________
Required continuing education	$______________
Other (specify) ______________________________	$______________
Lottery tickets	$______________
Charitable contributions / Church giving	$______________
Child(ren)'s allowance	$______________
Extraordinary travel expenses for visitation with child(ren)	$______________
Other (specify) ______________________________	$______________
Other (specify) ______________________________	$______________
Other (specify) ______________________________	$______________
TOTAL WEEKLY EXPENSES NOT DEDUCTED FROM PAY	$______________

VII. ASSETS

INSTRUCTIONS: List all assets including, but not limited to the following. If additional space is needed for any answer or to disclose additional assets an attached sheet may be filed.

A. REAL ESTATE

Real Estate -- Primary Residence

Address ____
(street address) (city or town) (state) (zip)

Title held ____

Outstanding 1st mortgage $__________
Outstanding 2nd mortgage or home equity loan $__________
Equity $__________
Purchase Price of the Property $__________
Year of Purchase __________
Current Assessed Value of the Property $__________
Date of Last Assessment __________
Fair Market Value of the Property $__________

Real Estate -- Vacation or Second Home (including interest in time share)

Address ____
(street address) (city or town) (state) (zip)

Title held ____

Outstanding 1st mortgage $__________
Outstanding 2nd mortgage or home equity loan $__________
Equity $__________
Purchase Price of the Property $__________
Year of Purchase __________
Current Assessed Value of the Property $__________
Date of Last Assessment __________
Fair Market Value of the Property $__________

B. **MOTOR VEHICLES**, including cars, trucks, ATV's, snowmobiles, tractors, motorcycles, boats, recreational vehicles, aircraft, farm machinery, etc.

Type __________
Make __________
Model __________
Purchase Price of Vehicle $__________
Year of Purchase __________
Fair Market Value $__________
Outstanding Loan $__________
Equity $__________

Type __________
Make __________
Model __________
Purchase Price of Vehicle $__________
Year of Purchase __________
Fair Market Value $__________
Outstanding Loan $__________
Equity $__________

VIII. ASSETS CONTINUED

C. PENSIONS

	Institution	Account Number	Listed Beneficiary	Current Balance / Value
Defined Benefit Plan				
Defined Contribution Plan				

D. OTHER ASSETS. List assets which are held individually, jointly, in the name of another person for your benefit, or held by you for the benefit of your minor child(ren). (List particulars as indicated, e.g., institution/plan name(s) and account number(s), named beneficiaries and current balances, if applicable)

	Institution	Account Number	Listed Beneficiary	Current Balance
Checking Account(s)				
Savings Accounts(s)				
Cash on Hand				
Certificate(s) of Deposit				
Credit Union Account(s)				
Funds Held in Escrow				
Stocks				
Bonds				
Bond Fund(s)				
Notes Held				
Cash in Brokerage Account(s)				
Money Market Account(s)				

	Institution	Account Number	Listed Beneficiary	Current Balance
U.S. Savings Bond(s)				
IRAs				
Keough				
Profit Sharing				
Deferred Compensation				
Other Retirement Plans				
Annuity (please specify whether a tax deferred annuity or tax sheltered annuity).				
Life Insurance Cash Value (please specify whether a term or a whole/universal life insurance policy).				
Judgments/Liens				
Pending Legacies and/or Inheritances				
Jewelry				
Contents of Safe or Safe Deposit Box				
Firearms				
Collections				
Tools/Equipment				
Crops/Livestock				
Home Furnishings (value)				
Art and Antiques				

TOTAL ASSETS $ ______

IX. LIABILITIES (List loans, credit card debt, consumer debt, installment debt, etc., which are not listed elsewhere)

INSTRUCTIONS: All payment figures must be listed by their WEEKLY amount. DO NOT list payments by their MONTHLY amount. In order to compute the weekly payment, divide the monthly payment by 4.3. For example, if your credit card liability is $500.00 per month, divide 500 by 4.3. This will give you a weekly payment of $116.28.

CREDITOR	KIND OF DEBT	DATE INCURRED	AMOUNT DUE	WEEKLY PAYMENT
TOTALS				

CERTIFICATION BY AFFIANT

I certify under the penalties of perjury that the information stated on this Financial Statement and the attached Schedules, if any, is complete, true and accurate. **I UNDERSTAND THAT WILLFUL MISREPRESENTATION OF ANY OF THE INFORMATION PROVIDED WILL SUBJECT ME TO SANCTIONS AND MAY RESULT IN CRIMINAL CHARGES BEING FILED AGAINST ME.**

________________ Date

________________ Signature

COMMONWEALTH OF MASSACHUSETTS

County of ________________

Then personally appeared the above ________________ and declared the foregoing to be true and correct, before me this ________ day of ________

________________ Notary Public

My Commission Expires: ________________

INSTRUCTIONS: In any case where an attorney is appearing for a party, said attorney MUST complete the Statement by Attorney.

STATEMENT BY ATTORNEY

I, the undersigned attorney, am admitted to practice law in the Commonwealth of Massachusetts -- am admitted pro hoc vice for the purposes of this case -- and am an officer of the court. As the attorney for the party on whose behalf this Financial Statement is submitted, I hereby state to the court that I have no knowledge that any of the information contained herein is false.

________________ Date

________________ Signature

Name of Attorney ________________
Please Print

Address ________________

Tel. No. ________________

BBO # ________________

INCOME ASSIGNMENT WORKSHEET

________________________________, SS.

PROBATE AND FAMILY COURT
NO. ____________________________

PLAINTIFF:

Name ________________________________

Address ______________________________

____

Telephone Number ______________________

Social Security No. _____________________

DEFENDANT:

Name ________________________________

Address ______________________________

____

Telephone Number ______________________

Social Security No. _____________________

Obligor's Place of Employment

Employer's Name ____

Address: ____

____

Telephone Number ____

Effective Immediately ❑

Suspended ❑

____
Date

Obligor to pay $ ____________________________ per week / month

as alimony and / or child support.

Arrearage $________________

Current Order $________________

Arrears Order $________________

Payment made payable to: ❑ Probation Department

❑ Spouse directly

Send to (to reimburse): ❑ Spouse

❑ DPW-______________________ office

❑ Other ____

Health Insurance:
Obligor's Insurer ______________________________ Policy No. ______________________

Commonwealth of Massachusetts
The Trial Court
The Probate and Family Court Department

______________________ Division Docket No. ____________________

____________________________________,
Petitioner/Plaintiff

and/v. Settlement/Separation Agreement

____________________________________,
Petitioner/Defendant

This agreement is made this _____ day of ______________, _____, by and between ____________________________________ of ____, ____________________________ County, Massachusetts (hereinafter called the "wife"), and ____________________________________ of ____, ____________________________ County, Massachusetts (hereinafter called the "husband"). All references to the "parties" shall mean the above-mentioned husband and wife.

Statement of Facts

The husband and wife were married at ____, ____________________________ County, ____________________________________ on ____________________, _____. The husband and wife are now living separate and apart.

❑ There are no minor or unemancipated children.

❑ There is/are ___ unemancipated minor child(ren).

❑ There is/are___ unemancipated child(ren), over the age of 18 years, but full time undergraduate student(s) under the age of 23 years, dependent upon the parties for financial support.

This agreement is made in order to settle finally and completely and determine:

a. The property rights of each of the parties;
b. What should be paid to the parties for their respective support in consideration of the provisions of Massachusetts General Laws, Chapter 208, Section 34;
c. Whether and to what extent all or any part of the estate of the husband or wife should be assigned to the other in consideration of the provisions of Massachusetts General Laws, Chapter 208, Section 34;
d. All other rights and obligations arising from the marital relationship, including, but not limited to child-related matters;
e. All other matters which should be settled finally and completely in view of the pending divorce action. Notwithstanding the foregoing, the parties acknowledge that any provisions relating to the unemancipated children shall remain subject to modification by the court upon a material change in circumstances of either parent, a child, or if a modification is consistent with the best interests of child.

I. General Understanding and Disclosure. The husband and wife declare and acknowledge that each understands the position, circumstances, income, financial resources, expenses, and prospects represented by the other; and the terms, provisions, and conditions of this agreement, and, based on the information received, believe that its terms, provisions, and conditions are fair, reasonable, and acceptable. The parties further state that they have negotiated the terms of this agreement directly and have had the opportunity to consult with legal counsel of their own choosing, and that after being fully and fairly informed as to all the facts and circumstances herein set forth, and after having read this agreement line by line, they freely and fully accept the terms, conditions, and provisions and enter into this agreement voluntarily and without any coercion whatsoever. The parties further acknowledge and declare that this agreement contains the entire agreement between the parties and that there are no agreements, promises, terms, conditions, or understandings, and no representations or inducements leading to the signing of the agreement, expressed or implied, other than those set forth herein, and that no oral statement or prior written matter extrinsic to this agreement shall have any force or effect. The parties represent and acknowledge that each has fully described his or her assets and liabilities to the other party to the best of his or her knowledge and ability, both orally and otherwise, and by the exchange of copies of current Massachusetts Rules of Domestic Relations Procedure Supplemental Rule 401 Financial Statements, duplicate signed copies of which shall be filed with the court.

II. Separate Status

A. From the date of this agreement, the husband and wife agree to respect the privacy of one another for the rest of their lives, as fully as if sole and unmarried.

B. The husband and wife warrant, represent, and agree that they have not in the past and shall not contract or incur any debt, charge, or liability whatsoever in the name of the other or for which the other, his or her legal representatives or his or her property or estate shall or may become liable hereafter, except as otherwise provided in this agreement. As of the date of this agreement, there are no outstanding bills, debts, charges, or liabilities incurred by the husband or wife for which the other party may be liable other than as provided in this agreement. The husband and wife further covenant at all times to hold the other free, harmless, and indemnified from and against all debts, charges, or liabilities hereafter contracted or incurred by him or her in breach of the provisions of this paragraph, and from any and all reasonable attorneys' fees, costs, and expenses incurred by the other as a result of any such breach.

III. Waiver of Estate Claim

A. Except as provided herein, the husband and wife hereby waive any right at law or in equity to take against any last will made by the other, including all rights of dower or of curtesy, and hereby waive, renounce, and relinquish to the other, their respective heirs, executors, administrators, and assigns forever, each and every interest of any kind or character, which either may now have or may hereafter acquire in or to any real or personal property of the other, whether now owned or hereafter acquired by either, to share in the other party's estate in the event of intestacy, or to act as executor or administrator of the other party's estate.

B. Except as provided herein, the husband and wife shall have the right to dispose of his or her property by will, or otherwise, in such manner as each, in his or her uncontrolled discretion, may deem proper as if no marriage between them ever existed; and neither one shall claim any interest in the estate of the other, except to enforce any obligation imposed by this agreement.

IV. Mutual Release. Except for any cause of action for divorce, or any enforcement of any Probate and Family Court judgment concerning dissolution of the marital relationship, or to enforce the provisions of this agreement in any court, or to enforce any existing abuse prevention case against either party, the husband and wife hereby release and forever discharge the other in connection with matters arising out of the marital relationship from any and all actions, suits, debts, claims, demands, and obligations whatsoever, both in law and at equity, which either of them has ever had, now has, or may hereafter have against the other or any third party, upon or by reason of any matter, cause or thing up to the date of this agreement, as the parties intend that henceforth there shall exist between them only such rights and obligations as are specifically provided in this agreement.

V. Full Satisfaction. The husband and wife agree to accept the provisions set forth in this agreement in full satisfaction and discharge of all claims, past, present, and future, which either party may have against the other, and which in any way arise out of the marital relationship.

VI. Exhibits. There are annexed hereto and hereby made a part hereof Exhibits ______________________.
The husband and wife agree to be bound by, and to perform and carry out, all of the terms of the exhibits to the same extent as if each of the exhibits were fully set forth in the text of this agreement.

VII. Agreement to Survive/Merge with Judgment of Divorce. At any hearing on the divorce complaint, a copy of this agreement shall be submitted to the court with the request that it be ❑ incorporated but not merge ❑ merged in the judgment of divorce and that it shall ❑ survive ❑ not survive as an independent contract. Notwithstanding the foregoing, any provisions relating to the unemancipated children shall remain modifiable by the court upon a material change in circumstances of a party or a child, or if a modification is consistent with the best interests of a child.

VIII. Strict Performance. The failure of the husband or of the wife to insist in any instance upon the strict performance of any of the terms hereof shall not be construed as a waiver of such terms for the future, and such terms shall nevertheless continue in full force and effect.

IX. Validity. In the event any part of this agreement shall be held invalid, such invalidity shall not invalidate the whole agreement, but the remaining provisions of this agreement shall continue to be valid and binding to the extent that such provisions continue to reflect fairly the intent and understanding of the parties.

X. Documents. Whenever called upon to do so by the other party, each party shall forthwith execute, acknowledge, and deliver to or for the other party, without further consideration, any and all deeds, assignments, bills of sale, or other instruments that may be necessary or convenient to carry out the provisions of this agreement, or that may be required to enable the other party to sell, encumber, hypothecate, or otherwise dispose of the property now or hereafter owned or acquired by such other party.

XI. Governing Law. This agreement shall be construed and governed according to the laws of the Commonwealth of Massachusetts.

XII. Modification. This agreement shall not be altered or modified except by an instrument signed and acknowledged by the husband and wife or by order of a court of competent jurisdiction.

Signed on the day and year first above written and executed in several counterparts.

________________________________ ________________________________

Signature of Wife Signature of Husband

________________________________, ss. ____________________, ______

Then personally appeared before me the above-named ________________________
________________________and acknowledged the foregoing to be her free act and deed,

Before me,

____

Notary Public
My commission expires:

________________________________, ss. ____________________, ______

Then personally appeared before me the above-named ________________________
________________________ and acknowledged the foregoing to be his free act and deed,

Before me,

____

Notary Public
My commission expires:

Exhibit A

Child Custody and Visitation

The parties shall have joint legal custody of the ________ minor child(ren) who shall reside primarily with the husband/wife. The other parent shall have reasonable access to the minor child(ren), including overnight visits at all reasonable times and places. The parties also agree to share equitably/equally all holidays, the child(ren)'s birthdays, school and summer vacations, and other special occasions, except that the husband shall be entitled to spend every Father's Day with the child(ren), and the wife shall be entitled to spend every Mother's Day with the child(ren).

Both parents shall have access to the child(ren)'s school and medical records. The party with primary physical custody shall ensure that the other parent has timely notice of school meetings and events.

Both parents shall encourage the child(ren)'s respect and affection for the other parent. Neither shall denigrate the other parent in the presence of the child(ren).

Exhibit B

Alimony, Child Support, and College Expenses

1. Alimony

- ❑ Both parties waive their rights to seek past, present, and future alimony from the other.
- ❑ Commencing ______________________________, _________, and on the first day of every month/week thereafter until the husband's/wife's remarriage, or the death of either party, the husband/wife shall pay the husband/wife the sum of $________________ as alimony. The parties agree that the husband/wife shall be/shall not be entitled to deduct alimony payments made, and the husband/wife shall be taxed/not taxed on alimony received. The husband's social security number is ________________________ and the wife's is ________________________.

2. Child Support

The husband/wife shall pay the wife/husband the sum of $______________ each and every month/week, commencing on ________________________________, and continuing each and every ____________________________________ until the emancipation of a child. Emancipation (defined below) of a child shall allow the reduction of child support by ____________________ a month/week. Child support is payable monthly/weekly until the last child's emancipation. So long as the husband/wife pays child support in a timely manner in the amounts required by this exhibit, he/she shall be entitled to claim the child dependency exemption, and the other party shall release the dependency exemption by signing and delivering IRS Form 8332, upon request.

Child support shall be adjusted annually upon review of the parties' respective incomes from all sources. Adjustments shall be made in keeping with the then current Child Support Guidelines for the Commonwealth of Massachusetts. The parties agree to exchange federal and state tax returns on or before ____________________, in order to implement the adjusted rate by ____________________ of each year. If the parties wish, they may provide a letter from a certified public accountant as to income from all sources in lieu of supplying tax returns.

3. Children's Education Expenses

The parties shall share ❑ equally ❑ in proportion to income from all sources the unemancipated child(ren)'s college education expenses not covered by scholarships, loans, grants, and the child(ren)'s savings, provided, however, that each party has been consulted as to the child(ren)'s choice of college, and given prior permission which shall not be withheld or delayed unreasonably. Both parents wish to promote the child(ren)'s interest in higher education, and shall cooperate with the other parent and the children in finding the best possible college in keeping with the child's interests and aptitude. The parties agree to cooperate with one another in applying for financial aid, including but not limited to scholarships and loans.

For purposes of this agreement, "emancipation" is defined as the first to happen to a child:

a. attaining the age of 18 unless the child has plans to enroll as a full time student in an accredited post-secondary school program, in which event, emancipation shall occur upon cessation of full time enrollment in an undergraduate program or the age of 23, whichever occurs first.

b. death.

c. marriage.

d. entry into the U.S. military, except that cessation of service shall require emancipation to be determined under the remaining provisions of this definition.

e. full time employment, excluding summer jobs or work during the school year.

f. living permanently away from both parents, excluding time away at summer camp or school.

For purposes of this agreement, "college expenses" is defined to include tuition, room, board, books, laboratory fees, _____ round trips from college to a child's home each school year, and all items customarily listed on college bills, and precollege expenses such as preparatory courses, test fees, reasonable travel to and from prospective schools, and application fees.

Exhibit C

Division of Marital Assets

1. **General Provisions.** The parties acknowledge that in entering into this agreement, they have considered the length of their marriage, their ages, health, stations in life, occupations, sources of income, vocational skills employability, assets, conduct, liabilities, financial needs, and the opportunity of each with regard to the future acquisition, preservation, and appreciation in the value of their assets, and the contributions of the parties as homemakers to the family unit.

2. **Personal Property.** The parties agree that they have divided all of their personal property (with the exception of those items on a list, if any, attached hereto), tangible and intangible, to their mutual satisfaction. The property in the name or possession of a party shall be his or hers absolutely, and the other party shall have no further claim.

3. **Real Estate (select one option and mark the appropriate box)**

❑ The parties agree that the husband/wife may use and occupy the marital domicile at ____, ____, ______________________________ County, Massachusetts, until such time as the house sells on or about ______________________________, _______, or the husband/wife chooses to move, whichever is sooner. In the interim, the husband/wife shall pay principal, interest, taxes, insurance, and general maintenance for the property. If the husband/wife no longer resides at the marital domicile, the parties shall share the foregoing expenses equally unless the husband/wife uses and occupies the marital domicile, in which event he/she shall be solely liable for those expenses.

The parties agree that the marital domicile shall remain on the market until sold. When sold, the net proceeds shall be divided ❑ equally ❑ with _____ percent to the husband/wife, and the balance to the other spouse.

"Net proceeds" shall be defined as the gross sales price reduced by a broker's commission, if any, and the principal balance of the first mortgage of approximately $__________________, in addition to reasonable seller's costs, including but not limited to attorneys fees associated with the transaction. Each party represents that there are no other encumbrances, and if either party causes voluntarily or involuntarily any encumbrance to be placed on the marital home, he or she shall use best efforts to remove the encumbrance and shall indemnify and hold harmless the other against any loss or liability in connection with the encumbrance.

Each party shall be liable for capital gain tax, if any, on his and her share of net proceeds received from the sale.

❑ **Alternate (for parties who agree for one spouse to buy the other spouse's share):** The parties agree that the husband/wife shall pay the wife/husband the sum of $________________ within ________ months of the date of this agreement, whereupon the wife/husband shall transfer all of her/his right, title, and interest in the marital domicile to the husband/wife, subject to the existing first mortgage. The husband/wife shall indemnify the wife/husband against any loss or liability in connection with the first mortgage, including but not limited to attorneys' fees and costs. The husband/wife shall refinance the existing first mortgage upon becoming the sole owner of the marital domicile, so as to remove the non-owner from any liability for payment.

4. **Liabilities**

Except as otherwise provided herein, the parties acknowledge that they currently have no outstanding joint liabilities incurred during the marriage. The parties agree that any other indebtedness incurred during the marriage by either the husband or the wife shall be the full and sole responsibility of the party incurring the liability.

Exhibit D

Medical and Life Insurance

1. Medical Insurance

The husband/wife presently has medical insurance as a benefit of his/her employment. So long as the husband/wife is eligible for his/her current medical and health insurance policy, or its equivalent, he/she shall maintain and keep in force such policy or its equivalent, for the benefit of the wife/husband until the wife/husband dies, remarries, or ceases to make timely payments, and for any additional cost for his/her coverage, and if the wife/husband is eligible under the policy. The husband/wife also agrees to continue coverage for the benefit of each unemancipated child, so long as a child remains eligible.

Both parties shall have all the rights and benefits set forth in Massachusetts General Laws Chapter 175, Section 110(I).

Each party shall be solely liable for each party's own uninsured health-related expenses, but shall share equally in any uninsured health-related expense of an unemancipated child. For purposes of this exhibit, uninsured health-related expenses shall be defined as any payment, deductible, or co-payment for medical or dental office or emergency room visits, prescription medication, surgery, orthodontia, eyeglasses, contact lenses, and other audiovisual aids, psychotherapy, physical or occupational therapy, and so forth. Neither party shall be liable for a child's uninsured health-related expense unless the party gives prior permission, except in an emergency. Permission shall not be withheld or delayed unreasonably. The parent with physical custody of a child in need of emergency medical or other health-related treatment shall be authorized to obtain such treatment without the other parent's prior permission, but shall notify the other parent as soon as possible.

2. Life Insurance

Both parties acknowledge and agree that each maintains life insurance for the benefit of the other and the unemancipated children with death benefits in the amounts of $________________ payable in the event of the husband's death for the wife and $______________________ for the children; and $________________ payable in the event of the wife's death for the husband and $________________ for the children.

Each shall maintain insurance in the amount stated above for the benefit of the children, so long as there are any unemancipated children, and the husband/wife shall maintain insurance in the amount stated above for the benefit of the other party, so long as he/she has any alimony obligation.

The parties may use insurance trusts for the benefit of the children, provided, however, that the terms and the trustee(s) shall be subject to the approval of the other party. Approval shall not be withheld or delayed unreasonably.

Exhibit E

Tax Returns and Legal Fees

1. Tax Returns

The husband and wife each hereby represent and warrant to the other that each has paid all income taxes, local, state and federal, on all joint returns filed by the parties; that to their knowledge no interest or penalties are due and owing, no tax deficiency proceeding is pending or threatened, and no audit is pending.

If there is a deficiency assessment in connection with any of the joint returns, the party receiving notice of such deficiency shall notify the other party immediately in writing. The party responsible for the act or omission which caused the deficiency assessment shall be solely liable for any deficiency assessment, penalty, and interest, and shall indemnify and hold the other harmless against any loss or liability in connection therewith. In the event neither party is responsible for the act or omission which caused the deficiency assessment, then the parties shall pay the assessment ❑ equally ❑ in proportion to their income for that tax year.

2. Legal Fees

The husband and wife shall be solely responsible for, and shall pay, his and her own expenses incurred in connection with the negotiation and preparation of this agreement and all related matters, including all court appearances and the prosecution of any complaints for divorce. Each agrees to indemnify and save harmless the other from any and all claims on account of such legal fees and expenses which the other shall be obligated to pay.

3. Legal Fees and Cost of Enforcement

After written notice, if either the husband or the wife is adjudicated in default of his or her obligations under this agreement, the defaulting party shall be required to pay any and all reasonable counsel fees and expenses incurred by the other party in enforcing any of the terms and provisions of this agreement.

THE TRIAL COURT
THE PROBATE AND FAMILY COURT DEPARTMENT

____________________ DIVISION DOCKET NO. ____________________

REQUEST FOR TRIAL — PRE-TRIAL ASSIGNMENT
THE FORM SHOULD NOT BE USED FOR MARK-UP OF TEMPORARY ORDERS AND MOTIONS

Please print or type

Please assign
for hearing: ____
Plaintiff

v.

____
Defendant

TYPE OF CASE ____________________ TIME REQUIRED ___________ HEARING AT ____________

( ) Uncontested

( ) Contested

- ( ) Merits
- ( ) Custody
- ( ) Support
- ( ) Visitation
- ( ) 208, §34
- ( ) Other _________________________

The following papers must be on file before cases can be assigned for hearing:

- ( ) Summons or Return of Service
- ( ) Marriage Certificate
- ( ) Statistical Form R408
- ( ) Financial Statement (Supp. Rule 401)
- ( ) Affidavits of Both Parties (1A Divorces)
- ( ) Notarized Agreement (1A Divorces)
- ( ) ____________________________________

Has Discovery Been Completed ( ) Yes ( ) No

Has This Case Been Pre-Tried ( ) Yes ( ) No

I hereby certify that, in my opinion, this case is ready for trial.

Requested by:		Opposing Counsel/Defendant
________________________	Name	________________________
________________________	Address, Zip	________________________
________________________	Phone No.	________________________

FOR REGISTER'S USE ONLY
ACTION

The above-entitled matter has been assigned for
________________________________ (Trial) ________________________ (Pre-Trial Conference)
at ________________________________ on __________________, ______, at __________ A.M.
____. Returned without action. Data Incomplete. See Above.

Register of Probate

Clerk's Initials

COMMONWEALTH OF MASSACHUSETTS

_______________ SS. PROBATE COURT

No. _______________

_______________ Plaintiff

v. Complaint for Divorce

_______________ Defendant

1) Plaintiff, who resides at _______________
was lawfully married to the defendant, who now resides at _______________.

2) The parties were married at _______________ on _______________,
and last lived together at _______________ on _______________.

3) The minor child(ren) of this marriage, and date(s) of birth is/are:

_______________ _______________

_______________ _______________

_______________ _______________

4) Plaintiff certifies that no previous action for divorce, annulling or affirming the marriage, separate support, desertion, living apart for justifiable cause, or custody of child(ren) has been brought by either party against the other except _______________.

5) On or about _______________, _____, the defendant _______________
____
____
____

6) Wherefore, plaintiff demands that the court:

❑ waive the 30 day requirement for filing this complaint

❑ grant a divorce for _______________

❑ prohibit defendant from imposing any restraint on plaintiff's personal liberty

❑ grant h_____ custody of the above-named child(ren)

❑ order a suitable amount for support of the plaintiff and said minor child(ren)

❑ order conveyance of the real estate located at _______________

❑ _______________ standing in the name of _______________

_______________ as recorded with _______________

Registry of Deeds, Bk. _______________ Pg. _______________

❑ allow plaintiff to resume her former name of _______________

❑ _______________

Dated: _______________

Signature of Attorney _______________

Plaintiff's Signature, if Pro Se _______________

Print name and address _______________

____

COMMONWEALTH OF MASSACHUSETTS

______________________ SS.

________________________________ Plaintiff

V. Complaint for Divorce

________________________________ Defendant

For Plaintiff:	Filed ______________________, ________
______________________________	Judgment ______________________, ________
Address ______________________	Temporary Orders ________________, ______
______________________________	______________________________
Tel No. ______________________	______________________________
For Defendant:	______________________________
______________________________	Documents filed:
Address ______________________	Marriage Certificate ❑
	Plaintiff's Financial Statement ❑
______________________________	Defendant's Financial Statement ❑
	Service on Summons ❑
Tel No. ______________________	

INSTRUCTIONS

Refer to Massachusetts General Laws Chapter 208 and Massachusetts Rules of Domestic Relations Procedure.

1) A certified copy of your civil marriage certificate must be filed with this Complaint.

2) Recite street address, city or town, and county in paragraphs one and two; city or town and county or state in paragraph five.

3) In completing paragraph four, please provide only the docket number and county.

4) The allegations in paragraph five must comply with General Laws Chapter 208, Sections 1 and 2 and Massachusetts Rules of Domestic Relations Procedure Rule 8.

5) All requests for temporary relief must be made by motion, although several prayers may be contained in one. For temporary restraining orders see Mass. R. Dom. Rel. P. Rule 65, affidavit requirement.

6) If attachment or trustee process is desired, a motion with affidavit must be filed. A certificate of insurance is normally not required in domestic relations cases. See Massachusetts Rules of Domestic Relations Procedure Rules 4.1 and 4.2.

7) Plaintiff must sign this Complaint if appearing pro se; otherwise plaintiff's attorney must sign and give his address in the space provided.

Commonwealth of Massachusetts
The Trial Court
The Probate and Family Court Department

______________________ **Division** **Docket No.** ____________________

_________________________________,
Plaintiff

Motion to Delay Filing of
Marriage Certificate

V.

_________________________________,
Defendant

Now comes the plaintiff in the above-entitled matter and respectfully states that:

1. Plaintiff intends to file a complaint for divorce, along with motions for temporary orders concerning the care and custody of the parties' minor child(ren).

2. Plaintiff does not have a certified copy of the parties' marriage certificate.

Wherefore, for the foregoing reasons and those more fully stated in plaintiff's affidavit filed herewith, plaintiff requests that the court enter an order allowing the delayed filing of a certified copy of the parties' marriage certificate and such other relief as this court deems just and appropriate.

Dated: ______________________

Respectfully submitted,

____

Name: ______________________________

Address: ____________________________

____

Telephone No.: _______________________

Commonwealth of Massachusetts
The Trial Court
The Probate and Family Court Department

______________________ **Division** **Docket No.** ____________________

_________________________________,
Plaintiff

V.

Affidavit in Support of
Motion to Delay Filing of
Marriage Certificate

_________________________________,
Defendant

Now comes the plaintiff in the above-entitled matter and under oath states as follows:

1. Plaintiff and defendant were married on __________________, _______, and last lived together at ____, on ____________________________, _________.

2. They are the parents of the ____ minor child(ren), whose name(s) and date(s) of birth is/are:

3. The child(ren) presently reside(s) with plaintiff at ______________________ ____________________________________, ____________________________________, ____________________________________ County, Massachusetts.

4. The plaintiff requires immediate temporary orders concerning the care and custody of the minor child(ren), including but not limited to temporary orders of support and maintenance of medical insurance for the benefit of the family.

5. The plaintiff used due diligence to locate and obtain a copy of the parties' marriage certificate from the state of ________________________________ where the parties were married.

6. The plaintiff has been informed that the request for a certified copy of the marriage certificate will take approximately _________________________ weeks to fulfill.

7. The plaintiff will file the certificate upon receipt.

Signed under penalties of perjury this _______ day of ________________, ______.

____
Signature of Plaintiff

Commonwealth of Massachusetts
The Trial Court
The Probate and Family Court Department

____________________ **Division** **Docket No.** ____________________

______________________________,
Plaintiff

V. Motion to Amend Complaint

______________________________,
Defendant

Now comes the plaintiff in the above-entitled matter and respectfully states that:

- ❑ Plaintiff filed a complaint for divorce against defendant in this court and did not include her request to resume her former name, and Plaintiff now wishes to resume her former name.
- ❑ The parties have reached a complete and final settlement and wish to proceed with a Joint Petition under M.G.L. Ch. 208, Sec. 1A and thus ask to strike the complaint for divorce and file in its place a Joint Petition and Affidavit in Support of the Joint Petition.

Wherefore, plaintiff respectfully requests that she be allowed to amend her complaint by:

- ❑ adding a request to resume her former name of ____________________________.
- ❑ striking the complaint and filing the attached Joint Petition and Supporting Affidavit.

Dated: ______________________

Respectfully submitted,

____

Name: __________________________

Address: _________________________

____

Telephone No.: ____________________

Commonwealth of Massachusetts
The Trial Court
The Probate and Family Court Department

____________________ **Division** **Docket No.** ____________________

________________________________,
Plaintiff

V. Answer and Counterclaim

________________________________,
Defendant

Now comes the defendant in the above-entitled matter and responds to the plaintiff's complaint for divorce as follows:

1. Admits the allegations in paragraph(s) ______________________________.
2. Denies the allegations in paragraph(s) ______________________________.
3. Denies

4. Denies that the plaintiff is entitled to:
   (a) a divorce on the ground of cruel and abusive treatment;
   (b) or any other relief pursuant to his/her complaint for divorce.

Counterclaim

1.____, the above-named defendant and plaintiff in the counterclaim (hereinafter referred to as the "husband"/"wife"), who resides at ____, ______________________________, ________________________County , ________________________ was lawfully married to ______________________________________, the above-named plaintiff and defendant in the counterclaim (hereinafter referred to as the "husband"/"wife") who now resides at ____, ______________________________, ________________________County , ________________________ .

2. The parties were married at ____, ______________________________ County, ______________________________, on ____________________, _____, and last lived together at __________________________, ________________________, ______________________ County, ____________________, on ____________________, ______.

3. The minor child(ren) of this marriage, and date(s) of birth is/are:

4. The husband/wife certifies that no previous action for divorce, annulling or affirming marriage, separate support, desertion, living apart for justifiable cause, or custody of child(ren) has been brought by either party against the other except: ____________________

____

5. On or about ______________________________, ________, the husband/wife

____

6. Wherefore, the husband/wife requests that this court:

- ❑ grant a divorce for____
- ❑ prohibit defendant/plaintiff from imposing any restraint on the husband's/wife's personal liberty
- ❑ grant him/her custody of the above-named child(ren)
- ❑ order a suitable amount for support of the husband/wife and the said minor child(ren)
- ❑ order conveyance of the real estate located ____________________________ standing in the names of ______________________________ as recorded with ______________________ Registry of Deeds, Book __________, Page _________
- ❑ allow the wife to resume her former name of ___________________________
- ❑ order an equitable distribution of marital assets under M.G.L. Ch. 208, Sec. 34, and such other relief as this court deems just.

Dated:_____________________

____
Signature of Party or Attorney

Address:_________________________________

____

Telephone No.:____________________________

Certificate of Service

____________________________ County ______________________________, _______

I, ____, certify that I served the foregoing answer and counterclaim on my spouse/spouse's attorney, by mailing a copy, first class mail, postage prepaid to my spouse's residence or attorney's office at ________________________

____.

Signed under penalties of perjury.

____
Signature of Party or Attorney

Commonwealth of Massachusetts
The Trial Court
The Probate and Family Court Department

______________________ **Division** **Docket No.** ____________________

__________________________________,
Plaintiff

V. Notice of Appearance

__________________________________,
Defendant

To the Register of the above-named court:

Please enter my appearance (pro se) as attorney for ______________________________ ____ in the above named case.

Dated: ________________________

____
Signature of Pro Se Party or Attorney

Address:__________________________________

____

Telephone No.:_____________________________

Certificate of Service

___________________________ County ______________________________, _______

I, ____, certify that I served the foregoing Notice of Appearance on my spouse/spouse's attorney, by mailing a copy, first class mail, postage prepaid to my spouse's residence or attorney's office at __________________ ____.

Signed under penalties of perjury.

____
Signature of Party or Attorney

Commonwealth of Massachusetts
The Trial Court
The Probate and Family Court Department

____________________ **Division** **Docket No.** ____________________

______________________________,
Plaintiff

V. Motion for Alternate Service

______________________________,
Defendant

Now comes the plaintiff in the above-entitled matter and respectfully states as follows:

1. The parties were married at ____________________, ______________ County, ____________________, and last lived together in the Commonwealth of Massachusetts at ____, ____________________, in the County of __________________________.

2. Since the parties last lived together, the plaintiff has had no communication with the defendant, and has no information as to where the defendant now resides.

3. The plaintiff wishes to proceed with a complaint for divorce.

Wherefore, the plaintiff requests that this court enter an order:

1. Allowing the plaintiff to serve notice of the complaint for divorce filed with this motion by publication in the local newspaper;

2. For such other relief as this court deems just.

Dated: ____________________

____
Signature of Party or Attorney

Print name:____________________________

Address:______________________________

____

Telephone No.:__________________________

Commonwealth of Massachusetts
The Trial Court
The Probate and Family Court Department

______________________ **Division** **Docket No.** ____________________

________________________________,
Plaintiff

V.

Motion to Proceed in
Forma Pauperis

________________________________,
Defendant

Now comes the plaintiff in the above-entitled matter and respectfully states as follows:

1. The plaintiff wishes to file the complaint for divorce filed with this motion.

2. The plaintiff is without adequate means to pay the fees required to file the complaint; and also lacks the means to pay for serving the complaint upon the defendant in a manner reasonably calculated to give notice.

Wherefore, for the foregoing reasons and those more fully outlined in the supporting affidavit of indigency filed herewith, the plaintiff requests that this court enter an order:

1. Waiving the filing fee and costs; and

2. Providing service on defendant of the plaintiff's complaint for divorce in a manner reasonably calculated to give notice, and that costs of service be paid by the Commonwealth pursuant to M.G.L. Ch. 261, Sec. 27A-D, and Rule 403 of the Supplemental Rules of the Probate and Family Court.

Dated: ______________________

____
Signature of Party or Attorney

Print name:______________________________

Address:_________________________________

____

Telephone No:____________________________

Commonwealth of Massachusetts
The Trial Court
The Probate and Family Court Department

__________________ **Division** **Docket No.** __________________

______________________________,
Plaintiff

V.

______________________________,
Defendant

Affidavit of Indigency and Request for Waiver, Substitution or State Payment of Fees and Costs

Pursuant to M.G.L. Ch. 261, Sections 27A-G, the applicant, ______________________________
______________________________, swears (or affirms) as follows:

1. Applicant is indigent in that he/she is a person [check only one]:
   - ❑ (a) who receives public assistance under the Massachusetts Aid to Families with Dependent Children, General Relief, or Veteran's Benefits programs, or receives assistance under Title XVI of the Social Security Act, or the Medicaid Program, 42 USC 1396, et seq., or
   - ❑ (b) whose income, after taxes, is 125% or less of the current poverty threshold annually established by the Community Services Administration pursuant to Section 625 of the Economic Opportunity Act, as amended, or
   - ❑ (c) who is unable to pay the fees and costs of the proceeding in which he/she is involved, or is unable to do so without depriving him/herself or his/her dependents of the necessities of life, including food, shelter, and clothing. [Note: If the applicant checks (c), he/she should fill in the information called for in the "Supplement to Affidavit of Indigency."]
2. Applicant requests that the following normal fees and costs (e.g., filing fee, service of process costs, etc.) either be waived, substituted, or paid by the state.
   [Note: In filling in blanks in this paragraph and paragraph 3, be as specific as possible as to fees and costs known at time of filing this request. A supplementary request may be filed at a later time, if necessary.]
   ____
   ____
   ____
3. Applicant requests that the following extra fees and costs (e.g., cost of transcribing a deposition, expert assistance, etc.) either be waived, substituted, or paid by the state.
   ____
   ____
   ____

Signed under the penalties of perjury.

Date: __________________ ______________________________
Signature of applicant
Printed name: ______________________________
Address: ______________________________
____
Telephone No.: ______________________________

Commonwealth of Massachusetts
The Trial Court
The Probate and Family Court Department

______________________ **Division** **Docket No.** ____________________

______________________________________,
Plaintiff

V.

Supplement to
Affidavit of Indigency

______________________________________,
Defendant

If the applicant checks (c) on the affidavit of indigency, he/she should fill in the information called for on this supplementary form.

Note: Pursuant to M.G.L. Ch. 261, Sections 27A-G, the applicant, ____, swears (or affirms) as follows:

(a) Date of birth: ____
(b) Highest grade attained in school: ____________________________
(c) Special training: ____
(d) List any physical or mental disabilities: ______________________
____
(e) Number of dependents: ____________________________________
(f) Income, expense, asset & liability information:

Gross Income (specify whether monthly or weekly):
$__________________ per ___________________
If from employment, list your occupation and your employer's name and address: ____
____
____
Source of income, if not from employment: ______________________
____
If applicant's spouse is employed, list occupation and name and address of his/her employer: ____
____
____
Applicant's gross annual income for preceding year: $_______________
Deductions:

Federal tax: ____________
State tax: ____________
Social Security: ____________
Health insurance: ____________
Pension: ____________

Other: ____________
Total: ____________

Net Income (specify whether monthly or weekly):

$__________________ per __________________

Expenses (specify whether monthly or weekly):

Rent: ____________
Food: ____________
Clothing: ____________
Utilities: ____________
Other expenses: ____________

Net income minus expenses (specify whether monthly or weekly):

$__________________ per __________________

Assets:

Own car? __________________ year and make __________________

Market value: ____________
Balance due: ____________

Bank accounts: ____________
Other property: ____________

Liabilities:

____

____

____

(g) Other facts which may be relevant to applicant's ability to pay fees and costs?

____

____

Signed under penalties of perjury.

____

Signature of applicant

Print name: ______________________________

Address: ________________________________

____

Telephone No.: ____________________________

Commonwealth of Massachusetts
The Trial Court
The Probate and Family Court Department

______________________ Division **Docket No. ____________________**

__________________________________,
Plaintiff

V.

Motion for Temporary Orders of Custody, Support, and Maintenance of Insurance Benefits

__________________________________,
Defendant

Now comes the plaintiff/defendant in the above-entitled matter and respectfully states as follows:

1. The parties have been married for _____ years, and last lived together at _______________ __________________________________, ______________________ County, Massachusetts.

2. ❑ There are no minor children.

   ❑ There is/are ______ unemancipated child(ren) of the marriage, namely:
   Name Date of Birth

3. ❑ The plaintiff/defendant is without adequate means of support for himself/herself, and thus requires alimony.

   ❑ The plaintiff/defendant is living with the unemancipated children, and requires child support.

4. The plaintiff/defendant does not have his/her own medical insurance.

5. The plaintiff/defendant has a life insurance policy with ____________________________ __________________, Policy No. ____________________, with a face amount of $_____________.

6. Other:

Wherefore, the plaintiff/defendant requests that this court enter the following orders for the foregoing reasons and those more fully outlined in a supporting affidavit filed with this motion:

❑ 1. That plaintiff's/defendant's spouse be ordered to pay alimony of $__________ per week, commencing on ____________________________, _________, and continuing thereafter each and every __________________________.

❑ 2. That the parties be given joint legal custody of the child(ren) with primary physical custody to plaintiff/defendant, and reasonable time with the other parent, including overnight visits at all reasonable times and places.

❑ 3. That plaintiff/defendant's spouse be ordered to pay child support of $___________ per week, commencing on________________________, ________, and continuing thereafter each and every _______________________________.

❑ 4. That plaintiff/defendant's spouse obtain/maintain medical insurance for the benefit of the family at the sole cost of the _________________, and that the parties share equally all uninsured medical and dental expenses of the unemancipated child(ren).

❑ 5. That plaintiff/defendant's spouse obtain/maintain life insurance on his/her life with ____, Policy No. ______________________, with a face amount of $______________, for the benefit of the plaintiff/defendant/unemancipated child(ren).

❑ 6. Other:

7. Such other orders as the court deems just.

Dated: ___________________

____
Signature of Pro Se Party or Attorney

Print name:______________________________

Address:_________________________________

____

Telephone No.:___________________________

Certificate of Service

____________________________, ss. ____________________________, ______

I, ____________________________________, certify that I served the foregoing motion and supporting affidavit on the plaintiff/defendant by mailing a copy, first class mail, postage prepaid, to the plaintiff/defendant or opposing counsel at ___________________________________ ____________________________________, together with notice that I scheduled a hearing on the motion on __________________, _______, at ________ ____.m. at the _______________ County Probate and Family Court at ____.

____
Signature of Pro Se Party or Attorney

Commonwealth of Massachusetts
The Trial Court
The Probate and Family Court Department

______________________ **Division** **Docket No.** ____________________

_________________________________,
Plaintiff

V.

_________________________________,
Defendant

Affidavit in Support of
Motion for Temporary Orders of
Custody, Support, and Maintenance
of Insurance Benefits

Now comes the plaintiff/defendant in the above-entitled matter, under oath, and deposes as follows:

1. The parties were married at ________________________, ____________ County, ________________________, on __________________, _______, and last lived together at ____, ______________________________________, ________________________ County, Massachusetts, on __________________, _______.

2. Plaintiff now resides at ____, ____________________________, __________________________ County, Massachusetts, and the defendant resides at ____, ____________________________, __________________________ County, Massachusetts.

3. ❑ There are no minor children of the marriage.

❑ The _____ unemancipated child(ren) of the marriage, namely:

Name	Date of Birth

reside with the plaintiff/defendant.

4. During the marriage, the plaintiff/defendant was the primary caretaker of the child(ren), and continues in that roll. The child(ren) is/are doing well as a result of plaintiff's/defendant's child care.

5. The plaintiff/defendant is without adequate means to provide support for the family, and requires:

❑ alimony
❑ alimony and child support
❑ child support

from the plaintiff's/defendant's spouse.

6. On information and belief, the plaintiff's/defendant's spouse is employed full time, and has sufficient means to provide for the spouse's own support and the support of the family.

7. On information and belief, the plaintiff's/defendant's spouse has medical and life insurance as a benefit of employment, and can maintain benefits at reasonable cost for the family.

8. Other:

Signed under penalties of perjury this ______ day of ______________________, _________.

____
Signature of Party

Certificate of Service

__________________________ County ______________________________, ______

I, ____, certify that I served the foregoing affidavit on my spouse/spouse's attorney, by mailing a copy, first class mail, postage prepaid to my spouse's residence or attorney's office at ______________________________
____.

Signed under penalties of perjury.

____
Signature of Party or Attorney

Commonwealth of Massachusetts
The Trial Court
The Probate and Family Court Department

_____________________ **Division** **Docket No.** ____________________

________________________________,
Plaintiff

Motion to Preserve Marital Assets Without Notice to Spouse

V.

________________________________,
Defendant

Now comes the plaintiff/defendant in the above-entitled case and respectfully states as follows:

1. The parties have been married since _______________________, ______, and last lived together at ____, _____________________ County, Massachusetts, on _______________________, ______.

2. On or about _______________________, ______, the defendant _______________ ____ ____.

3. The defendant/plaintiff is an employee of _______________________________, and has employment benefits such as health, dental, disability, and life insurance, in addition to various retirement benefits.

4. The plaintiff/defendant will suffer irreparable harm without an immediate order being entered for the preservation of marital assets and the maintenance of benefits for him/her through the defendant's/plaintiff's employment, including but not limited to:

a. the following specific assets:

b. such other assets not specifically named herein, but which may be subject to an equitable division between the parties.

c. maintenance of all health-related benefits.

d. maintenance of any and all past, present, and future benefits of the defendant's/plaintiff's employment for third parties, including but not limited to any death benefits of life insurance and retirement plans.

Dated: ____________________

____
Signature of Party or Attorney for Party

Address:____________________________

____

Telephone No.:______________________

Commonwealth of Massachusetts
The Trial Court
The Probate and Family Court Department

____________________ **Division** **Docket No.** ____________________

_______________________________,
Plaintiff

Affidavit in Support of Motion
to Preserve Marital Assets

V.

_______________________________,
Defendant

Now comes the plaintiff/defendant in the above-entitled matter, under oath, and deposes as follows:

1. Throughout the parties' marriage the plaintiff/defendant has been dependent upon the plaintiff/defendant for financial support, as the plaintiff/defendant has been the stay-at-home parent of the parties' _____ minor child(ren).

2. On information and belief, the plaintiff/defendant:

3. On information and belief, the plaintiff/defendant will suffer irreparable harm without an immediate order being entered for the preservation of marital assets and maintenance of benefits, in that the plaintiff/defendant will have an opportunity to conceal assets, and possibly terminate medical coverage for plaintiff/defendant, and __________________
____
____.

Signed under penalties of perjury this _______ day of ______________________,
________.

____
Signature of plaintiff/defendant

Commonwealth of Massachusetts
The Trial Court
The Probate and Family Court Department

______________________ **Division** **Docket No.** ____________________

______________________________,
Plaintiff

V.

______________________________,
Defendant

Petition for Writ of
Habeas Corpus

Now comes the plaintiff/defendant, of ____________________, ____________________ County, Massachusetts, in the above-entitled matter and respectfully represents that:

1. The parties were married at ____________________, ________________County, ____________________, and last lived together at ____________________________, ______________, ______________ County, Massachusetts, with the _____ minor child(ren) of the marriage, namely:

Name Date of Birth

2. On or about ____________________, ______, the parties separated. The plaintiff/defendant and ____ minor child(ren) continue to reside at ______________________________, ____________________, ________________ County, Massachusetts.

3. From date of separation until the present, the plaintiff/defendant spends significant time with the _______ minor child(ren), and has a close loving relationship with the child(ren).

5. The plaintiff/defendant recently discovered that the plaintiff/defendant ____________________ ____.

6. Plaintiff/defendant would be compelled to commence litigation in ____________________ for the return of the children, causing unnecessary expense, confusion, delay, and irreparable harm to the plaintiff/defendant.

Wherefore, the plaintiff/defendant asks under M.G.L. Ch. 208, Sec. 32 that this court:

1. Issue an order directing the Sheriff and the Sheriff's deputies to have before this court the minor child(ren), ____, and to summon the plaintiff/defendant to appear and show cause why the child(ren) is/are imprisoned and restrained by the plaintiff/defendant.

2. Enter such other orders as this court deems just and consistent with the best interests of the minor child(ren), including but not limited to granting plaintiff/defendant a temporary order of custody of the ______ minor child(ren).

Dated: ____________________

____
Plaintiff's/Defendant's signature
Print name:____________________
Address:____________________
____
Telephone no.:____________________

Commonwealth of Massachusetts
____________________ County

Date:____________________

Then personally appeared the above-named ______________________________ and acknowledged that the foregoing statements are true.

____
Notary Public
My commission expires:

The Commonwealth of Massachusetts
DEPARTMENT OF PUBLIC HEALTH
REGISTRY OF VITAL RECORDS AND STATISTICS
CERTIFICATE OF ABSOLUTE DIVORCE OR ANNULMENT
(Chap. 208, Sec. 46 G.L.)
R-408

HUSBAND

HUSBAND NAME FIRST MIDDLE LAST 1.			
USUAL RESIDENCE - STREET ADDRESS 2a		CITY, TOWN OR LOCATION 2b	
COUNTY 2c.	STATE 2d.	DATE OF BIRTH *(Mo., Day, Yr.)* 3.	NUMBER OF THIS MARRIAGE *(1st, 2, Specify)* 4.

WIFE

WIFE - NAME FIRST MIDDLE LAST 5a.			MAIDEN NAME 5b.
USUAL RESIDENCE - STREET ADDRESS 6a.		CITY, TOWN OR LOCATION 6b.	
COUNTY 6c.	STATE 6d.	DATE OF BIRTH (Mo., Day, Yr.) 7.	NUMBER OF THIS MARRIAGE *(1st, 2nd, Specify)* 8.

DATE OF THIS MARRIAGE *(Mo., Day, Yr.)* 9.	NUMBER OF CHILDREN BORN ALIVE OF THIS MARRIAGE 10a.	NUMBER OF CHILDREN UNDER AGE 18 IN THIS FAMILY 10b

FOR COURT USE ONLY

JUDGMENT

COUNTY OF JUDGMENT 11.	TITLE OF COURT 11b.	
DATE OF JUDGMENT NISI *(Mo., Day, Yr.)* 12.	TYPE OF JUDGMENT - DIVORCE OR ANNULMENT *(Specify)* 13.	DATE OF JUDGMENT 14.
DOCKET NUMBER 15.	NAME OF PLAINTIFF 16.	CAUSE FOR WHICH GRANTED 17.
SIGNATURE OF CERTIFYING OFFICAL 18a.	TITLE OF OFFICIAL 18b.	

Commonwealth of Massachusetts
The Trial Court
The Probate and Family Court Department

_______________________ **Division** **Docket No.** ____________________

______________________________________,
Plaintiff

Motion to Compel Production
and Order for Sanctions

V.

______________________________________,
Defendant

Now comes the plaintiff in the above-entitled matter and states as follows:

1. On or about ______________________________, _________, the plaintiff served a ____ ____ on defendant, requiring defendant to file and serve a response on or before ____________________________, ________.

2. As of the date of this motion, defendant refuses or fails to respond.

3. Plaintiff cannot adequately negotiate or prepare for trial without the response(s).

Wherefore, plaintiff requests that this court order defendant to respond within _______ days or be subject to such sanctions as this court deems just, including but not limited to prohibiting the defendant from raising any issues concerning ___________________________ ________________________________ which is the subject of the discovery plaintiff seeks.

Dated: _______________________

____
Plaintiff's signature
Print name: ______________________________
Address: ________________________________
____
Telephone No.: ___________________________

Certificate of Service

______________________________, ss. ____________________________, ________

I, __________________________________, certify that I served the foregoing Motion to Compel Production and Order for Sanctions on defendant by mailing a copy, first class mail, postage prepaid, to: ____ ____, together with notice that the motion has been scheduled for hearing at the _______________________ County Probate and Family Court on ______________________________, ________, at _______ ___.m.

____

COMPLAINT FOR PROTECTION FROM ABUSE (G.L. c. 209A)

FOR COURT USE ONLY | DOCKET NO. | TRIAL COURT OF MASSACHUSETTS

PART 1
☐ BOSTON MUNICIPAL COURT
☐ DISTRICT COURT ____________ DIVISION
☐ PROBATE & FAMILY COURT ____________ DIVISION
☐ SUPERIOR COURT ____________ COUNTY

PART 2
NAME OF PLAINTIFF (the person seeking protection)

PART 3

3A Write your address here if you are NOT asking the Court to keep it confidential

____

____

Daytime Phone No. (   )

3B Write your address here only if you are asking the Court to keep it CONFIDENTIAL (that is, impounded)

____

____

Daytime Phone No. (   )

PART 4
If you left a former residence to avoid abuse, write that address here:

____

PART 5
Your attorney (if any)

Name ____________________

Address ____________________

____

PART 6
I ☐ am ☐ am not under the age of eighteen.
The defendant ☐ is ☐ is not under the age of eighteen.

PART 7
NAME & ADDRESS OF DEFENDANT (the person causing abuse)

____

____

____

Daytime Phone No. (   )

Date of Birth *(if known)*

PART 8
CHECK AS MANY AS APPLY: The defendant and I:

☐ are currently married to each other.
☐ were formerly married to each other.
☐ are not married but we are related to each other by blood or marriage; specifically, the defendant is my
____
☐ are the parents of one or more children.
☐ are not related but we now live in the same household.
☐ are or were in a dating or engagement relationship of the following nature:

Date relationship began: ____________________
Nature of relationship: ____________________
Frequency of contact during relationship: ____________________
____
If it has ended, date relationship ended: ____________________

PART 9
Are there any prior or pending court actions in any state or country involving you and the defendant for divorce, annulment, paternity, child custody or support, guardianship, separate support, legal separation, or abuse prevention?
☐ No ☐ Yes If Yes, give court, type of case, date and *(if available)* docket number: ____________________
____

PART 10

On or about (dates) ____________________ I suffered abuse when the defendant:

☐ attempted to cause me physical harm.
☐ caused me physical harm.
☐ placed me in fear of imminent serious physical harm.
☐ caused me unwillingly to engage in sexual relations by force, threat of force, or duress.

Therefore:

☐ 1. I ask the Court to order the defendant to stop abusing me.

☐ 2. I ask the Court to order the defendant not to contact me, or any child(ren) listed below, unless authorized by the Court.

☐ 3. I ask the Court to order the defendant to leave and remain away from my residence which is located at:
____________________.

If this is an apartment building or other multiple family dwelling, check here. ☐

☐ 4. I ask the Court to impound my address to prevent its disclosure to the defentant, the defendant's attorney, or the public.
Do not check item 4 if you wrote your address in Part 3A above.

☐ 5. I ask the Court to order the defendant to leave and remain away from my workplace which is located at:
____________________.

☐ 6. I ask the Court to award me temporary custody of the following children under 18.

NAME	DATE OF BIRTH

You may not obtain an Order from the Boston Municipal Court or a District or Superior Court covering items (6) or (7) in Part 10 if there is a prior or pending Order for custody or support from the Probate and Family Court.

☐ 7. I ask the Court to order the defendant, who has a legal obligation to do so, to pay temporary support ☐ for me ☐ for any child(ren) in my custody ☐ for both

☐ 8. I ask the Court to order the defendant to pay me $____________ in compensation for the followoing losses suffered as a direct result of the abuse ____________________

☐ 9. I ask the Court to order the following ____________________
____

10. I ask the Court to order the relief I have requested above, except for items (7) and (8), without advance notice to the defendant because ther is a substantial likelihood of immediate danger of abuse. I understand that if the Court issues such a temporary Order, the Court will schedule a hearing within 10 court business days to determine whether such a temporary Order shoud be continued, and that I must appear in court on that day if I wish the Order to be continued.

PLAINTIFF'S SIGNATURE

AFFIDAVIT	Describe in detail the most recent incidents of abuse. State what happened, the dates, who did what to whom, and describe any injuries. Also describe any history of abuse.

On or about ________________, 199___, the defendant

If more space is needed, attach additional pages and check this box: ☐

I declare under penalty of perjury that all statements of fact made above, or in any additional pages attached, are true.

DATE SIGNED	PLAINTIFF'S SIGNATURE X ____________________	
WITNESSED BY	PRINTED NAME OF WITNESS	TITLE/RANK OF WITNESS

Commonwealth of Massachusetts
The Trial Court
The Probate and Family Court Department

____________________ **Division** **Docket No.** ____________________

__________________________________,
Plaintiff

v. Interrogatories

__________________________________,
Defendant

In answering these interrogatories, you must furnish all requested information, not subject to a valid objection, that is known by, possessed by, or available to, you or any of your attorneys, consultants, representatives, or other agents. You must serve a copy of your answers and objections within 30 days of the date of these interrogatories unless I have served you with interrogatories at the same time as I served the complaint and summons, in which event you must serve your answers and objections within 45 days of the date of these interrogatories.

If you are unable to answer fully any of these interrogatories, you must answer them to the fullest extent possible, specifying the reason(s) for your inability to answer the remainder, and stating whatever information, knowledge, or beliefs you have concerning the unanswerable portion. An evasive or incomplete answer is deemed to be a failure to answer under Mass.R.Dom.Rel.P. 33 and may render you or your attorney or both liable for expenses of a motion to compel pursuant to Mass.R.Dom.Rel.P. 37.

Each lettered subpart of a numbered interrogatory is considered a separate interrogatory for the purpose of objection. You must object separately to each subpart and if you object to less than all of the subparts of a numbered interrogatory, then you must answer the remaining subparts. In addition, if you object to an interrogatory or a subpart thereof as calling for information which is beyond the scope of discovery (e.g. "not reasonably calculated to lead to the discovery of admissible evidence," "work product," "unduly burdensome, " etc.), nevertheless you must answer the interrogatory or subpart thereof to the extent that it is not objectionable.

You must supplement responses to these interrogatories when so requested by me prior to trial. In addition, without being requested to do so by me, you must supplement reasonably the answers to all interrogatories requesting the identification of persons expected to be called as expert witnesses at trial. Without being requested to do so by me, you must also amend any answer when it is discovered to have been incorrect when made or when it is discovered to be no longer true and circumstances are such that a failure to supplement is in substance a knowing concealment.

DEFINITIONS

1) "Identify" or "state identity of" with respect to a document means give the following information if known:

a) a general description thereof [e.g., letter, memorandum, report, etc.];

b) a brief summary of its contents;

c) the name and address of the custodian of the original;
d) the name and address of the person(s), if any, who drafted, prepared, compiled, or signed it; and
e) any other descriptive information necessary in order to adequately describe it in a subpoena duces tecum, or in a motion or request for production thereof.

2) As used herein, the words "record," "records," "document," or "documents," include the original and any copies of any written, printed, typed, or graphic matter of any kind or nature, however produced or reproduced, any book, pamphlet, periodical, letter, memorandum, contract, agreement, invoice, bill, receipt, cancelled check, telegram, report, record, study, handwritten note, working paper, paper, chart, graph, drawing, sketch, index, tape, data sheet, or data processing card of any other written, recorded, transcribed, punched, taped, filmed, or graphic matter, now in possession, custody, or control of the present or former agents, representatives, or employees of yours, or any and all persons acting in your behalf, including documents at any time in the possession, custody, or control of the present or former agents, representatives, employees of yours, or any and all persons acting in your behalf, including documents at any time in the possession, custody, or control of such individuals or entities, or known by you to exist.

3) "Oral communication" refers to any oral expression, exchange, or transmission or thoughts, messages, information, or the like, at any time or place, and under any circumstances whatsoever.

4) "Persons" refers to any individual person (whether living or deceased), partnership firm, corporation, association, joint venture, or other entity.

5) The words "you" or "your" mean you and each of your present and former agents, employees, and all other persons acting or purporting to act on behalf of you, but the use of such terms shall not be construed so as to limit the information provided to that which is within the personal knowledge of such party.

6) "Plaintiff/Defendant" refers to you, and all of your attorneys, consultants, representatives, and other agents.

7) "Plaintiff/Defendant individually" refers to the you as an individual and not to any of your attorneys, consultants, representatives, or other agents.

8) "Quote or Paraphrase" when used herein, requires that solely on the basis of your personal recollection, state the exact wording of the oral statements which you also are to "quote or paraphrase." If this is not possible, then you should so indicate and provide instead a paraphrasing of the oral statement which connotes the substance of what was said, as accurately as possible. In addition, if you definitely recall that particular words were used, you should include these words in your answer, indicating that you definitely recall those words were used.

INTERROGATORY NO. 1: State your name, address, social security number, occupation, current employer, and marital status.

INTERROGATORY NO. 2: List all schools and other educational institutions you have attended since _______, and indicate:

a) the dates attended;

b) any diploma or degree received;
c) major concentration, if any;
d) grade point average, if any;
e) honors earned, if any; and
f) reason(s) for leaving.

INTERROGATORY NO. 3: List each and every employer you have had since ______, including their names, addresses, telephone numbers, the title of each position you held, the salary earned, and the reason(s) for leaving each position.

INTERROGATORY NO. 4: Please set forth an itemized list of all income, gifts, loans, support in cash or kind, and all things of any value of any kind, valued at more than $300.00, which you have received from anyone since _______, other than the support provided to you by your spouse.

INTERROGATORY NO. 5: Identify each occasion since __________, upon which you have traveled outside Massachusetts, for vacation or pleasure purposes, and as to each occasion describe:

a) your destination(s)
b) by whom you were accompanied, and
c) the funds by which the travel was financed.

INTERROGATORY NO. 6: For the calendar year _________, please state the amounts spent by you for living expenses for yourself or for persons legally dependent on you for the following:

a) rent or mortgage payments
b) utilities
c) food
d) clothing
e) cleaning and laundry
f) transportation
g) education
h) medical, psychological and dental care
i) insurance
j) contributions to pension or retirement fund
k) travel/vacation
l) gifts, other than those for dependents
m) charity
n) debt repayment
o) household help
p) furnishings
q) home repairs/improvements

INTERROGATORY NO. 7: Please identify by source and amount each inheritance which you have received during your marriage to ____, and every inheritance which you presently have a reasonable expectancy of receiving.

INTERROGATORY NO. 8: Set forth the name, address, account number, and amount presently in any savings accounts, stock accounts, checking accounts, certificates of deposit, individual retirement accounts, safety deposit boxes, or any other financial vehicle or institution, whether owned individual, jointly, or held by another person or entity in trust for you or your children.

INTERROGATORY NO. 9: List all assets, including real estate, stock, jewelry, furs, coins, antiques, automobiles, furniture and furnishings, silver, crystal, china, artwork, or any other tangible item valued in excess of $200.00, in which you claim an ownership interest.

INTERROGATORY NO. 10: State whether anyone owes you money. If so, state the name and address of the debtor, the amount of the debt, the form of the obligation, the date the obligation was incurred, the date the obligation becomes due and owing the conditions for payment of the obligation, and the consideration given for the obligation.

INTERROGATORY NO. 11: State whether you incurred any debts to another person. If so, state the name and address of the creditor, the amount of your debt, the form of the obligation, the date the obligation becomes due and owing, the condition for payment of the obligation, and the purpose of your incurring the debt.

INTERROGATORY NO. 12: State the names and addresses of any and all proposed expert witnesses and annex true copies of all written reports rendered to you by any such proposed expert witness(s).

DATED: ____________________ By Plaintiff or Defendant

____
Signature

Address:______________________________________
____

Telephone No.:________________________________

CERTIFICATE OF SERVICE

____________________________, SS. ________________________, ______

I, ____, certify that I served the foregoing Interrogatories on defendant by mailing a copy of the Interrogatories, first class mail, postage prepaid, to his/her attorney of record,____
____ or to the defendant
at ____.

____
Signature

Commonwealth of Massachusetts
The Trial Court
The Probate and Family Court Department

_______________ **Division** **Docket No.** _______________

_______________________,
Plaintiff
v.
_______________________,

Request for Production
of Documents

Plaintiff/Defendant, _______________________, hereby requests, pursuant to Rule 34 of the Massachusetts Rules of Domestic Relations Procedure, and Rule 34 of the Massachusetts Rules of Civil Procedure, that you produce the documents hereinafter described and permit me and my attorney, if any, to inspect them and copy such of them as we may desire. Plaintiff/Defendant requests that the documents be made available for this inspection and copying at the Plaintiff's/Defendant's office or the office of Plaintiff's/Defendant's lawyer at _______________________ Massachusetts on _______________, _______, at _________ ____.m. and from day to day thereafter as may be required.

This request is intended to cover all records and documents in the possession of you, or subject to your custody and control, whether they are located in your principal or secondary place of residence, any principal or secondary office, at the offices of your attorneys or any accountant, or at any other place or in the possession of any other person with records and documents subject to your custody and control.

As used in this request, the terms "documents" and "records" shall mean the original, all copies and drafts of writings of any kind, including, without limiting the generality of the foregoing, correspondence, memoranda, reports, notes, letters, messages (including reports, notes and memoranda of telephone conversations and conferences), calendar and diary entries, contracts, records, data, agreements, checks and canceled checks, check registers, bank statements, brokerage account statements, and any other designated documents, records, statements or other writings and printed materials specifically referred to in the following numbered requests.

All documents and records specified in each of the numbered paragraphs which follow shall be for the period from January 1, ________ , up to and including the present date, unless a different date is specified.

1. Any and all records concerning your present employment, employment status, business or professional status, or personal status relating to any other business entity, including without limitation, wages, salaries, bonuses, stock options, commissions, earnings (including over-

time), income, employment contracts or agreements, pay raises, promotions, payroll deductions, other deductions of any kind, monies, credit union account, deferred compensation rights, pension plan, pension fund, retirement plan, retirement fund, stock plan and stock fund, and other benefits or deductions of any kind which are, were previously, or which may be in the future paid, available, accepted, rejected, credited, offered, withheld for any purpose by any individual, agency, department, company or otherwise, or to which you are, were, or may become entitled in the future at any time.

2. Specific reference and demand for production is made for any deferred income plans, wage continuation plans, and any deferred compensation plan, whether any of the above plans are qualified or nonqualified plans, including, but not limited to the following:

A. All records and documents in your possession or control or in the possession or control of any of your agents or available to you from your employer(s) concerning all deferred compensation plans or arrangements as hereinafter defined, in which you (hereinafter the "participant") are now or were at any time during the applicable time period, or at any time prior to the applicable time, which concerns any issue in this litigation in any manner whatsoever, an active participant and under which you have or had at any of the above-referenced time periods actual or potential rights to future benefits. The plans or arrangements are defined herein to include, without limitation, the following:

1) Pension, profit sharing, or stock bonus plans which qualify for special tax treatment by virtue of meeting the requirements of Section 401(a) of the IRC; including any such plans containing cash or deferred arrangements described in IRC Section 401(k); including any HR-10 or "Keough" plans; and including any plans sponsored by an agency of the federal or state government.
2) Annuity plans described in IRC Section 403(a);
3) Tax-sheltered annuity plans described in IRC Section 403(b);
4) Individual Retirement Accounts or annuities (IRA's) or Simplified Employee Pensions (SEP's) described in IRC Section 408;
5) Stock option or stock purchase plans described in IRC Sections 422, 422(a), 423, or 424;
6) Deferred compensation plans for government employees described in IRC Section 457;
7) Excess benefit plans as defined by Section 3(36) of the Employee Retirement Income Security Act of 1974, as amended;
8) Deferred compensation plans of any kind, whether written or unwritten, whether or not funded through dedicated investments, and whether or not financed by reduction of the participants' regular salary or wages.

B. The records, documents, and data requested herein include specifically, without limitation, the following for each and every plan identified under Part (A) above:

1) All documents evidencing or describing the plan, such as plan documents, trust agreements, resolutions of Boards of Directors, etc., including all amendments to such documents to date, even those intended to be adopted within the immediate forthcoming year but which have not yet been formally adopted;

2) Copies of any and all descriptive material or announcements prepared for, or issued to, participants within the last six (6) years;
3) Copies of any filings or correspondence between the plan or its administrator, actuary, or other fiduciary with the Internal Revenue Service, the Department of Labor, the Pension Benefit Guarantee Corporation, the Securities and Exchange Commission, and/or any other regulatory agency within the last six (6) years; including all attachments to said documents or exhibits submitted in connection with such correspondence;
4) Any and all documents, tables, rates, worksheets, interpretive rules, calculation methods, or other data which would be required in addition to the plan documents requested above by a knowledgeable person not otherwise familiar with the day-to-day operation of the plan to be able to compute the amount of any type of benefit under the plan;
5) Copies of all documents of any nature evidencing any optional rights or benefits under the plan, including any such elected, however, including all such rights or benefits whether elected or not and specifically including, but not limited to, the following:
    a. Salary reduction agreements;
    b. Survivor option elections or waivers;
    c. Elections of employee contribution rates;
    d. Special elections under stock option or stock purchase plans;
    e. Elections to suspend or delay benefits;
    f. Election of various benefits under a "cafeteria" plan;
    g. Waiver of any elections previously made.

3. Copies of any original, amended, or restated partnership agreement, whether limited or general, in which you now have or had any interest either as a general or limited partner during the stated years.

4. All books and records showing any benefit now or previously available to you from any business entity in which you have or had a legal or equitable ownership interest, including without limitation, automobile expenses, travel expenses, personal living expenses, entertainment expenses, life insurance, bonuses, health, and accident and hospital insurance.

5. All articles of organization, by-laws, buy-sell agreements, business property, and liability insurance policies, business operating accounts, contracts between you and any business entity not publicly traded in which you have any interest, and books of accounts, of any such business entity in which you have any interest, including but not limited to cash receipts, cash disbursements, accounts receivable and accounts payable, capital accounts maintained by you or on your behalf by any business entity, commercial leases entered into by you or on your behalf as landlord or tenant, license agreements, purchase and sale agreements as buyer or seller by you or on your behalf by any such business entity in which you have any interest.

6. All savings or credit union passbooks or other passbooks of yours, or any card or any other evidence of any savings account, credit union account, special notice account, NOW account or equivalent, certificates of deposit, or any other form of deposit, including but not limited to the following accounts: ____,
____ including but not limited those held by you in your name, or in your behalf, or in your name jointly with any person or entity, or by some other person or entity in trust for you, or in your name as trustee for another person, during the years specified to the present date, including any such accounts in your name as custodian for any minor under the Uniform Gift of Minors Act or otherwise for the same period; showing any and all savings deposits and withdrawals of every kind and nature; and whether or not said accounts or passbooks are now opened or closed. Copies of all records, documents, monthly statements, deposits and withdrawal slips, and cancelled checks for all savings and checking funds during the period specified.

7. Copies of any and all records, accounts, monthly, quarterly or annual brokerage or other account statements, or other evidences of ownership, including but not limited to, securities, bonds, mutual funds, other funds of any kind or nature, commodity futures, other futures of any kind or nature, foreign currency, precious gems and metals, gold bullion, treasury notes and bills, municipal securities and bonds, warrants, rights to purchase, puts and calls, annuities, copyrights, patent rights, trademarks, trademark rights, royalties, rights to trade secrets, any other form of intangible right including any economic rights whether for tax write-off purposes or not, or other investments owned by you individually or owned by you jointly with any person or entity, or owned in your behalf jointly with any other person or by you as trustee, or by you as guardian or custodian during the years specified.

8. Copies of any and all records, lists, accounts or statements, or other evidence of ownership, indicating or evidencing all investments owned by you, either individually or jointly with any other person or entity, and not reflected in any brokerage or other account records or statements during the years specified.

9. All records relative to all trusts from which benefits have been received, are being received, or will be received by you, or in your behalf, whether such trusts are revocable or irrevocable, during the years specified or any time in the future.

10. Copies of any declarations of trust, whether revocable or irrevocable, and minute books, if any, for all trusts to which you are a party now or were a party, either as donor, trustee, or beneficiary.

11. Copies of any and all personal financial statements prepared by you or by an accountant or by any other person for you or in your behalf in reference to your personal finances or financial status, or for any business in which you have or had any interest during the stated years.

12. Copies of all financial statements, records, or documents containing financial information of any nature which have been submitted by you or in your behalf to banks or lending

institutions or to any persons or business entities in connection with any application by you for credit or loans during the stated years.

13. Copies of all records, documents, or statements showing or evidencing the present or previous cash surrender values of any and all life insurance policies, including but not limited to ______________________ policy number ________________, or certificates of life insurance insuring your life, currently in existence, and on any and all life insurance policies or certificates of life insurance in existence during the stated years.

14. All records, documents, vouchers, and receipts pertaining to the transfer by sale or gift or otherwise of any personal or real property to you or on your behalf or by you to any other person, business, or business entity during the years specified.

15. Copies of any and all wills and trusts wherein you are named as trustee or executor or wherein you are given any beneficial interest, including but not limited to, all wills and trusts of your parents and close relatives.

16. Copies of any trusts and accounts in which your children are named beneficiaries, either contingent or vested.

17. Copies of all present and past wills, and any codicils thereto, executed by you as the testator.

18. Copies of any and all federal and state tax returns filed by you individually or jointly with another or on your behalf, including but not limited to individual returns, corporate returns for any business entity not publicly traded in which you have an interest, partnership returns for any partnership in which you have an interest, or fiduciary returns filed by you or on your behalf as a fiduciary. Include accompanying worksheets, vouchers, receipts, and all other records substantiating the returns, together with profit and loss statements for any and all partnerships, corporations, trusts, joint ventures, or other corporate or business associations in which you have held or hold any legal or beneficial interest.

19. Copies of all deeds and records showing any purchase or sale of any real estate in which you (or any partnership, corporation, trust, or any other entity in which you have any interest), held or now hold any ownership interest, legal or equitable, either individually, as trustee, or as mortgagee, including without limitation, adjustment sheets, showing purchase price and other settlement costs, canceled checks, mortgage, mortgage records, and settlement statements.

20. Copies of all sales agreements and/or options for any real estate, including but not limited to ____ owned by you and those held by you in your name, or in your name jointly with any other person or in your name in trust, or in your name as guardian for any other person.

21. All leases or documents evidencing your status as lessee, whether individually or in a business capacity.

22. All leases or documents evidencing your status as lessor, whether individually or in a business capacity, including but not limited to the property known and numbered as ____.

DATED: ____________________ By the plaintiff

____
Signature
Address: ______________________________
____
Telephone No.: ______________________________

Certificate of Service

____________________________ County ______________________________, _______

I, ____, certify that I served the foregoing Request for Production of Documents on my spouse/spouse's attorney, by mailing a copy, first class mail, postage prepaid to my spouse's residence or attorney's office at ____________ ____.

Signed under penalties of perjury.

____
Signature of Party or Attorney

Commonwealth of Massachusetts
The Trial Court
The Probate and Family Court Department

______________ **Division** **Docket No.** ______________

______________________,
Plaintiff

V.

DIVORCE
Pre-trial Memorandum

______________________,
Defendant

This Pre-trial Memorandum is submitted by ________________, Plaintiff/Defendant (hereinafter Husband/Wife) in the above-captioned matter, in accordance with the Pre-trial Notice and Order of this Court assigning this matter for Pre-trial Conference on ______________, at _________ o'clock at ______________ Court in ______________________________ before Judge ________________.

I. PARTIES AND COUNSEL

Names, Address (if your address has been impounded or made confidential by court order, you do not have to list it below), and Telephone Numbers of Parties/Counsel:

Plaintiff: ______________________
____
____
____

Attorney: ______________________
(If Any) ______________________
____
____

Defendant: ______________________
____
____
____

Attorney: ______________________
(If Any) ______________________
____
____

II. GENERAL DESCRIPTION OF CLAIMS AND DEFENSES OF THE PARTIES

1. The (Wife/Husband) filed a complaint for divorce on ____________________, in the ______________ Division of the Probate and Family Court Department, Docket Number __________. The (Husband/Wife) duly filed an answer on ________________.

2. The (Wife/Husband) filed a counterclaim/complaint for divorce on ______________ in the ______________________ Division of the Probate and Family Court, Docket Number __________.

3. The grounds for the original Complaint are:

   ❑ Irretrievable Breakdown of the Marriage
   ❑ Cruel and Abusive Treatment

- ❒ Adultery
- ❒ Impotency
- ❒ Utter Desertion
- ❒ Gross and Confirmed Habits of Intoxication
- ❒ Grossly, wantonly and cruelly refuses or neglects to provide suitable support

4. The Complaint is requesting the following relief:

- ❒ a divorce;
- ❒ an order prohibiting the Wife/Husband from imposing restraint on her personal liberty;
- ❒ custody of the minor children of the marriage;
- ❒ orders of suitable alimony and child support;
- ❒ conveyance of the Husband's/Wife's interest in the marital real estate located at [ADDRESS], which now stands in the names of the Husband and Wife as tenants by the entirety; and
- ❒ an equitable division of marital assets pursuant to M.G.L., c. 208 §34.

5. The grounds for the Counterclaim or Cross Complaint are:

- ❒ Irretrievable Breakdown of the Marriage
- ❒ Cruel and Abusive Treatment
- ❒ Adultery
- ❒ Impotence
- ❒ Utter Desertion
- ❒ Gross and Confirmed Habits of Intoxication
- ❒ Grossly, wantonly and cruelly refuses or neglects to provide suitable support

6. The Counterclaim or Cross Complaint is requesting the following relief:

- ❒ a divorce;
- ❒ an order prohibiting the Wife/Husband from imposing restraint on her personal liberty;
- ❒ custody of the minor children of the marriage;
- ❒ orders of suitable alimony and child support;
- ❒ conveyance of the Husband's/Wife's interest in the marital real estate located at ____________________, which now stands in the names of the Husband and Wife as tenants by the entirety; and
- ❒ an equitable division of marital assets pursuant to M.G.L., c. 208, §34.

7. Restraining Orders:

If you or your spouse currently have a Restraining Order, please check below:

- ❒ Divorce M.G.L., c. 208, §18
- ❒ Abuse Prevention Petition M.G.L., c. 209A

at ______________________________ Court. If pending at a different Court, attach copy.

III. UNCONTESTED FACTS

The parties have not stipulated as to any uncontested facts. It is anticipated, however, that the following facts will not be contested at trial:

1. The parties were married at ______________________________ on ________________.
   (city or town where marriage took place) (Date)
2. This was the ____________ marriage for the Wife.
3. This was the ____________ marriage for the Husband.
4. There were ______________ children born of this marriage.
   They live with ________________ and their names are:

Child's Name:________________________
Date of Birth:________________________
Age:__________
Grade & School ______________________

Child's Name:________________________
Date of Birth:________________________
Age:__________
Grade & School ______________________

Child's Name:________________________
Date of Birth:________________________
Age:__________
Grade & School ______________________

Child's Name:________________________
Date of Birth:________________________
Age:__________
Grade & School ______________________

5. The Husband and Wife last lived in the same house/apartment together on _____ ________________. The house/apartment is located at ______________________ ____.
   (give street address, city/town and state)
6. The Wife now lives at ____ ____.
   (give street address, city/town and state unless impounded)
7. The Husband now lives at ____ ____.
   (give street address, city/town and state unless impounded)

IV. CONTESTED ISSUES OF FACT

The parties are unable to agree on the following issues of fact (check boxes that apply):

- ❒ The suitability of each party as legal and physical custodial parent of the minor children.
- ❒ Alimony, the financial needs and liabilities of the Wife.
- ❒ Alimony, the financial needs and liabilities of the Husband.
- ❒ The amount of support needed for the benefit of the minor children and the amount to be contributed by each party.
- ❒ The contribution by each party to the acquisition, preservation and appreciation in the value of the marital estate.
- ❒ The current value of marital assets.
- ❒ The contribution of each party as a parent and homemaker.

- ☐ The educational, employment, vocational skills and employability of each party.
- ☐ The opportunity of each party for future acquisition of capital assets and income including inheritances.
- ☐ The health of the parties.
- ☐ The conduct of the parties during the marriage.
- ☐ The present and future needs of the children.
- ☐ Other ____.

V. CONTESTED ISSUES OF LAW

- ☐ What custody/parenting/visitation arrangements should be entered for the parties in keeping with the best interests of the child/children pursuant to M.G.L., Chapter 208, §31.

- ☐ What amount of support should be provided by each of the parties for the benefit of the minor children pursuant to M.G.L., c. 208, § 28.

- ☐ Whether alimony is required by either party in consideration of the provisions of M.G.L., c. 208, § 34.

- ☐ What share of their marital assets should be awarded to each party in consideration of the provisions of M.G.L., c. 208, § 34.

VI. STATUS OF DISCOVERY

The Wife has filed:

- ☐ Interrogatories
- ☐ Request for Production of Documents
- ☐ Deposition Notices of ______________________________.
- ☐ None of the above

The Husband has responded to ______________________________
____.

The Husband has filed:

- ☐ Interrogatories
- ☐ Request for Production of Documents
- ☐ Deposition Notices of ______________________________
- ☐ None of the above

The Wife has responded to ______________________________
____.

VII. SCHEDULE OF EXHIBITS

Information needing to be exchanged between the parties (Exhibits).
List the documents or information that you need to get from the other party to prove your argument.

The Wife/Husband intends to introduce the following exhibits at trial:

- ☐ 1. Financial Statement(s) of the Wife.
- ☐ 2. Financial Statement(s) of the Husband.
- ☐ 3. Federal and state income tax returns of the parties for the past five years (unless the marriage is of shorter duration).
- ☐ 4. Documents showing the Wife's contribution to the purchase and financing of the marital home including: the source of down payment of $_______________.
- ☐ 5. Documents showing the Wife's contribution (financial and otherwise) relating to the acquisition, preservation and appreciation in value of marital assets including without limitation the marital home, savings and retirement funds.
- ☐ 6. Documents showing the Husband's contribution to the purchase and financing of the marital home including: the source of down payment of $_______________.
- ☐ 7. Documents showing the Husband's contribution (financial and otherwise) relating to the acquisition, preservation and appreciation in value of marital assets including without limitation the marital home, savings and retirement funds.
- ☐ 8. Documents relating to and reflecting the Wife's/Husband's segregation of and use of her/his earned income during the marriage.
- ☐ 9. Documents relating to pension and profit sharing plans participated in by the Wife/Husband.
- ☐ 10. Documents relative to value of real estate held by the parties.
- ☐ 11. Report of: (Guardian ad litem) (Family Service Office) (Social Worker) (Psychologist) (Psychiatrist) (Department of Social Services DSS).
- ☐ 12. Other Exhibits (list):

____
____
____
____
____

The Wife/Husband reserves the right to introduce additional exhibits.

VIII. LIST OF WITNESSES

The people I want to testify in court for me (witnesses).

The Wife/Husband intends to call the following witnesses at trial:

- ☐ The Wife
- ☐ The Husband
- ☐ Other Witnesses (list):

  ____
  ____
  ____

The Wife/Husband reserves the right to call rebuttal witnesses as necessary.

IX. LIST OF EXPERT WITNESSES

The Wife/Husband intends to retain and call the following expert witnesses at trial:

- ☐ Real Estate Appraiser
- ☐ Pension Plan Evaluator
- ☐ Personal Property/Jewelry Appraiser
- ☐ Social Worker/Psychiatrist/Psychologist/G.A.L./Family Service Office
- ☐ Other Expert Witnesses (list):

  ____
  ____
  ____

X. CURRENT FINANCIAL STATEMENT

A current Financial Statement of the Wife/Husband is submitted herewith pursuant to Rule 401 of the Supplemental Rules of the Probate Court.

XI. ESTIMATE OF TRIAL TIME

Estimate how long you think it will take for you to present your evidence to the court and for the opposing side to present his/her evidence, i.e., 1/2 day, 1 day.

The Wife/Husband anticipates that the trial this matter will take [NUMBER] _____ days.

XII. WRITTEN OFFER OF PROOF REGARDING FACTORS PURSUANT TO M.G.L. c. 208, § 34

1. Length of the marriage.

Please state the date and location of your marriage. If this is not the first marriage for either you or your spouse, please indicate prior marriages, the length thereof and how terminated. As to children of the prior marriage, please indicate with whom the children currently reside and whether child support is received or paid. Is alimony paid to a prior spouse? Include as child support or alimony not only amounts of weekly support but other special fees such as tuitions, uninsured medical expenses and provision of insurances, if applicable.

The parties were married on _______________ and have been married to each other for ______ years. They were married at ____________________.

____
____
____
____
____

2. The conduct of the parties during the marriage.

Please describe in detail, providing dates and circumstances where applicable, your marital history. Emphasis should be placed on the changing nature of the relationship between the parties from the onset of the marriage to the time of separation setting forth the sources of stress, difficulties in communication, differing lifestyles, goals and objectives, lack of affection and/or sexual intimacy, conflict, incidents of cruel and abusive treatment including description of conduct, dates and locations and witnesses, if any, substance abuse or other habits interfering with home, family life and the marital relationship.

Please indicate also how you coped with these matters during the marriage and indicate as well if either you or your spouse or both of you engaged in any form of professional counseling identifying the physician, therapist or other counselor and the periods of time involved. What were the results of such counseling?

Please describe the circumstances leading to your present separation and any prior separations that have occurred during the marriage.

Does either you or your spouse have an interest in reconciliation?

Please describe any other significant problems which have developed since the marital separation.

3. The age of the parties.

a. The Wife's birth date is _________; she is ____________years old.
b. The Husband's birth date is____________; he is ______ years old.

4. The health of the parties.

Please indicate any physical and mental health problems, either isolated or chronic illnesses or conditions that required hospitalizations or other treatment by you and/or your spouse as well as by any of your children that have occurred during the marriage. Please also describe any special needs posed by your children during the marriage and describe the manner in which these needs have been addressed, again providing the names of physicians, therapists, counselors, educational specialists who have been consulted with respect to these matters.

a. The Wife's health is ____
(explain past/present medical history, the doctor's prognosis and any long term effects)

b. The Husband's health is ____
(explain past/present medical history, the doctor's prognosis and any long term effects)

5. The station in life of the parties.

Please describe your station in life (wealthy, middle, low income lifestyle) as it developed or changed during your marriage. Indicate if you and/or your spouse held memberships in clubs or organizations which were integral to your lifestyle. Likewise, any form of volunteer work or civic association should be noted as a possible factor in enhancing your or your spouse's professional growth and current status.

Please describe your use of leisure time including activities which you pursued as a couple or individually. Please describe the pattern of vacationing or other travel during the marriage(i.e., the family would go to Cape Cod for one week each summer/ the parties would take a winter vacation.)

____
____
____
____
____
____
____
____
____
____

6. <u>The vocational skills of the parties and current employment and employability</u>.

Please provide a description of your educational background and that of your spouse including high school, vocational school, college, graduate schools, dates attended and degrees received. If such education was attained during any part of the marriage, state the source of funds for payment of school tuitions and related fees as well as the source of funds relied on during this period for living expenses and acquisition of assets, if applicable.

____
____
____
____
____
____
____
____
____
____

7. <u>The amount and sources of your income; employment and employability.</u>

Please set forth a complete list of your current income and that of your spouse indicating the source of each component (salary, wages, overtime, bonus, part-time job), amounts received and frequency of receipt.

Please set forth your employment record and that of your spouse during the marriage and note, if applicable, particular skills of either you or your spouse which suggest potential for current or future employment. Are there any factors currently interfering with your ability or your spouse's ability to work?

____
____
____
____
____
____
____
____

____
____
____
____

8. The respective estates of the parties and the marital estate.

Please set forth a listing of all assets held, in whatever form, by you, by your spouse and by you and/or your spouse jointly indicating the source of funds used for acquisition and the dates acquired.

As to real property held during the course of the marriage, please describe each parcel and indicate the reason acquired, i.e., residence or investment, the dates owned and the source of monies used for down payment, monthly carrying cost, costs of improvements, together with description of financing.

Estate

a. The parties own the following items:

1. Marital Home (Joint):
   Fair Market Value $__________
   First Mortgage $__________
   Home Improvement Loan $__________
   Equity $__________
2. Annuities/Stocks/Bonds $__________
3. Furniture and Furnishings, Jewelry $__________
4. Savings Accounts/Certificates of Deposit $__________
5. Checking Account $__________
6. Motor Vehicles: Estimated Value $__________
   ______________ Outstanding Loan $__________
   Year/Make
7. Full life insurance, cash surrender value $__________
8. Workman's compensation/personal injury or other pending litigation $__________
9. Business Interests $__________
10. Other (list) $__________
    ______________ $__________
    ______________ $__________
    ______________ $__________

b. The parties have the following bills and loans to repay:

☐ Bills:

Visa	Total amount due __________
Master Card	Total amount due __________
Discover Card	Total amount due __________
American Express	Total amount due __________
__________	Total amount due __________
__________	Total amount due __________
__________	Total amount due __________
__________	Total amount due __________
__________	Total amount due __________

___________ Total amount due ___________

☐ Loans:

School Total amount due ___________

___________ Total amount due ___________

___________ Total amount due ___________

___________ Total amount due ___________

___________ Total amount due ___________

9. The liabilities and needs of the parties.

This is reflected on your financial statement and your spouse's statement.

a. The Wife's weekly expenses are $___________. See her Financial Statement.

b. The Husband's weekly expenses are $_________. See his Financial Statement.

c. The health insurance is covered by ______________________________

____

(if this is an employee policy state whether or not it can continue)

____

____

____

____

____

10. The opportunity of each party for future acquisition of capital assets and income.

Please indicate the extent to which you **and/or your** spouse have opportunity for future **acquisition** on an increase in income and capital assets including not only income from salary, **investments**, rental income, trust income, pension or retirement plans, but also anticipated **inheritances** from parents or other relatives. **Potential litigation should also be listed.**

11. Present and future needs **of the dependent** children of the marriage. In fixing the nature and value of the **property to be so assigned**, the Court shall also consider the present and future needs of **the dependent** children of the marriage.

Please describe the particular **needs of children requiring** recognition in dividing assets **between the parties**; for example, do **the needs of the children** dictate that they remain in the **marital home with** the custodial parent, **delaying possible division and sale** of that asset. Do the **children require** that additional sums be **provided to the custodial parent** for the purpose of future **education. Do the** children have long-**term needs requiring** assistance beyond their minority. **Explain the child's** school, grade, and the **type of student he or she is.** Discuss the general health of the child, including any special medical, psychological, educational treatment or counseling to which the child goes.

____
____
____
____
____
____
____
____
____
____

12. <u>The contribution of each of the parties in the acquisition, preservation or appreciation in value of their respective estates</u>.

Please describe in detail the contribution of you and your spouse toward purchasing what you and your spouse own and include any contributions that were made during the marriage by your family or your spouse's family or any other source. Please indicate if you or your spouse entered the marriage with significant assets and, if so, how these were used.

____
____
____
____
____
____
____
____
____
____

13. <u>The contribution of each party as a homemaker and parent to the family unit.</u>

Please describe your role and that of your spouse as to homemaking, home management and child rearing and care during the marriage. Did either you or your spouse contribute primarily to these functions and, if so, what secondary functions and assistance, if any, did the other party provide.

If you were not the party primarily responsible for homemaking, home management and child care, please describe what assistance you provided during the marriage in these areas. Please indicate as well responsibilities assumed as to maintenance, improvement, renovations to your homes including yard and exterior maintenance as well as the tasks of cleaning, laundering, meal planning, preparation, etc.

As to care of the children, please indicate who was responsible for infant and toddler care including supervision and recreation and if, during the course of your marriage, child care, domestic or other services were used.

Please set forth in as much detail as possible your contributions toward parenting, the emotional growth and development of your children, including their schooling, health care, recreational, extracurricular and religious upbringing.

If applicable, please describe your role and contribution as step-parent.

Please state your children's educational history indicating schools and colleges attended, whether private and source of funds applied for education expenses.

XIII. REPRESENTATION OF GOOD FAITH NEGOTIATION

☐ The parties have negotiated in good faith but have been unable to reach a settlement agreement.

☐ A meeting pursuant to the pre-trial order to negotiate a settlement is not required since a **Restraining Order** (a Domestic Relations Protection Order under M.G.L. ,c. 208, §18 or an Abuse Prevention Order under M.G.L. c. 209A) has been entered in this matter.

Submitted by:

____

(Sign name)

____

(Print name)

Date: ________________

GLOSSARY

MASSACHUSETTS DIVORCE LAW DICTIONARY

abandonment. *See* **desertion.**

abuse. *See* **cruel and abusive treatment.**

abuse prevention. *See* **restraining order.**

admissible; admissibility. Describing any testimony, document, or demonstrative material officially considered by the court, i.e., allowed or admitted into evidence, generally in compliance with the rules of evidence.

admissions; request for admissions. One party to a case may require the other party to admit or deny in writing and under oath various assertions; e.g., "wife asks husband to admit or deny husband was guilty of cruel and abusive treatment on December 14, 1997."

adultery. Sexual intercourse between a married person and a third party. One of seven fault grounds for divorce in Massachusetts, but rarely used.

affidavit. A written statement, voluntarily signed under oath, usually in support of a motion or joint petition for a no-fault divorce.

alienation of affection. Any intentional, malicious interference with a marital relationship; no longer recognized by the Massachusetts courts.

alimony. Spousal support paid by agreement of the parties or by court order. The payments are usually periodic, but sometimes in a lump sum. In the absence of a separation agreement, courts must consider the same statutory factors considered in property divisions. *See* **equitable division of property.**

annulment. The court's judgment that a so-called "marriage" was never legally valid or invalid after the marriage.

answer to complaint and counterclaim. A responsive pleading that answers allegations made in the complaint. A counterclaim sets forth the defendant's allegations against the plaintiff, as if the defendant were asking for a divorce in the first instance. The defendant is sometimes called the *plaintiff-in-counterclaim* since he or she makes his or her initial claim for divorce in this pleading.

best interest of the child. The legal standard or doctrine for making child-related decisions.

burden of proof. The party asserting a claim must prove such claim is true—in civil cases the party must prove the claim by a preponderance of evidence. In criminal cases, proof must be beyond a reasonable doubt.

capias. A civil arrest warrant ordering the sheriff or other officer to take a person into custody and deliver him or her to court. This procedure is used when a party refuses to appear in court.

common law. A body of law, sometimes referred to as *case law*, developed by judges over many years which establishes how courts interpret statutes and handle matters not specifically covered by statutes.

common law marriage. A judicially-recognized marriage (but not recognized in Massachusetts) generally based on cohabitation.

constable. A private individual who is legally empowered to serve process.

constructive service of process. The service of process through alternative means such as publication in a newspaper when the defendant resides out of state or whose whereabouts are unknown.

contested and uncontested divorce. In contested divorces, the parties are adversarial, they cannot agree on the terms of divorce, such as alimony, custody, visitation, child support, and division of assets. In uncontested divorces, the parties agree to all matters, and present an executed separation agreement to the court for approval. Whether a divorce is contested or uncontested should not be confused with whether the divorce is fault or no-fault. The following chart illustrates the difference.

	Contested	Uncontested
Fault	grounds and property and/or support are in dispute; trial necessary if not settled.	unusual since uncontested divorces avoid conflict; insisting on fault destroys the cooperative nature of uncontested matters.
No-Fault	property and/or support in dispute; if no agreement is reached, the case goes to trial.	signed agreement presented to the court for its approval.

contingency fee. In divorce cases, an unethical type of fee agreement providing the lawyer with a percentage of your settlement or judgment.

co-respondent. A third-party co-defendant in a divorce action accused of committing adultery with the defendant.

court docket. The formal court record of all pleadings, orders, and judgments entered into a docket book available for public inspection.

court order. A written instruction from the court carrying the weight of law, i.e., the knowing violation of which constitutes contempt of court.

coverture. The period of time during which a person is married.

cross-examination. Following the direct examination of a witness by his or her own lawyer, cross examination is the follow-up questioning by the opposing lawyer.

cruel and abusive treatment. Ground for divorce in a fault divorce, wherein the plaintiff must prove physical or emotional harm to her or himself.

custody—legal. A legal status, or *custodianship*, vesting authority to approve all major decisions affecting a minor child. Chapter 208, Sec. 29 defines legal custody as follows:

sole legal custody. Where one parent has the right and responsibility to make decisions regarding the child's welfare, including matters of education, medical care, and emotional, moral, and religious development.

shared legal custody. Where there is the continued mutual responsibility and involvement by both parents in major decisions regarding the child's welfare, including matters of education, medical care, emotional, moral, and religious development. Sometimes separation agreements use terms such as *joint legal custody*, which means shared legal custody.

custody—physical. Relates to the physical location of the child. Chapter 208, Sec. 29 defines physical custody as follows:

sole physical custody. Where a child resides with, and is under the supervision of, one parent, subject to reasonable visitation by the other parent, unless the court determines that visitation would not be in the best interest of the child.

shared physical custody. Where a child has periods of residing with, and being under the supervision of, each parent; provided, that physical custody be shared by the parents in such a way as to assure the child frequent and continued contact with both parents.

Such terms as *sole, primary, shared,* and *joint* are used to describe various parenting and visitation plans.

de facto. Latin meaning "in fact." Acting in a certain manner, usually as if complying with what a court might order, without such order being in place. For instance, if one parent is making voluntary child support payments pursuant to the guidelines, he or she is paying *de facto* guideline support, even though no court has so ordered.

Department of Revenue. The Massachusetts agency responsible for child support enforcement.

Department of Social Services (DSS). The Massachusetts agency responsible for the health and welfare of children.

desertion. One of several grounds for a fault divorce. Massachusetts requires the plaintiff to prove several of the following factors: 1) the defendant left the marital home for over one year; 2) the parties failed to agree to such departure; 3) the party who left failed to pay support; and 4) the reason for the departure was not caused by the plaintiff.

discovery; pretrial discovery. Discovery is the formal procedure for gathering information pursuant to rules of court. The primary methods are requests for financial statements under Supplemental Rule 401, requests for production of documents, written interrogatories, depositions, and subpoenas to third parties.

domicile. A person's "legal" home, i.e., where the person spends most of his time, or intends to return, if currently living elsewhere.

equitable distribution of property. Massachusetts is an *equitable distribution* state, meaning that all property, whenever or however acquired, regardless of legal title, is subject to "fair" (equal or unequal) division.

evidence. Any testimony, document, or demonstrative material. *See* **rules of evidence.**

exhibit(s). Any evidence attached to a pleading or introduced at trial, for example, a party's pay stub attached to a motion for temporary support.

ex parte (hearing, motion, order). *Ex parte* means without notice to, or attendance of, the opposing party. The motion session of the Probate and Family Court is referred to as the *Ex Parte Session,* although both parties are usually present.

expert witness. In divorce cases, most experts are called to testify as to the value of the marital home, pensions, and privately-held businesses. In child-related disputes, mental health professionals are often called to testify.

Family Service Office; Family Service Officer. Sometimes known as the Probation Department, this office and its employees, also known as probation officers, assist the court with dispute resolution.

fault and no-fault divorces.

In **fault** divorces, the complaint for divorce must state grounds for divorce. They include cruel and abusive treatment, adultery, abandonment, and other types of misconduct.

No-fault complaints for divorce merely allege an "irretrievable breakdown" of the marriage. The court must find that the marriage has "irretrievably broken down," leaving no chance of reconciliation.

find; findings. After considering the evidence presented, a court or jury interprets the evidence and sets forth what it believes, i.e., finds, are the actual facts. Courts have great latitude in weighing evidence and in believing or disbelieving witnesses. The court's findings, along with its *conclusions of law,* form the basis for the court's decision. *See* **judgment.**

Investigator-Attorney. A court-appointed lawyer who investigates matters pursuant to judicial order and reports his or her findings to the court.

impeach; impeachment of testimony. Discrediting a witness by proving lies, inconsistencies in stories told, and untrustworthiness. The witness may be impeached during cross-examination or by the direct testimony or evidence of another witness. *See* **direct-examination** and **cross-examination.**

impoundment of pleadings. You can ask the court, via motion, to impound your papers for good cause, such as certain inflammatory matters might be read by the children.

in camera hearing. A closed-door hearing in judge's chambers, usually concerning sensitive child-related issues.

infant. A person who has not reached legal majority, usually eighteen years of age. Also, referred to as a *minor,* or *unemancipated child.*

injunction; injunctive relief. A court order prohibiting certain activity. *See* **temporary order** and **temporary restraining order.**

interlocutory hearing. Any court hearing at which a pretrial order or ruling is requested.

interrogatories. Interrogatories consist of written questions propound to a person (who must be a party to the case). Answers must be in writing and made under oath pursuant to rules of court. *See* **discovery** and **pretrial discovery.**

irretrievable breakdown. The legal ground for no fault divorce, also known as "1-A" divorces because they are granted under Chapter 208, Section 1A of the Massachusetts General Laws.

joint custody. *See* **custody-legal** and **custody-physical.**

joint petition. When both parties ask the court to do the same thing, usually to grant a no fault divorce.

judgment of absolute divorce. The court's final judgment after expiration of the judgment nisi period. Upon this date you are legally divorced and can remarry. Generally, the final decree occurs automatically upon termination of the waiting period. Additional court filings and appearances are not required.

judgment nisi. The initial, temporary judgment of divorce. When courts grant divorces, their judgments are not final until the expiration of a statutory "waiting period" known as the *nisi* period. It begins when the judgment *nisi* enters and ends upon entry of the "judgment absolute" on the docket.

jurisdiction. The court's legal authority to hear your case and issue legally enforceable orders and judgments. The Probate and Family Court in the county where you last lived together has jurisdiction over the divorce, unless neither party currently lives in such county.

legal separation. Massachusetts courts do not grant legal separations, but all separations are legal in the sense that people have the right to live apart without a court order. *See* **separate support** for rights of separated parties where neither party files a complaint for divorce.

mandatory factors (to be considered by the court). The factors a court must consider before making a final decision relating to property division and alimony. *See* **equitable distribution.**

marital property. In the absence of a prenuptial agreement, all property in which either party has an interest, including property acquired before marriage, inheritances, gifts, and property held in only one spouse's name.

marriage certificate. The official certification (with raised seal) of your marriage issued by a civil authority which you need to file with the court for a divorce.

memorandum of law. A legal document filed along with pleadings or other court papers setting forth your lawyer's legal research in support of a request to the court.

merged agreement. *See* **separation agreement.**

motion. A written request asking, or *moving,* the court to grant a temporary order, or rule on a legal matter.

negotiated settlement; negotiated agreement. The parties, usually with counsel, develop a separation agreement. These agreements are not mediated; the parties, without any neutral third-party settle their controversy through negotiation.

notice; legal notice. The procedure for informing a party that a legal action or motion is pending before a court.

pendente lite. Latin for "during the litigation."

perjury. Knowingly lying under oath.

pleadings. Includes the complaint (or petition), answer, and counterclaim.

prejudice; with and without prejudice. The concept that what happens in court or by stipulation of the parties will affect future proceedings. Generally, temporary orders are said to be *without prejudice,* which means that the parties have a right to a trial on all matters, including those decided by temporary orders. In contrast, *with prejudice* means that even at trial the earlier order determines the outcome. If your complaint for divorce is dismissed without prejudice, you may file again. If it is dismissed with prejudice, you may not refile.

preliminary hearing. Any court proceeding that occurs prior to trial.

premarital assets. Assets acquired by either party before marriage. These assets are part of the marital estate in Massachusetts. (*See* **marital property**.) By contrast, in many states, assets acquired by one party before marriage remain the separate property of that party.

prenuptial agreement. A written, premarital contract dealing with death and divorce, setting forth the rights and responsibilities of the parties upon occurrence of these events. The agreement must be "fair and reasonable" at the time it is signed and also at the time a party seeks to enforce it.

pretrial conference. A court-mandated meeting of all parties and counsel with the trial judge.

privilege. Refers to evidence based on private communications made within legally recognized "confidential relationships," such as husband-wife, attorney-client, patient-psychiatrist, and priest-penitent. Also refers to the privilege against "self incrimination" which can be asserted by a party accused of adultery—a criminal offense in Massachusetts.

Probate and Family Court. The Massachusetts trial court with jurisdiction over divorce.

production of documents. Under a rule of court the plaintiff or defendant is allowed to demand documentary evidence to be produced by the other party. *See* **discovery**.

pro se; pro se appearance. When a party handles his or her own case, i.e., represents himself or herself, she is said to appear *pro se*."

Proposed Findings and Rulings; Proposed Orders, Proposed Judgment. A document prepared by you or your lawyer and submitted to the court setting forth your best case scenario, i.e., how you want the judge to find the facts, make *conclusions of law*, and decide the case.

QDRO (Qualified Domestic Relations Order—pronounced "kwahd-row"). A court order directed to a "plan administrator" or "custodian" allocating retirement benefits between spouses.

rehabilitative alimony. Short-term spousal support designed to help the recipient "get started" with his or her new life. *See* **alimony.**

restraining order. A temporary court order prohibiting a party from certain activities. Issued in response to a motion, restraining orders often are issued to protect marital assets and to protect against domestic violence. Violating a domestic restraining order is a criminal offense.

Rules of Domestic Relations Procedure. The rules that govern court procedure or steps you must follow in a court case.

rules of evidence. The statutory rules governing the admissibility of testimony, documents, and demonstrative materials.

sanctions. Under the *Rules of Domestic Relations Procedure*, courts may penalize or sanction a party or counsel for improper behavior, such as making frivolous claims or withholding evidence.

separate property. Property not considered marital property (i.e., part of the marital estate). In some states, property owned prior to the marriage, and possibly inheritances or gifts received during marriage, are not considered marital property. In Massachusetts, all property is marital property.

separation agreement. A legally enforceable spousal contract settling all matters. A *merging* separation agreement is modifiable by court order after divorce upon a *material change* in circumstances. A *surviving* separation agreement cannot be modified by court order unless something more than a material change occurs, for example, if one party is on welfare.

service; service of process. The legal process of informing, i.e., "giving notice," that a complaint or motion is pending.

Special Master. A court-appointed individual, usually an attorney, who assists the court as a private judge during certain aspects of the case, such as discovery.

stipulation; stipulated agreement. A written agreement intended to be entered as a court order upon filing an "assented to" motion of the parties.

strike; motion to strike. Upon motion of a party, a court may remove pleadings and evidence from the record if it finds the material is irrelevant, scandalous, or without proper notice.

subpoena; subpoena duces tecum. An order, usually of a notary public, issued to a party or non-party to a case, to attend a legal proceeding such as a trial or deposition. If documents also are requested, the subpoena is called a subpoena *duces tecum*, Latin for "bring with you." *See* also **discovery.**

surviving agreement. *See* **separation agreement.**

temporary order, temporary restraining order (TRO). A pretrial order compelling a party to do something, or prohibiting him from certain activities.

trial memoranda; pretrial memoranda. A "sales" document filed with the court, setting forth each party's theory of the case, what they want, and why they should get it.

uncontested divorce. A divorce in which the parties agree on all matters as set forth in their separation agreement.

vacate the marital home, motion to. A request to the court made by motion asking that one party be forced to vacate the marital home.

venue; change of venue. The location of the court, in contrast to jurisdiction which determines whether a court has legal authority to hear a case. Venue is where a court, with proper jurisdiction, will hear the case. When a case is transferred to a new location within the same jurisdiction (county or state), the transfer is called a *change of venue*.

visitation; supervised visitation. Pursuant to stipulation, agreement, or court order, visits of unemancipated children with their non-custodial parent. Visits are supervised by a responsible adult when the non-custodial parent is accused of child abuse or neglect.

wage assignment. A court order to a third party, usually an employer, requiring the employee's wages to be attached (automatically deducted from a paycheck) and assigned (paid) to another party.

INDEX

A

B

C

D

E

F

G

H

I

J

L

M

N

O

P

Q

R

S

T

U

V

W

Your #1 Source for Real World Legal Information…

SPHINX® PUBLISHING

A Division of Sourcebooks, Inc.®

- Written by lawyers
- Simple English explanation of the law
- Forms and instructions included

How to File Your Own Bankruptcy (4th Edition)

Whether you are considering filing for bankruptcy or are looking to avoid it at all costs, this book can help you. Includes instructions and forms necessary for filing Chapter 7 (debt discharge) and Chapter 13 (payment plan) bankruptcy and much more!

208 pages; $19.95;
ISBN 1-57071-223-9

How to Buy a Condominium or Townhome

Provides information on forms of ownership, rights and duties of owners and associations,finding the right property, purchase documents, closing procedures, privacy issues, determining what you can afford, sample forms and state-by-state listings of statutes.

176 pages; $16.95;
ISBN 1-57071-164-X

How to Write Your Own Premarital Agreement

With the divorce rate of over 50 percent, although unpleasant, it is wise to consider drafting your own premarital agreement. With this book, you can also cancel or modify an existing premarital agreement. Includes inheritance and divorce laws, with forms and instructions

180 pages; $19.95;
ISBN 1-57071-344-8

Other Massachusetts Legal Survival Guides

How to Probate an Estate in MA	$19.95	Landlords' Rights & Duties in MA	$19.95
How to Start a Business in MA	$16.95	How to Make a MA Will	$9.95

See the following order form for books available for other states. Coming in 1999—Ohio!

What our customers say about our books:

"Your real estate contracts book has saved me nearly $12,000.00 in closing costs over the past year." —A.B.

"…many of the legal questions that I have had over the years were answered clearly and concisely through your plain English interpretation of the law." —C.E.H.

"If there weren't people out there like you I'd be lost. You have the best books of this type out there." —S.B

Legal Survival Guides are directly available from Sourcebooks, Inc., or from your local bookstores.

For credit card orders call 1–800–43–BRIGHT, write P.O. Box 372, Naperville, IL 60566, or fax 630-961-2168

SPHINX® PUBLISHING ORDER FORM

BILL TO:		SHIP TO:	
Phone #	Terms	F.O.B. Chicago, IL	Ship Date

Charge my: ❒ VISA ❒ MasterCard ❒ American Express

❒ Money Order or Personal Check

Credit Card Number

Expiration Date

Qty	ISBN	Title	Retail	Ext.
		SPHINX PUBLISHING NATIONAL TITLES		
____	1-57071-166-6	Crime Victim's Guide to Justice	$19.95	____
____	1-57071-342-1	Debtors' Rights (3E)	$12.95	____
____	1-57071-162-3	Defend Yourself Against Criminal Charges	$19.95	____
____	1-57248-001-7	Grandparents' Rights	$19.95	____
____	0-913825-99-9	Guia de Inmigracion a Estados Unidos	$19.95	____
____	1-57248-021-1	Help Your Lawyer Win Your Case	$12.95	____
____	1-57071-164-X	How to Buy a Condominium or Townhome	$16.95	____
____	1-57071-223-9	How to File Your Own Bankruptcy (4E)	$19.95	____
____	1-57071-224-7	How to File Your Own Divorce (3E)	$19.95	____
____	1-57071-227-1	How to Form Your Own Corporation (2E)	$19.95	____
____	1-57071-343-X	How to Form Your Own Partnership	$19.95	____
____	1-57071-228-X	How to Make Your Own Will	$12.95	____
____	1-57071-331-6	How to Negotiate Real Estate Contracts (3E)	$16.95	____
____	1-57071-332-4	How to Negotiate Real Estate Leases (3E)	$16.95	____
____	1-57071-225-5	How to Register Your Own Copyright (2E)	$19.95	____
____	1-57071-226-3	How to Register Your Own Trademark (2E)	$19.95	____
____	1-57071-349-9	How to Win Your Unemployment Compensation Claim	$19.95	____
____	1-57071-167-4	How to Write Your Own Living Will	$9.95	____
____	1-57071-344-8	How to Write Your Own Premarital Agreement (2E)	$19.95	____
____	1-57071-333-2	Jurors' Rights (2E)	$9.95	____
____	1-57248-032-7	Legal Malpractice and Other Claims Against...	$18.95	____
____	1-57071-400-2	Legal Research Made Easy (2E)	$14.95	____
____	1-57071-336-7	Living Trusts and Simple Ways to Avoid Probate (2E)	$19.95	____
____	1-57071-345-6	Most Valuable Bus. Legal Forms You'll Ever Need (2E)	$19.95	____
____	1-57071-346-4	Most Valuable Corporate Forms You'll Ever Need (2E)	$24.95	____
____	1-57071-347-2	Most Valuable Personal Legal Forms You'll Ever Need	$14.95	____
____	0-913825-41-7	Neighbor vs. Neighbor	$12.95	____
____	1-57071-348-0	The Power of Attorney Handbook (3E)	$19.95	____
____	1-57248-020-3	Simple Ways to Protect Yourself from Lawsuits	$24.95	____
____	1-57071-337-5	Social Security Benefits Handbook (2E)	$14.95	____
____	1-57071-163-1	Software Law (w/diskette)	$29.95	____
____	0-913825-86-7	Successful Real Estate Brokerage Mgmt.	$19.95	____
____	1-57071-399-5	Unmarried Parents' Rights	$19.95	____
____	1-57071-354-5	U.S.A. Immigration Guide (3E)	$19.95	____
____	0-913825-82-4	Victims' Rights	$12.95	____
____	1-57071-165-8	Winning Your Personal Injury Claim	$19.95	____
		CALIFORNIA TITLES		
____	1-57071-360-X	CA Power of Attorney Handbook	$12.95	____
____	1-57071-355-3	How to File for Divorce in CA	$19.95	____
____	1-57071-356-1	How to Make a CA Will	$12.95	____
____	1-57071-408-8	How to Probate an Estate in CA	$19.95	____
____	1-57071-357-X	How to Start a Business in CA	$16.95	____
____	1-57071-358-8	How to Win in Small Claims Court in CA	$14.95	____
____	1-57071-359-6	Landlords' Rights and Duties in CA	$19.95	____
		FLORIDA TITLES		
____	1-57071-363-4	Florida Power of Attorney Handbook (2E)	$12.95	____
____	1-57071-403-7	How to File for Divorce in FL (5E)	$21.95	____
____	1-57071-401-0	How to Form a Partnership in FL	$19.95	____
____	1-57248-004-1	How to Form a Nonprofit Corp. in FL (3E)	$19.95	____
____	1-57071-380-4	How to Form a Corporation in FL (4E)	$19.95	____
____	1-57071-361-8	How to Make a FL Will (5E)	$12.95	____

Form Continued on Following Page

SUBTOTAL ____

To order, call Sourcebooks at 1-800-43-BRIGHT or FAX (630)961-2168 (Bookstores, libraries, wholesalers—please call for discount)

SPHINX® PUBLISHING ORDER FORM

Qty	ISBN	Title	Retail	Ext.
		FLORIDA TITLES (CONT'D)		
____	1-57248-056-4	How to Modify Your FL Divorce Judgement (3E)	$22.95	____
____	1-57071-364-2	How to Probate an Estate in FL (3E)	$24.95	____
____	1-57248-005-X	How to Start a Business in FL (4E)	$16.95	____
____	1-57071-362-6	How to Win in Small Claims Court in FL (6E)	$14.95	____
____	1-57071-335-9	Landlords' Rights and Duties in FL (7E)	$19.95	____
____	1-57071-334-0	Land Trusts in FL (5E)	$24.95	____
____	0-913825-73-5	Women's Legal Rights in FL	$19.95	____
		GEORGIA TITLES		
____	1-57071-387-1	How to File for Divorce in GA (3E)	$19.95	____
____	1-57248-047-5	How to Make a GA Will (2E)	$9.95	____
____	1-57248-026-2	How to Start and Run a GA Business (2E)	$18.95	____
		ILLINOIS TITLES		
____	1-57071-405-3	How to File for Divorce in IL (2E)	$19.95	____
____	1-57071-415-0	How to Make an IL Will (2E)	$12.95	____
____	1-57071-416-9	How to Start a Business in IL (2E)	$16.95	____
		MASSACHUSETTS TITLES		
____	1-57071-329-4	How to File for Divorce in MA (2E)	$19.95	____
____	1-57248-050-5	How to Make a MA Will	$9.95	____
____	1-57248-053-X	How to Probate an Estate in MA	$19.95	____
____	1-57248-054-8	How to Start a Business in MA	$16.95	____
____	1-57248-055-6	Landlords' Rights and Duties in MA	$19.95	____
		MICHIGAN TITLES		
____	1-57071-409-6	How to File for Divorce in MI (2E)	$19.95	____
____	1-57248-015-7	How to Make a MI Will	$9.95	____
____	1-57071-407-X	How to Start a Business in MI (2E)	$16.95	____
		MINNESOTA TITLES		
____	1-57248-039-4	How to File for Divorce in MN	$19.95	____
____	1-57248-040-8	How to Form a Simple Corporation in MN	$19.95	____
____	1-57248-037-8	How to Make a MN Will	$9.95	____
____	1-57248-038-6	How to Start a Business in MN	$16.95	____

Qty	ISBN	Title	Retail	Ext.
		NEW YORK TITLES		
____	1-57071-184-4	How to File for Divorce in NY	$19.95	____
____	1-57071-183-6	How to Make a NY Will	$12.95	____
____	1-57071-185-2	How to Start a Business in NY	$16.95	____
____	1-57071-187-9	How to Win in Small Claims Court in NY	$14.95	____
____	1-57071-186-0	Landlords' Rights and Duties in NY	$19.95	____
____	1-57071-188-7	New York Power of Attorney Handbook	$19.95	____
		NORTH CAROLINA TITLES		
____	1-57071-326-X	How to File for Divorce in NC (2E)	$19.95	____
____	1-57071-327-8	How to Make a NC Will (2E)	$12.95	____
____	0-913825-93-X	How to Start a Business in NC	$16.95	____
		PENNSYLVANIA TITLES		
____	1-57071-177-1	How to File for Divorce in PA	$19.95	____
____	1-57071-176-3	How to Make a PA Will	$12.95	____
____	1-57071-178-X	How to Start a Business in PA	$16.95	____
____	1-57071-179-8	Landlords' Rights and Duties in PA	$19.95	____
		TEXAS TITLES		
____	1-57071-330-8	How to File for Divorce in TX (2E)	$19.95	____
____	1-57248-009-2	How to Form a Simple Corporation in TX	$19.95	____
____	1-57071-417-7	How to Make a TX Will (2E)	$12.95	____
____	1-57071-418-5	How to Probate an Estate in TX (2E)	$19.95	____
____	1-57071-365-0	How to Start a Business in TX (2E)	$16.95	____
____	1-57248-012-2	How to Win in Small Claims Court in TX	$14.95	____
____	1-57248-011-4	Landlords' Rights and Duties in TX	$19.95	____

SUBTOTAL THIS PAGE ____

SUBTOTAL PREVIOUS PAGE ____

Illinois residents add 6.75% sales tax
Florida residents add 6% state sales tax plus applicable discretionary surtax ____

Shipping— $4.00 for 1st book, $1.00 each additional ____

TOTAL ____